ACCLAIM FOR THE WISDOM OF
The Journey Toward Complete Recovery

Recovery takes on new meaning in Dr. Michael Picucci's *The Journey Toward Complete Recovery*. He expands our hearts and opens our minds to the wonders, the growth and the tremendous rewards of a holistic, ongoing approach in recovering the lost parts of our Self. Anyone touched by the dis-ease of addictions or "blocked energy," will be awakened and transformed by this work, as I have. He gives both promise and hope.

CAROLYN CRAFT, Director and Host
Wisdom Channel Radio and Television Network

The Journey Toward Complete Recovery helps us reframe the word "healing" in such a fundamental way that it opens our minds to amazing new possibilities.

CHARLES GARFIELD, PH.D.
Professor of Psychology, University of California at San Francisco
author, *Peak Performers*, co-author, *Wisdom Circles*,
A Guide to Self Discovery and Community Building in Small Groups,
and Founder, AIDS Shanti Project

Michael Picucci has "walked his walk." In presenting his community-based vision, he writes from a deep, impassioned experience of personal recovery.

MIKE LEW
author, *Victims No Longer: Men Recovering from Incest
and Other Sexual and Child Abuse*
Co-Director, The Next Step Counseling & Training, Brookline, Mass.

Michael Picucci's Authentic Process Therapy "A.P.T." includes the psychological and spiritual stages to achieve holism. His workshop in Orlando exploring the Sexual-Spiritual Split was powerful. It totally affected everyone who attended in an incredibly dynamic way. Great Work! I can't wait to incorporate these principles in my own private practice as a marriage and Family Therapist.

MAUREEN WARMAN, MPA, LMFT
President, "Life Enhancement Series, Inc.," Orlando, Fl.

This book charts a visionary course for therapeutic healing that is radically inclusive of the mind, body, and soul. A profound contribution to the healing arts!

COLLIN BROWN, Director
Body Electric School, Oakland Ca.

A wonderful Journey into the wholeness of healing!

DON CLARK, PH.D.
author, *Loving Someone Gay*, Twentieth Anniversary Edition

Picucci's Authentic Process Therapy (APT) is an exciting update on the timeless insight that "we are all medicine for each other." This book celebrates people!

EVAN T. PRITCHARD
author, *No Word for Time: The Way of the Algonquin People*

Everyone, at some time in their lives, is ready to make the leap from alienation and / or addiction to a celebration of possibilities. I have been witness to Michael Picucci's personal adventure. As it has evolved, he has embraced and expanded the concept of healing. What began over 60 years ago as a daring and isolated experience for Bill W. (the founder of Alcoholics Anonymous) is now accessible to a much wider community. People anxious to replace inner turmoil with creative serenity are given a place to start.

DAVID ROTHENBERG
Founder, The Fortune Society

The Journey Toward Complete Recovery is testimony to the power of community healing. Michael Picucci's understanding and wisdom on healing the sexual-spiritual split is invaluable to all of us seeking healthy relationships.

BARBARA WARREN, PSY.D., CASAC
Director, Mental Health & Social Services
New York Lesbian & Gay Community Services Center

An exciting and perceptive book for lay people and therapists alike.

AUDREY DELAMATRE
Reviewer, *The Phoenix*

The Journey Toward Complete Recovery is fresh air. The truth does, indeed, set you free. A field guide in the art of maturing. A must read!

BARRY WALKER, M.ED.
Director and Senior Faculty Member
North German Psychotherapy Community, Germany

This book is a richly detailed, experientially based, process of recovery that is guided by a humane, holistic, and interactive vision of psychotherapy.

J. GARY LINN, PH.D.
Tennessee State University

The Journey Toward Complete Recovery is a generous offering to all who are on a healing journey in life. Michael Picucci presents a powerful map for navigating this terrain. His work is honest, insightful, rich, and provocative in its integration of mind, body, and spirit. More than a map, it is a powerful invitation to healing.

THOMAS HERINGTON, MD, PSY.D. CAND
San Anselmo, Ca.

I heartily applaud Michael Picucci's method that addresses the "whole" person on an emotional, physical and spiritual level. I compare it to the Eleventh Step of AA. This book provides Good Orderly Direction (GOD)!

SANDRA ABOUZEID, CAP, ICADC
President, Voices of Wellness Productions

I've been an avid reader and practitioner of holistic health for over 20 years. *The Journey Toward Complete Recovery* has taught me a lot more.

CINDY SPRING
co-author, *Wisdom Circles* (with Charles Garfield and Sedonia Cahill)
and *Sometimes My Heart Goes Numb: Love & Caregiving in a Time of AIDS*
(with Charles Garfield)

This valuable new book is a gentle, loving roadmap to one's authentic self.

MICHAEL GRABILL
reviewer, *In the Life*

The
Journey Toward
Complete Recovery

The
Journey Toward
Complete Recovery

MICHAEL PICUCCI

North Atlantic Books

Published by
North Atlantic Books
P.O. Box 12327
Berkeley, California 94712

Cover design by Susan Quasha
Book design by Vicki Hickman
Photo of author by Dave Bussick

Printed in the United States of America

The Journey Toward Complete Recovery is sponsored by the Society for the Study of Native Arts and Sciences, a nonprofit educational corporation whose goals are to develop an educational and cross cultural perspective linking various scientific, social, and artistic fields; to nurture a holistic view of arts, sciences, humanities, and healing; and to publish and distribute literature on the relationship of mind, body, and nature.

Library of Congress Cataloging-in-Publication Data
Picucci, Michael.
    The journey toward complete recovery : reclaiming your emotional, spiritual & sexual wholeness / Michael Picucci.
       p. cm.
    ISBN 1-55643-286-0 (pbk. : alk. paper)
     1. Compulsive behavior -- Treatment. 2. Psychic trauma -- Treatment
    3. Self-help techniques. 4. Conduct of life. 5. Self-actualization
    (psychology) I. Title.
RC533. P49 1998
616.86′06--dc21   98-7069
                                    CIP

    1 2 3 4 5 6 7 8 9 10

Dedicated to my partner in life,
Elias J. Guerrero, Jr.

Contents

Introduction

An Authentic Process Toward Complete Recovery

This book presents a bold new vision of psychotherapeutic healing. This type of therapy is called *An Authentic Process Toward Complete Recovery* or simply *"Authentic Process Therapy."* It has organically grown out of my personal experience, the experiences of my clients, the countless workshops I've conducted over the years, the wisdom of the maturing recovery movement, and insights from diverse cultural perspectives.

Authentic Process Therapy (APT) is a significant healing approach for *all* human beings who want to enrich their lives. It is not just for addicts, ex-addicts, and those who identify themselves as adult survivors of a traumatic childhood. While the research comes from the reclaiming of health, happiness, and fulfillment for the most broken of us, the application of these healing strategies is beneficial to *every* person seeking a richer life. Those who have experienced the depths of despair have used these healing techniques, emerging from their personal process with profoundly illuminating insights for all of us. APT is a multi-staged system for recovering your emotional, psychological, cultural, spiritual and sexual wholeness through community healing. The goal (also, the result, I trust) of your commitment to the process is complete recovery, or holism as described in Chapter One.

What makes Authentic Process Therapy bold, new and distinct from other modes of healing? I feel that there are several important factors:

- It was developed out of the *experience* of those being healed, rather then from an academic or medical perspective.
- It incorporates from many disciplines and cultures that which has consistently demonstrated the ability to effect transformational change.
- It incorporates the "community healing approach" used in addictions recovery (Twelve-Step, Therapeutic Communities,

etc.) but shifts the focus to breaking down the barriers to
feeling whole and complete experienced by *all* people.

- It merges clinical, scientific, and psychotherapeutic discoveries
  and places them within the spiritual community context.
- The healing process is clearly defined from the onset. This
  awareness of the "big picture" of one's journey brings comfort
  and grace to the healing. However, it allows unlimited flexibility providing for individual adaptation.
- The personal "powers" and tools required for the journey are
  described in simple terms.
- The process is pragmatic because anyone who dedicates
  themselves to the journey will *experience* concrete results with
  each engagement.

The benefits of committing one's self to the process are glimpsed
before the process has begun. The *living map* presented in this book invites you to move towards concreteness and adequacy, towards facts,
towards action and towards personal power. It invites the reader to
make good sense out of what has previously been an ambiguous process. For example, this book presents a list of universally "shared desires"— what most people really want from therapy — then provides
tools and insights for fulfilling those desires, culminating in complete
recovery.

At the heart of this new vision is the healing technique which itself is
called Authentic Process. In this approach, the therapist/facilitator, op-
erates without clinical distance. The facilitator teaches an efficient system of healing while simultaneously guiding individuals through their
own process. Therapists and clients work together without hierarchy
towards mutual authenticity and community. Everything is discussed,
nothing is hidden. It is not esoteric in nature, not elitist, and not "medical." People are simply encouraged to speak from the heart.

Authentic Process is one of the "Four Powers That Dissolve Barriers
to Complete Recovery" that are available in APT. These powers are:

1. The Power of Community-based Healing
2. The Power of Shared Intentionality
3. The Power of Shared Belief
4. The Power of Authentic Process.

These are all fully described in Chapter Four. We use the Four Powers to move through various "stations of experience" (thoroughly depicted in Chapters Two, Six, and Seven) toward fulfilling the "constellation of shared desires" that are inherent in the human condition. Along the way, as the Tree of Awareness blossoms, it can produce wonderful and sometimes totally unexpected fruit. These rewards are described in Chapter Eight.

There are markers or navigational points that help us steer our course on our journey toward complete recovery. Eleven of them are in Stage One (outlined in Chapter Two) and twelve more in Stage Two (fully described in Chapters Six and Seven). I call these markers "stations." In doing so I seize upon the paradoxical definitions of the word "station." It can mean an "assigned post or position where a person stands," and can also have the transitional meaning of "a stopping place along a route." Both meanings apply. Each station has a transitional nature in that you move in and out of it time and again. At the same time each station also creates an experiential foundation that serves as an emotional platform. Imagine a space station that is designed to become the hub for future expansion. You can move among the stations and return to any one of them again and again as you continue your transformation.

Please avoid confusing the Twelve Stations of Stage Two with the Twelve Steps of AA and similar programs, or the twelve stations on the way to crucifixion in Catholicism. While all three philosophically suggest a death-rebirth experience, the common number of twelve is "coincidental" — or perhaps synchronicity.

The fact that I have been in focused co-creation of these concepts for fourteen years does not mean that other therapists are not doing similar work. I am happy to report that more and more of my colleagues are finding their own way to comparable healing approaches. What this book does is offer a map of the journey for the traveler. I use the metaphor of a tree to help present this map. To draw on that metaphor for a moment, you could say that Authentic Process Therapy is at the present time in its sapling stage of development. The living application of this healing, in the form presented in this book, is only four years old. The exciting results are being demonstrated at The Institute for Staged Recovery in New York City which was founded for this purpose. The Institute creates psychospiritual community workshops for individuals who desire to heal into wholeness and has already begun to train therapists to facilitate this process. This sapling will sprout deeper roots as more individuals intuitively, organically, and serendipitously draw to it and take root with it.

About the New Edition

The first hardcover edition of this book, entitled *Complete Recovery: An Expanded Model of Community Healing,* was primarily used as support for the "Getting Where You Want To Go" workshops we conduct at the Institute. These workshops gave me an opportunity to see the synergy of these ideas and experiences in action, setting the stage for a concise revision of the book for major distribution. By observing people using the book interactively, I could see the benefit in making the text less theoretical and more grounded in concrete, everyday terms. This has been accomplished. Much new material has been added from the workshop process and from the lives of the participants as well.

Also, in the earlier edition I chose not to share some important aspects of myself. At the time of the first writing, the ideas synthesized were so commanding that I felt these personal stories were less important and perhaps distracting from the main theme. I later realized that they are germane. I happen to be living as a gay man (though I feel much more complex than that label generally implies) who is HIV positive. Technically speaking, I have had AIDS since 1983, survived two cancers, intensive chemotherapy, numerous complications and surgeries, and a near-death experience; however, today I am blessed with health and vitality.

As the first edition of this work went to press, I had a heart attack (totally unrelated to my other health conditions) with accompanying triple bypass surgery. I have also lost two life partners, one female and one male, and many friends whom I dearly loved to AIDS. I have been both numbed and awakened by those losses. I share all this with you because I want you to know that the *fragility* of this experience we call life rarely escapes me. I have an ongoing desire for the recovery and enrichment of the human spirit and feel a deep pressing concern and compassion for our species and our world. With this comes a fascination with the nature of human consciousness. To me, nothing could be more interesting than the heart and mind and how they work.

The honest representation of my own sexual diversity is essential to the understanding of this healing work, as it was central to its creation and development. Certainly, this does not mean that one has to be gay, lesbian, or bisexual to benefit from this empowering journey; quite the contrary is true. *All* human beings can reclaim their emotional, spiritual, and sexual wholeness by engaging in the healing stations outlined in this book. What's important is to acknowledge that the many years of research and development this book represents were carried out by a population which was approximately 80 percent sexually diverse (gay, lesbian, bisexual, transgender), while the remaining 20 percent were heterosexually self-identified.

There is a natural and historic inclination toward new and experimental healing and transformative practices within the sexually diverse community. Not only have they been oppressed and misunderstood by the conventional healing and spiritual establishments, they have born the scars of all oppressed people: with a high rate of drug and alcohol abuse, as much as three times the national average. It is now three decades since the "sexual revolution" which marked the beginning of the gay liberation and feminist movements (which have become so much more than anyone suspected at the time). It is time that all sexual beings, whatever our present orientation and gender, completely drop the shackles of shame as we enter a new age where new forms of healing will become more important. Sexually diverse people have always been out front in the world of new ideas. They can reconcile polarities at each of the important crossroads and bring fresh perspectives and sensitivities to relationship, gender and cultural biases. In some Native American cultures, they were referred to as the *berdache, winkte,* or *two-spirit* people. In many indigenous cultures, they were the healers and seers of the existing and emerging order.

In some Native American traditions, sexually diverse people were the shamans, and when they were not the shamans they were often sought out by shamans for advice. Anthropologist and Fulbright scholar Walter Williams, in his book *The Spirit and the Flesh* says: "The *berdache* received respect partly as a result of being a mediator.... Since they mix the characteristics of both men and women, they possess the vision of both. They have double vision, with the ability to see more clearly than a single gender perspective can provide. This is why they are often referred to as 'seer,' one whose eyes can see beyond the blinders that restrict the average person.... By the Native American view, someone who is different offers advantages to society precisely because she or he is freed from the restrictions of the usual."

The point being made is that it is natural for gay and lesbian developments in healing and recovery to bear fruit for all people. The healing experience being offered to *all* in this book is a gift from the entire recovering community with special insights and contributions from its sexu-

ally diverse brothers and sisters. Together, we constitute the whole —
the healing is for all.

Likewise, though I feel that my own struggle with drugs and alcohol
was the central impetus to develop this work, you do not have to have a
primary addiction or Twelve-Step experience to be "in recovery." You
must merely recognize the potential in your life for greater authenticity
of expression and interaction with the world around you, and be willing
to examine the wounds that isolated you to begin with. Fortunately, as
this book goes to press, a transformation and expansion in the meaning
of the word "recovery" is occurring worldwide.

In making the distinction between addictions recovery and the larger
recovery of spirit that this book addresses, let me share my perspective
and where it comes from. I do not speak for or represent any Twelve-
Step program, but as one informed voice from the center of the vortex
that we have come to call addictions recovery. In that I have been a
grateful member of a Twelve-Step addictions program for more than
twenty years, my voice has been influenced by my own recovery, the
recovery of others, and years of experiential and psychospiritual research that led to my doctorate in "The Psychology of Addictions Psychotherapy."

To make this new nomenclature work, we need to separate the process in to two distinct stages: primary and complete recovery. I see *primary* addictions recovery as the recovery from life-threatening, involuntary attachments to alcohol, drugs, food, sex, and gambling (depending
on circumstances, other cravings may also be considered primary if they
are life-threatening). The healing from a primary addiction requires a
committed, singular focus for at least one to two years, more for some.
In this book, Stage One recovery addresses this healing and honors the
Twelve-Step and other recovery programs. The healing of a primary
addiction is the dissolving of the first barrier to the complete recovery of
spirit.

Expanding now beyond primary addictions, we acknowledge other
involuntary habitual behaviors, thinking, and feelings that are roadblocks or barriers to the fullness of who we are. In a humorous way, you
might think of them as heavy pieces of luggage; suitcases filled with
medieval suits of armor, swords, flintlock rifles, Winchester repeaters,
and a selection of dueling pistols. These *very* heavy suitcases are hinder-
ances to our completing the journey; to our full self-expression, the
shame-free presentation of ourselves, the intimacy we seek, and the gift
of serenity which is inherent in our spiritual existence. (When I say

"spiritual" I mean the joy of feeling our spirit connecting with the spirit of others, nature, and our universe.) I speak here of cultural, behavioral, psychological, and emotional addictions. You might recognize them as codependence, self-diminishing thinking, depression, self-sabotaging behavior, underachieving, over-achieving, physical self-injury, fear of encroachment, fear of abandonment, negative projections, being sexually unfulfilled, lacking love, black and white or right and wrong thinking, and all other outer manifestations of internalized dilemmas. All of these, and more, are highly injurious defensive weapons, outdated and heavy, burdens that keep us from what we want the most: mutual trust, love, and respect.

By definition, complete recovery includes freedom from all the above. We drop the armor and weaponry piece by piece, compassionately understanding why they were necessary in bringing us to our present ground of being. We come to see all addictions, personal as well as cultural ones, as ways the organic system creates equilibrium and a feeling of safety when faced with chaotic, traumatic conflicts beneath the conscious surface. We learn that with education and "inner statesmanship," these underlying conflicts can present themselves for healing. As we are able to make it "okay" for them to come out of hiding, our aliveness grows with each exposure and addictions fall away. Keep in mind that until the underlying chaos is released and cleared up, our inner defense system will update old addictions and defenses with other primary or secondary addictions, to keep equilibrium, or to keep up the imagined balance of power. Although this is progress, the real work is always the spiritual, cognitive, emotional work that changes the addictive state to the holistic one.

Making the connection between the struggle for freedom from addiction and the struggle for spiritual freedom in our lives is a big jump for some. But that is where many of us have come to on the journey, and can't turn back. Recently, I was invited to speak at a Unitarian-Universalist church on Authentic Process Therapy. When I was asked what the title of my talk would be, the words "Recovery of Spirit" came mysteriously from my mouth. At that pivotal moment in the process, all my thinking and feeling shifted from "recovery *from*" addictions and childhood trauma, to *"recovery of"* fulfillment, wisdom, serenity, and emotional, spiritual and sexual wholeness.

I could no longer comfortably talk in terms of "recovery from," and from then on the term "recovery of" seemed like a natural evolution. Everyone at the institute felt immediately at home with this new perspective. Suddenly and spontaneously, everything had been turned right side up. We felt ourselves moved from a problem-oriented process to a solution-oriented process. It was (and still is) refreshing.

Even more important, our journey now feels inclusive for our brothers and sisters who never had a primary addiction problem or Twelve-Step experience. They had been coming to workshops also wanting help and inspiration in their search for meaning, purpose, and intimacy in their lives. The dynamic energy of the "recovery from" movement had lured them, yet they often felt slightly out of place. Now, with this incredible, spontaneous transformation, the "recovery from" movement has matured and expanded to fully include them and the "recovery of" process they know they must undertake.

What is Complete Recovery?

The definition of complete recovery continues to grow and expand with each person who adopts it as their process. In the essential experience of complete recovery: 1. we integrate many of the split-off aspects of ourselves so that we *feel* whole; 2. we reclaim our emotional, spiritual, and sexual wholeness; 3. we present ourselves to the world free of toxic shame; 4. we experience a rich open-hearted spiritual connection with ourselves, others, and the pulse of the universe; and 5. we identify more with our spirit than with our conditions, realizing that we are always larger than whatever our present challenges may be.

At the core of complete recovery is a state of *being* that is in a constant, conscious evolutionary process of completing itself. To the best of our ability we stay up to the moment in taking care of our inner and outer needs, continually discovering what those needs are. In this state one makes an effort to appropriately and authentically express the fullness of oneself. One knows what it is to have an open heart, and is conscious of when, how and where one chooses to experience this opening. In Chapter Eight you will read about the many rewards of this journey, each one continuing to define aspects of complete recovery, although your own definition will ultimately be more important than any that I may give you. I encourage people to make this term their own and define it as they wish.

I'm aware that the concept of complete recovery may be jarring to those currently in programs based on total abstinence. The concept does not mean that one is cured of addictive tendencies but rather that one feels complete and whole as a human being, a being who is entitled to the joy of living and who can be authentic and sincere in their expression of it. This occurs when we have accepted and corrected unconscious self-delusions and integrated the many aspects of the self.

In the Twelve-Step programs it is said that *anonymity* is the spiritual foundation for each program, a tradition born in Alcoholics Anonymous. In Authentic Process Therapy, the foundation is the ongoing desire for completion, for feeling complete and whole and resolved concerning this lifetime and our purpose for being here. That is the binding spiritual glue that brings us together and makes the healing possible.

I sometimes think of this feeling of completion as always being prepared for the possibility of my demise. Have I done everything I needed to do? Are my relationships up-to-the-moment and emotionally complete to the best of my ability? Asking these questions helps us focus on our life as a whole to see exactly what remains unresolved. Far from being a death-wish, it is a buoyant freedom to *live* with. It is a gift I received from my several encounters with my mortality.

The following "promises" are excerpted from *Alcoholics Anonymous,* the pivotal book that galvanized AA and inspired the other Twelve-Step programs:

> We are going to know a new freedom and a new happiness. We will not regret the past nor wish to shut the door on it. We will comprehend the word "serenity" and we will know peace. No matter how far down the scale we have gone, we will see how our experience can benefit others. That feeling of uselessness and self-pity will disappear. We will lose interest in selfish things and gain interest in our fellows. Self-seeking will slip away. Our whole attitude and outlook upon life will change. Fear of people and economic insecurity will leave us. We will suddenly realize that God is doing for us what we could not do for ourselves.

I, and many others in Twelve-Step programs, fully realized these promises only when we expanded our recovery objectives. Authentic Process Therapy is an expanded perspective which offers these additional tools.

In Authentic Process Therapy, we also expand on these promises: We will know true intimacy, and connect in meaningful ways with others. We will finally heal the schism between our spiritual and sexual nature. Fear of authority figures will disappear as we put our faith in an inner, higher authority. In presenting ourselves shame-free to the world, we will discover our purpose for being. We will realize that God is the Great Spirit within us and beyond us. When we open our hearts we will know that we are the Spirit, represented in an energetic feeling we call love. We will experience and know the feeling of complete recovery.

Similar to the Twelve-Step path to healing, this is a journey of attraction; grab onto it if it feels like a clear, safe, and secure path to where you want to go. Or, if you are lost and this direction seems more suitable for you than others, climb aboard. Bring yourself to it only if it feels right to you, and even then, take what works for you and leave what does not, remembering we all have different needs at different times. There is no right or wrong way to grow and evolve — there is only your way.

Today, recovering people are finding the emotional freedom to experience intimacy, joy, creativity, feelings of accomplishment, serendipity, and connection with spirit through Authentic Process Therapy. This freedom to experiment with joy is a giant step beyond traditional definitions of recovery; it is something many "normal" or "healthy" people have difficulty with.

These same techniques which empower former addicts toward states of wholeness and happiness can likewise work wonders for those outside of the recovery community who somehow feel empty and unfulfilled. People with chemical or process addictions and those whose addictions are less obvious can benefit equally from this process. For example, we all mix together things that should be clearly separated, such as adult needs and childhood needs, and separate as contradictory things that should remain connected, such as spirituality and sexuality. To reach deep enough within to be able to re-sort and redefine these concepts is the main milestone in Authentic Process Therapy.

My own evolution towards developing this approach has been a long, painful, and rewarding one, working through my own blocks, blind spots, and addictions, as well as those of hundreds of clients. I wasn't satisfied with mere self-control, and realized there was another step, and another, and yet another. Peeling back the layers of self-deceptions I went through many stages of recovery, as did my clients. Somewhere along the line, the paradigm shifts, and many of us end up in a place we don't expect to be. This new "place" seems to be a holistic state of being, rooted where we are in our lives, but being connected to a much greater whole; optimally capable of dealing with joy, bliss, serenity and creativity, as well as emotional traumas, loss, disease and injury. This text reflects that evolution.

As we journey toward complete recovery, the self expands to include our larger world and universe. The healing of this new transpersonal self occurs when one nears completion of their own personal biographical healing, the point at which the blocks to perceiving that holistic connection with life finally dissolve, and our own healing merges with the transformation of the world around us. Complete recovery, then, involves the shame-free presentation of the self through community healing, the experience of personal wholeness, and finally the transpersonal breakthrough into what I call "holism."

Stories That Heal

In writing this book, I have made every attempt to authentically portray events and emotions. However, the case histories I present are purely representative "composite" creations. These vignettes accurately reflect the experiences of many different recovering people that I've worked with over the last fifteen years, but they are not to be considered a portrait of any single individual. Some readers may not identify with these stories because they find the situations too extreme. However, most will identify with the feelings beyond the stories, and many of us can describe similar situations.

One such profile appears at the end of each chapter, illustrating a number of relevant concepts introduced earlier in the section. Many can draw parallels to their own situations and learn from these stories. In some cases I have tried to simplify very complex spiritual concepts and psychotherapeutic constructs to make them accessible to everyone. Readers who want to explore some of these in greater detail should refer to the bibliography at the end for a list of books that inspired this one.

The Healer in Recovery

It is significant that this research and writing has been done by a psychotherapist who is in addictions recovery himself, and is also an addictions counselor; this is my personal journey. I have included historic and ongoing experiences as well as my professional experience with clients and workshop participants. Motivation to write within the context of my role as therapist was inspired by the works of Carl Rogers, Alice Miller, Viktor Frankl, and John Bradshaw. In their writings I heard an important voice, an interactive voice grounded in the authenticity of the healing experience. This voice embraced a human struggle in which the therapist and the client conjointly sought a greater sense of personal freedom and fulfillment. Because of my own personal engagement in the process of recovery, I feel comfortable influencing the future in addictions healing, research and education. Recovery has very much been my world and it has helped me reformulate my experience of family. This research, it could be said, is my own way of attempting to interact with and nurture my own family.

For me, this text is somewhat of a completion experience, and writing it a healing ritual. It sums up the holism of my recovery thus far and expresses the fulfillment of many of my needs. I know it will bring me joy to continue teaching, expanding, and integrating these concepts. During my years of intense study on this staged community approach, I have worked with many clients and conducted numerous workshops, and I am always greatly encouraged by the thirst people have for a fuller life. Although sometimes I feel jarred by the enormity of the issues, for me these shared traumas serve as a clarion call to examine the realities that shape our world and histories.

To the clients and workshop participants over the years, I say a heartfelt thank you. It is the work, struggle, trust, healing and commitment of you courageous pioneers that provides the content and spiritual vitality that runs through this book. Out of our growth, perseverance and determination for a fuller recovery, we are reshaping the structures, theories and institutions that serve us. This is necessary. We are the specialists in defining our own recovery and discovery needs. We can heal each other and we can train those whom we empower to help us. May we continue to persevere.

Cautions and Thoughts on the Use of This Text

Please never use this text to diminish your own process or experience. These words are intended to present new possibilities, ideas, behaviors and ways of being. They were never meant to suggest you should already be there. If you feel disheartened or daunted by all the work, that's appropriate. It is a great deal to absorb at one time. Think of it as a process where every delicious morsel of progress is continually rewarding you with the flavor of new possibilities. Remember to watch for the feeling of wholeness as it gradually enters and changes your life through its bounty. Validate each stage as it happens. Use this *living map* as it serves you along the way. Change it to suit yourself, or create from it a new map, all your own. This map really works, but only if you make the journey. It confirms the reality that wholeness and complete recovery are not only within our grasp, but ours *within the wink of an eye*. If we can accept the basics of this map—that we are not inherently flawed, and that our conditions and weaknesses have historical and cultural precedent — then we are immediately freed of the weighty tendency to feel ashamed, fearful, and self-diminishing. We are free to embrace this process in a way that is suitable to us, always holding the larger experience of wholeness in our body-mind.

Special Populations

Some may find doing this healing work in community more challenging than others. This is particularly true if one's dissociative tendencies are very severe, relative to the early traumas one was exposed to. People with more severe dissociation challenges often have been given psychiatric labels such as Borderline Personality, Dissociative Identity Disorder (Multiple Personality), Bipolar, etc. My experience is that such individuals greatly benefit from this living map of staged recovery but may experience distinctive challenges in healing communities. These problems arise when we compare ourselves to others. Those of us with more severe dissociation must realize that it may be harder for us than for others to grow in the obvious ways, and our timing may appear slower. Healing does occur nonetheless, and in actuality, it is hard to say how quickly we are progressing, since the complete scope of our psychic injuries may not be apparent to anyone, not even ourselves. As we relinquish our shame for our more dissociative tendencies, we might feel empowered to do some of this same work with others who share similar levels of dissociation. Though I have not yet seen this done, I can only imagine the awesome healing potential. Frankly, I have had no experience applying these principles to people who have been diagnosed as being schizophrenic, but it would make sense to do so. It would be interesting to explore the healing possibilities of this kind of work on the post-traumatic aspects involved with the various conditions lumped together under the term schizophrenia.

Age is also a factor. In most of the healing communities that I have facilitated, participants range in age from 24–60, mostly in the 30–42 range. Older people in particular have a difficult time accepting a new approach, fearful that their whole life has been wasted. This is never the case. I have also found that people born prior to 1945 have a handicap in these healing communities. Culturally, their mindsets were more established prior to the social and cultural revolution of the 1960s (which I believe is presently having its more mature, seasoned manifestation). Even so, as Jean Houston, Ph.D, author of *The Possible Human*, once said,

"our education prepares us to be straight white males living in 1926."
We are all archaic by the time we finish college, but the reality lag is
even greater for those who are over sixty. This being the case, older people often cannot synthesize new information and values with the speed
younger people do. There are also different issues and perspectives that
one focuses on as one heads into one's fifties. I am keenly aware of the
demarcation line in age because I was born as the war came to a close in
1945 at the very cusp of the baby boom. Starting at the year of my birth
an enormous energy wave of consciousness, in the form of new babies,
came onto this earth. Things have been speeding up ever since in an
evolutionary burst. People born before 1945 often do not feel connected
to this process. Although I have seen older people do brilliant healing in
workshops shoulder to shoulder with younger people, I look forward to
the day when we can also create age and culture-appropriate healing
communities. Healing for these seniors would soar in its own special
way without the distraction and confusion of the younger mindset being
present. All in good time. We continue to learn.

To My Colleagues

This manual is written for my friends, known and unknown, who are in
the process of recovering the fullness of their lives. It is also written for
my professional peers: counselors, therapists, psychologists and
psychospiritual facilitators and educators. I have written as one voice
from within several communities and represent many views: that of a
formerly addicted person, of a professional within the psychology/
psychotherapy/addictions community, and of a human being living in
today's complex society. By sharing what I have learned and experienced, I offer a living map to help others. This manual, coupled with the
research of The Institute for Staged Recovery, aims to help people explore their psyches and spirit with compassion and without judgement.

The Institute, founded in New York City in 1994, is an expansion of,
and adjunct to, my private practice and experiential workshops. My co-
founders, Elias Guerrero, M.D., and John McCormack, C.A.S.A.C., and I
established the Institute to develop and provide both psychological and
cultural education for issues related to recovery, intimacy, sexuality,
spirituality, and personal fulfillment. Today it stands as a lively demonstration and model of the healing outlined in this book.

This text owes its existence to the people in recovery who have
forged a courageous journey through numerous layers of psychic darkness and confusion. The content has been improved by scores of profes-

sional training sessions I have conducted, in which therapists and counselors gave me generous feedback on the development of this work. I
am honored that so many of my colleagues found these ideas refreshing.
To the mental health and addiction professionals who work with recovering people, I suggest a willingness to at least temporarily suspend
preconceived ideas and loyalties to any single approach to addictions
counseling and/or psychotherapy while working with this book. Look
at the process through the eyes of the specific recovering person who
comes to you for help, bringing your own experience into the process.
Of course, this approach demands a great deal of you as a healing professional, yet it can bestow great rewards. I hope these chapters help
nurture this capacity.

The
Living
Map

Within and around the earth,
within and around the hills,
within and around the mountains,
your authority returns to you.

ALFONSO ORTIZ
Earth Prayers From Around the World

W hen friends come to visit me in the Big Apple, I like to take them to the observation deck on top of the World Trade Center. From there, 103 flights and a quarter of a mile up, we look down over New York City's arterial system of streets and avenues bound by two rivers, with Central Park at its heart. Before us spreads a bird's-eye view, a living map. Of course a map is useful in any new place, but a first encounter with the streets of New York can be daunting without one, for the looming skyscrapers block the sun, as well as one's instinct as to what lies ahead or behind, to the right or the left. My friends tell me the overview helps them plant themselves in this town and makes them less intimidated by the awesomeness of it all. They shed their fear and replace it with a growing sense of adventure.

A flat map from the corner newsstand may tell them how to get from one place to the next, but with this multi-dimensional living map, they feel how the pulse of the city beats throughout its sprawling body, and they feel that pulse in their own bodies as well. That way, when they go back down to street level again, they are no longer strangers in a strange land; they feel themselves part of the scene, part of a teeming whole.

My intention in writing this book is to offer such a living map. In this case, the terrain is not a city; it is the topography of healing: healing for the individual, for the community of humankind, and for the Earth. By healing I mean wholeness, freedom from those haunting feelings and fears of not being enough, not having enough, not doing enough. This healing I speak of does not entail a helpless, lonely stay in a hospital ward where one may well lose an organ or limb; this healing is an active, wondrous reclaiming of parts of the truly Godlike, as well as human, potentials with which each of us is born. And this reclaiming is only enhanced by — in fact it requires — the company, support, and participation of others.

This map shows a way to wholeness. It is not the only map, nor is it *the* definitive map to wholeness — such a map most likely doesn't exist — but it works. Take what you like and leave the rest, and then, only when you are ready. If you like, make your own map. No matter how many explorers set out to chart this journey, there will always be more wilderness to discover, and better paths to cut.

This is a *living* map because, just as the view from the top of the World Trade Center embraces Manhattan island in all its dimensions, the heights, sights, sounds, and smells, this map is designed to embrace the healing process and each of us involved in it physically, emotionally, mentally, sexually, and spiritually, in all *our* dimensions. As well as showing the way to specific resources and landmarks, this kind of map tends, like the view from the World Trade Center, to evoke within you the pulse of the terrain before you, so that you may know it as the pulse of your very own being.

I believe the human adventure is by definition a journey to wholeness, and this journey is underway whether we like it or not. So it can only help to outfit yourself with the right tools for the expedition: a compass and a map, for example. You already have the compass, your intuitive sense of direction (although you may have forgotten where you packed it); here is a map.

1

In Search of Holism

Have you ever seen a powerful movie, listened to a great piece of music or finished a really good book and, coming away with a feeling of profound happiness, said to yourself, "Everything makes so much sense. I wish life were like that —" only to wonder if perhaps it *could be* like that if only you could see things a little more clearly? Have you ever felt like everything in your life probably made sense, but you were missing some of the puzzle pieces, and so it remained a mystery to you?

If the answer is yes, then perhaps you have glimpsed the underlying holism that surrounds us all the time, but which we are so often blinded to by the sorrows that accompany even the happiest life. The quest for this holism can take a lifetime, but it is worth the trip. And whether you are recovering from trauma, incest, sexual abuse, cultural oppression and confusion, or addiction, if you are seeking complete recovery, you are in fact seeking to rediscover the holistic state. They are one and the same. But what exactly is holism?

1. The Possibility of Holism: Envisioning the Reward

Holism is the goal of Authentic Process Therapy (APT). It encompasses not only the feeling of being whole and complete in oneself, but also of being integrated into the cosmos, one with nature, and connected with all humanity. If we are able to envision for ourselves such a state or at least accept that it is possible, we can recognize the need for a complete recovery process which goes beyond healing addictions and compulsions. Holism is a place of great joy, bliss, love, empowerment, creativity, respect for all life, and peace, a place from which we can meet future challenges with grace and wisdom. We come from a new integration, having brought parts of ourselves (physical, emotional, psychological, and spiritual) together at the deepest level of inner knowing. This leads to integration and balance with every part having significant value and importance.

Holism is the understanding that reality is made up of organic and unified wholes that are greater than the simple sum of their parts. At the core of this experience is what I call "shame-free presentation of the self." When we reach a holistic state, we know who we are and no longer feel ashamed or embarrassed by our difficult personal history. Of course we will still be discriminating with regard to when and where we share certain aspects of ourselves, but we will experience and radiate the essence of true empowerment, entitlement and spiritual connectedness, whether we express it verbally or not.

Authentic Process Therapy is a highly effective way of releasing crippling toxic shame by exploring unconscious material and making it conscious. When this happens, it releases an energy that appears to enhance relationships with others and with the natural world. Carl Jung called this phenomenon "transcendent function." He explained that when unconscious content becomes conscious we experience a sense of clarity, a fuller understanding of ourselves, an experience that goes beyond ordinary, everyday consciousness. I refer to this as a glimpse of holism — a stroke of our own genius. It's almost like jumping to the top of the World Trade Center!

In interviews with individuals who experience holism, it is not uncommon to hear someone say, "I am awed," or "I never believed life could be this special." This was certainly the case for me. It was not just a passing euphoric feeling. It became established in my ground-of-being. Once, the awe surrounding my own life experience was so great that I sought out a therapist solely because I needed a safe place to humbly share it. I needed a place where I knew I would be heard and would not be triggering someone else's feelings of deprivation. It was a very special sharing between the therapist and me, and I have since been able to integrate awe and bliss as components of my everyday life. I, too, would never have believed it.

Recovering people are often embarrassed and reluctant to share blissful feelings because they are afraid they will be misunderstood, or that the feelings will not last. It is vital to find what I call "cultural safety:" safe friends, communities, or professionals with whom to share these feelings. Sharing further enlivens and validates them and makes them a real part of our daily experience. Small, validated experiences of bliss become the foundation for more intense and enriching ones. These loftier experiences, and the recognition of them in others, help create the desire to bring them forth more fully. Knowing that they are realizable motivates us to do the committed work which is part of Stage Two of complete recovery, as you will see in Chapter Three.

Nonetheless, for most people, there is a large gap between the deep holistic state and their "ordinary" awareness. With APT, this will lessen in time, but there will always be some feeling of transition between the two. To begin to get a grasp of how profoundly "different" the holistic state can be, it might be helpful to explore what author Stanislav Grof, M.D. calls "non-ordinary" states of consciousness.

In his Holotropic Breathwork trainings, people are taught to breathe in a very specific manner until they reach a "non-ordinary" state in which they begin to have physical, emotional, and sensory experiences that empower them with a larger view of life. Often they discover repressed traumatic conflicts or unfinished business from the past. These events tend to be very healing, unleashing new energy and clarity.

Community healing, as discussed later, also produces a non-ordinary state of consciousness. This is where deep healing occurs. When we enter into such a community setting, we leave the everyday world behind — the world of right and wrong, good and bad, "more thans" and "less thans" — and we find and integrate our complex, more complete selves. In the holistic perspective, there is no "normal" or "abnormal." We are diverse by design. As the author Jean Houston once said, "A normal person is someone you don't know very well."

An encounter with the holistic state of being may also bring with it feelings of "non-ordinary" calm and detachment. When we expand our perception of time, we see the impermanence of things and trust that it's okay. My friends who practice Buddhism have been able to articulate to me many of the finer points of nonattachment and impermanence. For me, this has come to mean that as much as I may want to cling to certain things, relationships, or even life itself, deep down in my soul I know that I am okay without them. Somehow, my inner sense of knowing and my experiences of transcendent spiritual calm give me something to fall back on when other realities appear to desert me — or at least the part of me that wants to hold on. Similarly, in the experience of holism, people report feeling less dependent on the "things" of life to feel whole and content. They relax their sense of "holding on."

There is a look, or aura, that I perceive in people who have this personal sense of awareness. I see it in some of the elders in the recovery movement. I see it in some of the dynamic teachers and leaders in our society. I see it in depictions of Buddha and Jesus and in the faces of some of the wise people of many cultures. There is a kind of otherworldly respect and knowing in their eyes. They seem content to feel their serenity in privacy, even without verbalization. They have a *presence* that goes beyond ordinary time and space. Psychologist Christina Grof, in *The Thirst for Wholeness,* summarizes this beautifully:

> As we become freer and more accepting, we awaken to our own wholeness. The word "whole" means healthy, free from wound or injury, healed. Wholeness is also defined as the unity or totality of complex components. This is what we have been thirsting for — and it is possible to find it in our everyday world. As we experience the spiritual awakening... we unite with the divine, we retrieve that core of wholeness within. A life of wholeness is a life of health and balance. In the process of healing from our wounds, we begin to harmonize our physical, emotional, mental, and spiritual parts. During our... spiritual practice and through our action in the world, we more easily integrate the small and the deeper Self. The immanent divine meets the transcendent divine, and we become aware of the miracle of our lives.

2. Barriers to Holism: Recognizing the Blindspots

Once we can envision our personal variation on the holistic state, we can begin to identify areas in which that experience is blocked for us, perhaps because some areas are too painful to examine and bring into connection with the rest of our life. Some of these roadblocks might include a lack of connection with ourselves and the world around us, a lack of community or an inability to communicate with others. Addiction (which is the way most people today cover up emotional pain) is perhaps the most common wedge between us and the truth of things. Stage One recovery, which we will describe later, deals with primary addictions, those which clearly affect all aspects of our life. However, there are countless more subtle forms of addiction most people never notice. They are still roadblocks to holism, because their purpose is to distract us from what's in front of us emotionally.

The split that we believe exists between spirituality and sexuality not only separates us from our significant others, our spouses and loved ones, but separates us from our bodies and from the natural world as well. It is a major detour on the road to holism. It adds to the repression of the shadow self (the dumping ground for the parts of our personality we disown), and to the separation of the body, mind, and spirit. This can lead to shame, and poor grounding of personal energy, which are roadblocks in themselves.

Other barriers include ignorance of psychospiritual principles, lack of respect for self and/or others, cultural pain, repressed trauma (and the refusal to recognize our original pain and trauma), depression and anxiety, confusing adult and childhood needs, and censoring our own inner voice.

The Relationship Between Trauma, Addiction, & Holism

If you're like most people in recovery, you suffered traumas or loss early in life, and received little or no help at the time. In order to survive the pain, you began to dissociate, or cut yourself off from the part of yourself that was in pain. During the time you were dissociating (fantasizing, drinking, taking drugs, drowning your sorrows in any one of a number of addictions or compulsions) you were splitting yourself into safe little compartments, to hide the pain from others and from yourself. We've all done it in some form. You began to fabricate stories around your "shadow" parts to deflect attention from them. You began to create stories around your over-compensating expanded ego too, as a hedge, creating a "mask of composure," a façade that controlled what feelings you let people see — usually only those manipulative ones leading to personal gain.

The light and dark sides of your mind became separated, and you began to see every situation in black and white, with little or no shades of gray. If something was not ideal, it was "hopeless." If something was good, you "outlined" it, separated it from all other things, and attached yourself to it as if it was your only hope. In the end, you had lost all concept of what a whole self might be. Your fear had divided and conquered your own being. Naturally, you became separated from the cosmos. You became "disconnected from the stars," which in Latin was expressed as "disastros." This disconnection still spells disaster any way you put it.

Underlying our disconnection from the stars is disconnection with ourselves. Underlying that dissociation is always pain. Underlying the pain is fear, and underlying the fear is trauma. The trauma happened to us: we didn't cause it, it's done, it's over and we can't undo it. But there is a solution to your situation and to your suffering, one which will dramatically change your life. For simplicity's sake, let's call it applying the principles of Authentic Process Therapy and doing the healing work.

The antidote to traumatic memory is visualization. Redraw the picture in your mind of your wound. Deep within you is that child that was hurt, still the same age as when it all started. Visualize yourself as an adult going back and helping that child that you were. Love and protect that child that was traumatized. Watch over that child. Let him or her know they are not alone, and that it was not their fault.

The antidote to fear is skill. Through the techniques and concepts shared in this book and others that fall into your lap, realize that you are learning skills that relate to almost every situation that could come up, and that as you become more adept at handling these situations confidently, fear will disappear by itself.

Once fear lessens its grip, the pain will lessen as well. Once the pain diminishes, the need to dissociate will fade. Instead of running away in fear, you will begin to look forward to exploring new adventures; small ones at first, perhaps, but growing more and more bold as time heals your wounds. As so many have said, "It is never too late to have a happy childhood."

The chart on the next page shows in the simplest terms how addiction begins in pain and fear, and how it can be resolved back into a state of complete recovery or holism through learning self-healing and situational skills such as those presented in this book.

Understanding Repressed Trauma

As Buddha once said, "No one is free from suffering." Take a straw poll among your friends and you will see that these words are as true today as they were 2,650 years ago.

We all have repressed traumatic conflicts from childhood and adolescence. Some of us have been exposed to more serious and direct physical, sexual or emotional traumas. Does this mean we have to be in pain all the time? No, but repressing the memory does not eliminate the pain, it merely makes it harder to find, and gives it a life of its own. In Stage Two Recovery we re-engage with forgotten memories in the spirit of healing the pain.

Trauma is a global human phenomena. It means being wounded. It means enduring an emotional shock that creates substantial and lasting damage to one's psychological and emotional development. Humanity

THE RELATIONSHIP BETWEEN TRAUMA, ADDICTION, & HOLISM

*(Progressing from the Holistic State of infancy at the top
to the Holism of Complete Recovery at the bottom)*

Holistic State

IN INFANCY, OR IN PRE-NATAL / EMBROYONIC STATE

Traumas Encountered

Pain

Fear

Developing Defense Structure

Disconnection from Parts of the Self & the Universe

Dissociation/Repression

Black & White Views

ALL OR NOTHING THINKING

Addictions

DRUGS / ALCOHOL / SEX / OTHER STIMULUS
HIDING / DEPRESSION / ANXIETY / COMPULSIONS

Inner or Outer Intervention

Acknowledgment of Addiction/Depression

Surrender/Asking for Help

Self-Healing Skills/Coping Skills

Knowledge/Faith in Higher Power

Developing Psychospiritual/Interpersonal Skills

Self-Expression/Authentic Process/Community Healing

Less Fear/More Love

Integration of Missing Parts of the Self

Holistic Experiences of Complete Recovery

Fruits of the Tree

has endured trauma since pre-neolithic times, and it shows no signs of ending any time soon.

As children we have boundless interest, curiosity, energy, and a feeling of ownership and connectedness with all that is. Our natural instincts would be to let ourselves be molded by the land and the sky, for we are firstly animals imbued with spirit and secondly humans with thinking minds. Spared the influence of our civilization's dualistic thinking, we would naturally have taken on different values such as many indigenous, earthbased cultures have.

I am not diminishing the concept of civilization, but when we indoctrinate children into such civilized concepts as dualistic thinking, and make them adapt to what is not natural, we are traumatizing their organic instincts to see and feel things in an intuitive, non-linear manner. In many ways we crush their spirit and sense of wonder. This is an observation, not a judgment. The point is, we *all* have traumatic losses to heal on our path to wholeness. Addiction to substances and states of being has its early roots in such traumas. While these cultural traumas have now become universal, most of us have additionally suffered traumatic wounds of an individual and personal nature.

These repressed traumas surface as forgotten physical injuries and abuses, emotional neglect or torment, overt or covert sexual abuse or psychological and emotional wounds. During this work, most people will excavate from their depths an array of mild to serious wounds that shaped their survival defenses. Some recovering people grew up in environments characterized by alcoholism/addiction, emotional instability or mental illness. Others experienced traumatic losses involving death, adoption or divorce. Still others will discover what I refer to as "endurance-trauma." Devastating in its subtlety and continuity, this is a prolonged, day-in and day-out, low-grade threat to a person's sense of safety and security.

While often stirring up feelings of loss, these surprises from the unconscious also help us understand why we chose to become addicted. It can be an "aha" experience. Some people, in the midst of unblocking repressed trauma, develop their skill of sensory recall to the point where they can even return to the experience of their own birth and to the earliest months and years of their development, which can connect them with a unique holistic experience. People who have not been exposed to this process are bound to be skeptical at first. The only way to understand is to experience it firsthand. It is all wonderfully mysterious, but that does not make it unreal.

3. Steps Toward Complete Recovery: Dissolving Barriers to Holism

In Authentic Process Therapy, the process from addiction, to unfulfilled lives, to total recovery, is broken down into two multi-layered stages. Stage One involves recognizing our disconnected state and our addictions, and addressing them appropriately.

Stage Two involves the rediscovery of joy and connectedness through dissolving the roadblocks to holism.

Stage One Recovery: Addressing Primary Addiction

Addiction has its roots in the human condition. We all share the potential for becoming addicted, either to substances, processes, states, or behaviors. In each case, these addictions cover up the pain which caused us to fall out of grace with the cosmos in the first place. For those of us who have a primary addiction, if we are to achieve wholeness and integration, we need to allow this reality to surface and heal the wound. We cannot do this without addressing the primary addiction (or addictions) which disguise the pain and hide it from ourself and others.

There are eleven major steps or "stations" to Stage One Recovery:

1. Coming face-to-face with addiction/compulsion
2. Joining self-help groups
3. Finding a higher power and/or a new family of affiliation
4. Making a conscious decision to recover
5. Risking depending on others
6. Discovering new awareness, hope and motivation
7. Seeing support as a life saver
8. Recognizing more diverse feelings
9. Planting seeds for Stage Two work
10. Sharing family and personal secrets
11. Acknowledging and celebrating Stage One triumph

Stage Two Recovery: Expanding on What Works

Stage Two of our complete recovery is a community-based individual process by which we learn to dissolve the internal roadblocks to wholeness and holism not addressed by the Stage One healing process.

In this process, we learn to connect with others and with our environment through community. At the same time we learn to connect with our true self through unwrapping our pain with the facilitation of a therapist or counselor.

Regaining the holistic state requires both reaching out to others and reaching inward, perhaps at the same time, so that we realize our ultimate goal of holistic interconnectedness with life, as we have envisioned it. The stages within Authentic Process Therapy are experienced differently for each individual. In Chapter Three, we will define and examine the major tenets of Stage Two, and how they can guide us back towards the holistic state.

From time to time I will use the word "crisis." While it can be a scary word for many, it is also a very positive one. A crisis is a crucial or decisive point or situation; a turning point. Because it includes a change or shift in one's way of being, it sometimes carries with it a feeling of instability. This is why we have community support, education, and facilitation, allowing us to stay grounded while at the same time feeling unstable. The reality is that no real change can occur in our way of being in the world without such crises. They break down the old stagnant energy systems in our bodies, giving birth to a newer sense of ourselves.

There are twelve "stations" within Stage Two Recovery, six "fundamental" stations and six "emergent" stations. Each is a healing crisis that most people engaging in this work encounter at some point in time. The Six Fundamental Stations are:

1. Finding the unconscious through the "inner child"
2. Awakening your body: finding your grounding
3. Exploring the sexual-spiritual split: the cornerstone of self-recognition
4. Revisiting "adolescent awkwardness"
5. Re-experiencing original pain and trauma
6. Grieving unresolved losses

The real landmark, or milestone of these fundamental stations is, "Healing the Sexual/Spiritual Split." After the healing crisis stage of the fundamental stations is engaged, we can begin the Six Emergent Stations. These are points of deep realization that occur as the roadblocks to holism start to disappear. They are:

7. Letting go: the authentic presentation of self
8. Corrective experience: learning more effective behavior
9. Separating adult needs from childhood needs
10. Integrating the shadow self
11. Updating and re-tuning the unconscious
12. Experiencing self-love and self-assertion

The major milestone of the Emergent Stations is "Separating adult needs from childhood needs." These are all defined and described in more detail in Part Two.

The Experience of
Holism & Transpersonal Healing

Awareness
of Impermanence

Serendipity,
Grace
& Synchronicity

Ongoing
Maintenance
of Stages

Service
to Others

Awe & Bliss

Respect for
Self & Others

Personal,
Spiritual Intimacy

Feelings
of Accomplishment

Intuitive
Inner Knowing

Body/Mind/Spirt
Connection

Shame-free
Presentation of Self

Experience
of Empowerment

▲ Experiencing self-love and self-assertion
▲ Updating and re-tuning the unconscious
▲ Integrating the shadow self
▲ Separating adult needs from childhood needs
▲ Corrective experience:
learning more effective behavior
▲ Letting go: the authentic presentation of self
▲ Grieving unresolved losses
▲ Re-experiencing original pain
& trauma
▲ Revisiting "adolescent
awkwardness"
▲ Exploring the sexual-spirtual split:
the cornerstone of self-recognition
▲ Awakening your body:
finding your grounding
▲ Finding the unconscious
through the "inner child"

*Unconscious
Material
to be worked
though
in Stage Two*

▲ Acknowledging and celebrating Stage One triumph
▲ Sharing family & personal secrets
▲ Planting seeds for Stage Two work
▲ Recognizing more diverse feelings
▲ Seeing support as a life saver
▲ Discovering a new awareness, hope and motivation
▲ Risking depending on others
▲ Making a conscious decision to recover
▲ Finding a higher power and/or a new
family of affiliation
▲ Joining self-help groups
▲ Coming face-to-face with addiction/compulsion

*Conscious
Material
experienced
by most people
two or more
years into their
recovery*

STAGE ONE | STAGE TWO

Tree Diagram of The Staged Model of Recovery

Out of these Emergent Stations comes a growing feeling of integration and wholeness, and a more profound relationship with others, and with all life. Gradually, the process begins to bear fruit. The benefits of the holistic state sometimes become evident before we recognize that we ourselves are in touch with it. These fruits might include a feeling of empowerment, an integration of body, mind and spirit in ways that are suddenly tangible to us, a desire to serve our world, an increasing ability to rely on intuition and inner knowing, hunches, and "nudges," a feeling of accomplishment without self-flagellation or hurtful gloating, feelings of awe and bliss, a feeling of boundless creativity, spiritual intimacy, a sense of respect for the self and for others, an acceptance and consequent awareness of impermanence, a growing sense of serendipity, (combining grace and synchronicity), an awareness of undergoing transpersonal healing, and the ability to present oneself in a shame-free and honest manner.

The Fruits of the Tree

The tree diagram (see page 15) is both a flat map and a bird's eye view of the healing journey to complete recovery through Authentic Process Therapy. It becomes a living map with a pulse when we bring our hearts and minds to the process outlined in these page. Like looking at Manhattan Island from atop the World Trade Center, we get to look down on the terrain before going down into it.

This bird's eye view has several potential effects: It can make the emergence into the healing process less frightening because we know what to expect; we can see that others are sharing this adventure with us, see what the benefits of the adventure are, and when things get tough, we can pull ourselves out, go back to the bird's eye view and reassess our position. Most importantly, we get to refine or acquire new skills. Intuition is our compass; as we begin to trust it, we will be guided to wherever we need to be in the tree. It will also guide us to the people, communities, and processes that we need for our individual journey. This is what brings pulsing, teeming aliveness to the process.

If you look at the tree you will discover an interesting reality. All twelve of the Stage Two stations end in *ing* which means they all relate to *doing*. In other words, earnest effort must be applied. The fruits of the tree, or the rewards of the journey, are all states of *being*. States of being by their very nature do not require doing anything. They are without negative stress. (Positive stress does accompany the state of pure being and becoming, but its consequence is a feeling of aliveness rather than the depression that accompanies the negative stress of suppression/oppression.) When you experience the fruits of the tree, there is no conscious effort — just reward! Imagine reaping rewards for just being and becoming who you really are — it is really that wonderful.

You now have a bird's eye view of the living map, looking at the two-stage recovery process from the lofty vantagepoint of the holistic perspective. Now let's go down to street level, and walk around some of these concepts and try to get a handle on what's really going on, using all our imaginative faculties of sense and sight and feeling. Let's begin the journey itself.

2

Stage One Recovery
The Journey Begins

The Eleven Stations of Stage One Recovery

While everyone reading this book may not think of themselves as having a primary addiction, understanding primary addiction is nevertheless fundamental to the overall process. This understanding is meaningful for all human beings. It gives us insight into society and the human psyche and condition.

Those who consider themselves Adult Children of Alcoholics (ACOA) may not have a primary addiction themselves, but may be affected by the issues of their parents. For them, the complete recovery concept is particularly apt.

The urgency of our struggle to remove the roadblocks to holism from our path becomes much clearer when we equate it with the more visible and dramatic struggle to free ourselves from chemical addictions. Likewise, Stage One takes on new meaning when viewed from a Stage Two perspective.

As we move into the second stage of the process, we can look back, identify and teach others about what we have been through. There are eleven stations in Stage One:

1. Coming face-to-face with addiction/compulsion
2. Joining self-help groups
3. Finding a higher power and/or a new family of affiliation
4. Making a conscious decision to recover
5. Risking depending on others
6. Discovering new awareness, hope and motivation
7. Seeing support as a life saver
8. Recognizing more diverse feelings

9. Planting seeds for Stage Two work
10. Sharing family and personal secrets
11. Acknowledging and celebrating Stage One triumph

Let us look at each of these stations in order.

1. Coming face to face with addiction/compulsion

When a person begins to come out of their denial that an addiction or compulsion is running their lives, that is the first station of Stage One recovery. It is a time when they either choose, or are compelled by outside forces to address this life-sized challenge. For many, an intervention or crisis is absolutely necessary to pierce through the denial or avoidance mechanisms that have built up. Such a crisis may seem catastrophic at the time, but it can open the gateway to an incredible journey, a journey of the soul.

2. Joining self-help groups

Rarely do we achieve freedom from a primary addiction without support from an understanding healing community. Most often, this support is found within Twelve-Step groups or therapeutic communities. With commitment to the group an organic healing process begins on all levels.

3. Finding a higher power and/or a new family of affiliation

When we leave a primary addiction behind, we also leave a world behind. Whether it is a world of isolation or of other addicted people, it must be replaced by both a sense of a power greater than ourselves and a compassionate "chosen family of affiliation." This may be the power of the healing community itself, a spiritual force, or both. The reason we need to choose a new family of affiliation is because most addictions are both triggered and enabled by the family of our childhood, as are many other roadblocks to holism.

4. Making a conscious decision to recover

People first enter recovery in many ways: They enter through crises, pressure from loved ones, job jeopardy, court order, or just plain exhaustion and confusion. At some point, though they may feel they have fallen or been dropped into recovery, they must make a conscious choice. Without making a personal, conscious choice to recover, relapse is inevitable. Most make the conscious choice only after they've seen others achieve successful recovery results and begin to model themselves after them. A clear conscious choice is not made until we believe that recovery is truly possible. This foreshadows the power of "shared intention" and "shared belief" so important in Stage Two.

5. Risking depending on others

It takes humility to ask for help. Humility cannot be learned from a book, but it must be learned. Most addicted people do not feel comfortable depending on others for their growth needs or asking for help. Stage One is where we learn how to do this. For many, it is also the beginning of a spiritual life experience. When we risk asking for help, our protective ego defenses relax and love can enter our being. We can then become open to the assistance that is all around us, in all its many mysterious and commonplace forms. At the center of this part of the healing process is humility; without it there is very little chance of recovery. This deep humility makes us more open and receptive to the holistic state.

6. Discovering new awareness, hope and motivation

The first year or two of recovery is full of psychological, emotional, and spiritual "openings." By openings, I mean new awarenesses that are more than cerebral. These insights are multi-dimensional and multi-layered. The awareness radiates through us like the warmth of direct sunlight on our skin. Once felt, it is a truth that never needs to be proven, only lived. These awarenesses, often coming from healing interactions with other group members, inspire the hope and motivation necessary to continue moving toward recovery, first *from* the primary addiction, and secondly, *of* a loving, childlike joy in living.

7. Seeing support as a life saver

At some point, relatively early in the process, we make the humble realization that we cannot heal our addiction alone, that our future lives are dependent on grabbing on to who and what we intuit as supportive to our journey. This is the purpose of the "sponsor" in AA, to be that temporary life raft for someone else.

We consciously surrender to this idea that an interconnectedness with others is vital to our survival. There is relief and peace in this surrender, for until this point we truly believe that such help is out of our reach. With this realization, we discover that we no longer have to be alone. This opens the gateway to authentic process and ultimately to the totally interconnected state of holism, in which we see how every part of the universe "helps" every other part.

8. Recognizing more diverse feelings

Gradually, as we move away from the active addiction, a diverse array of feelings begin to emerge which we were previously unaware of, feelings that have been masked for many years by the addiction. The appearance of these feelings is baffling at first because they surface without warning and before we have a chance to develop a vocabulary for them. In early Stage One, feelings are put aside so that we stay focused on building our recovery from addiction. As we become more grounded in recovery, we begin, with support, to name and understand the emergent feelings. This prepares the way for Stage Two, a process in which yet deeper feelings will be explored.

9. Planting seeds for Stage Two work

As complex feelings begin to emerge, so do inherent limitations. These challenges are part of human nature, appropriate to our history. These limitations existed prior to the addiction. Indeed, they may be what the addiction was ministering to. Often fears, rages, insecurities and profound layers of shame block us from manifesting our full presence. As one discovers these inner challenges they can now be assigned to the Stage Two process. When recovery of the primary addiction is stablized, and the emotional equilibrium needed to consciously engage in the next stage of recovery is in place, Stage Two can begin.

10. Sharing family and personal secrets

As we become more comfortable in recovery, we begin to remember that there were emotional problems and insecurities before the addiction, though we may not have had a vocabulary for them or a safe place to express them. In the safety of supportive community, we begin to risk sharing early personal and family secrets, some of which were minor, and some of which were terrible secrets that should have been reported to the authorities by a responsible adult. As a child, we may have been too afraid to speak up. Again, this is an element of Authentic Process which will come up again in Stage Two healing.

11. Acknowledging and celebrating Stage One triumph

Healing from an addiction is an *extraordinary* experience. It takes courage, grit, trust, and spirit. Each of us that does so must always remember that our recovery is a badge of honor. In Stage One, many people still feel too shameful to fully appreciate this, yet somehow they know that they have made their most remarkable achievement in recovering. Affirming this is vital to all future growth. It is on the foundation of this affirmation and self-love that one builds the bridge unifying the whole of existence.

When we enter Stage One as recovering individuals, our entire world is changing. Prior to "hitting bottom" or professional intervention (whatever form that may have taken), most of our life was colored by, and hinged on, the satisfaction of a craving. It would have been impossible to perceive life without feeding that core agenda and all the side issues that arose as a result. Stage One marks a time of sweeping change, because a massive psychic shift is needed to overcome the self-delusions so prevalent during the years of addiction.

In the first years of recovery or APT, as we build a non-addictive foundation, we begin to feel more sure-footed, but we also experience more emotional conflict. Some may be plagued by a nagging, free-floating guilt for no apparent reason. Others experience deep sadness or waves of frightening, almost uncontrollable rage. A prolonged grief experience is common.

Many people feel a complete absence of feelings — a condition that has its own set of problems. Often the people who experience this numbing lack of emotions will feel their intellect racing with thoughts of self-flagellation. They condemn their own lack of emotion. During these times, when we are consumed by our feelings (or lack thereof), our consciousness becomes fertile ground for the seeds of Stage Two recovery. This often begins as we start taking risks with our fledgling feelings of trust and begin to share personal and family "secrets" (in therapy or in community settings). This second stage, to be explored in the following chapters, acts as a beacon guiding the person out of despair and depression.

The process of grounding in Stage One must never be hurried. From my experience, each person knows, deep within, when the timing is right to begin Stage Two. The timing will depend on the degree of psychic, physical, family, relationship and financial damage that the addiction has fostered. Individuals will often signal their readiness by beginning therapy or seeking out support groups, such as "adult child" groups, incest groups, groups related to sexual or cultural diversity, etc., that address complex issues.

Celebrating Stage One

Stage One must be cherished and celebrated, because it brings self-realization, transformation and reclamation of spirit. The world ought to stop and shout out in joy at such a profound human occurrence, but all too often, it doesn't. Therefore, it would be beneficial if each of us personally made the effort to grant ourselves recognition for everyday personal triumph. Recovering people tend to want to rush the process, and this desire is understandable. But it is important to recognize that recovering from addictions is very difficult work, and that the very reason for the addiction itself was a lack of recognition and appreciation of one's personhood. Therefore, self-appreciation of Stage One triumph is crucial to growth and fulfillment.

Once we are able to recover from our primary addiction, or have our compulsions in check, we begin to realize how limited other areas of our lives have been. Again, this process should not be rushed. Take as much time as you need in Stage One, for only you know what you need in order to progress on to Stage Two.

My message to my friends in primary addictions recovery is: Pat yourself on the back, run your fingers through your hair, give yourself a hug and tell yourself, "We did well!" ("we" referring both to the adult self and to the forgotten child self). Then, say it again: "We did great!" Keep saying it until you can feel it. You most certainly deserve it, and the self-respect and afterglow generated will help fuel your Stage Two work toward resolution and further empowerment.

Stories Help Us Heal

It is important to tell stories, and also important that these stories be heard. As the Native American teacher Black Elk said, "I am going to tell you the story of my life... and if it were only the story of my life I think I would not tell it." Stories evoke the power of experience. They remind us that unknown forces are at work in each and every one of us, no matter how ordinary we may feel or judge others to be. They remind us that no one gets by with a perfect, unscarred life, and now and then, everyone shines with the divine. Stories inform us of resources we otherwise do not know to look for. They tell us that, however the details differ, we all feel the same emotions. This informs us that we are not alone in our own private soup, that we all belong to the same human family. Stories connect us one to another. They provide pathways and solutions. They give us courage. Cultural anthropologist Joan Halifax writes, "Stories are medicine because they teach us about and prepare us for the experience of change. Through the story, we connect to a more realistic vision of who we really are."

Throughout this book, I will share composite stories of individuals I've known whose healing may serve to inform, inspire, or guide you. But for now, let me start with a bit of my own:

Lost Innocence

Twenty years ago, I confronted my own denial of a primary addiction. I had been on a lonely inner journey for years, blindly committing myself to various relationships, endeavors and therapies in the hope of easing a chronic, mysterious inner ache. Self-help groups gave me enormous support and healing, helping me overcome the addiction to drugs and alcohol so I could manage my day-to-day life. However, this brought only sporadic relief from an intense inner turmoil. I felt as though there was a big hole inside of me, and in that hole was a restless squirrel, one that was almost constantly squirming. Slowly I decided to make friends with this scared and frantic inner companion. Determined to bring my heart and mind to the process, I began the second stage of my recovery journey.

At four years old, after constantly having to endure my parents' violent relationship based on my mother's infidelities, I saw my mother vanish from my life. When she abandoned my father, my two brothers and myself, it was sudden and definitive: no more mother. My father, basically a good, duty-bound man, was filled with bitterness toward his failed marriage, and had little or no patience or capacity for raising three boys. "You better be good! If you are not good, I will put you in a home. Your mother didn't give a damn for you and I don't have time for it all," he would say.

Between the ages of four and eight, I was uprooted eight times. Ever since I can remember, my father's rage and confusion reigned supreme in our little family. He was overwhelmed by the responsibilities of single parenthood. His threats to put me in a home if I misbehaved and the thought of being separated from my brothers and father absolutely terrified me.

We moved from place to place, sometimes together and sometimes apart. My world, never stable to begin with, became physically and emotionally unsafe. There was no place to go with my fears and confusions. Having already had my world so shaken, I dared not do anything that might risk my being abandoned or make my little universe fall further apart. My brothers and father seemed lost in their own coping mechanisms, so I had to be strong and pull myself through this childhood. I did just that.

Because these fears and others inhibited my ability to articulate complex feelings, I was left with a very limited emotional vocabulary. After a while, left without a language to express my feelings, my understanding of my own inner needs and struggles was also impaired. This inability to understand, articulate, and express my emotions permeated my being, leaving me feeling hopeless and vulnerable. I created complex systems of self-protection or defenses by "editing" myself. Instead of telling someone I was lonely, I told anyone who cared to ask that I could take care of myself. In reality, my mother was gone; I was miserable with confusion, fear and loneliness. I deeply suppressed the loneliness and fear and instead presented a "false self" to the outside world. These defenses increasingly became the only way I could reduce my pain and confusion in dealing with reality. To support and hold these defenses in place, I covered them, layer upon layer, with denial and false concepts about myself.

As a teenager, I turned to alcohol and drugs to fuel my defenses and strengthen me (I thought) for my adolescent challenges. In the early days of my addiction, I was drinking beer, liquor and codeine-based cough medicine, and feeling so alone and so different from other people. For many years I denied my terror and lack of security. I had to — there was no place to go with it.

I was age fifteen and feeling folded, spindled and mutilated, constantly struggling with complexities that no one ever seemed to want to talk about. Typical adolescent concerns, as well as deeper emotional issues, confused me. Drinking allowed me to confront the world on what seemed to be its terms and made me feel less hidden and withdrawn. Sixteen years later, when I became sober and reflected on my addictions, I first thought that they were an escape, a cop-out I chose because I was ill-equipped or too weak-willed to live up to societal norms. However, years later, after I reached the second stage of my personal work and recovered more fully, I developed a richer understanding of, and respect for, how the addictions process takes hold.

I now see addiction as a coping mechanism to control the effects of early traumatic stresses, childhood deprivations, cultural prejudices, abuses and ignorance. Addictions and compulsions serve as self-medications to help us deal with, and further suppress, complex issues that lie repressed deep in our psyche. In my case, I was too afraid to express the intense and complex feelings that fermented inside of me. I had good reason to suppress my feelings, since I was raised in an unstable environment. During my adolescent years, when my emotional development began to overrun my carefully constructed defense system, I turned to addictive behavior to help shore up the defenses. Seen in this way, the onset of the addiction was a desperate, *resourceful* attempt to neutralize an internalized, painful dilemma — an infinitely more manageable choice when compared with other options such as mental and physical diseases, psychosis or suicide.

In my subsequent therapy, as my defenses relaxed, the repressed trauma from years of living in a world that did not feel safe surfaced. At the time, it almost overwhelmed me: I experienced the waves of terror and fear of everyday occurrences. Fortunately, by then I had found safe settings and created communities where I could take my fears and confusions. With help, safety and support, I was able to put my life in a new perspective and understand the emotions and energetic triggers that related to my "traumatic recalls." Slowly I processed many of these feelings and have grown out of the unconscious limitations that were caused by my repressed past.

I relate my story — and other composite stories in this book — in such detail so that you can see that the sometimes rangy inclusiveness of the work I describe grew from an organic source. It grew from my life, and from the lives of others I have shared the journey with. These struggles find their truest meaning when they serve to spare others time and pain during the healing process.

3

Stage Two Recovery
The Path of Community-Based Healing

What is Stage Two Recovery

Stage Two of Authentic Process Therapy is a community-based individual process by which we learn to dissolve internal barriers to wholeness and complete recovery not addressed by the Stage One healing process

In this process, we learn to connect with others and with our environment through healing community. At the same time we learn to connect with our true self through unwrapping our pain with the help of a facilitating therapist.

There are many experiences in Stage Two of complete recovery, and they are different for each individual. In this chapter, we will define and examine the major tenets of Stage Two and how they can guide us back to complete recovery of our emotional, spiritual and sexual wholeness.

In the medical and psychiatric models there is still no cure for alcoholism or other addictions. Yet since 1935, with the founding of AA, millions of us have healed from these addictions and other compulsions by turning to a compassionate spiritual community. This approach has taken us a long way. We can now extend this community concept a step further.

This approach combines different aspects of specific idioms. Instead of pursuing one therapeutic approach as far as it will go, APT uses a more expansive strategy. It borrows the most useful current concepts of many different schools of thought and brings them together under one roof to create a possibility of complete recovery.

As individuals, we in recovery have very specific needs, and as a community, we have special interests. Traditional psychiatric approaches focus on the individual, but have their limitations, especially in terms of interpersonal dynamics. Traditional community-based therapy focuses on the recovering community, but is limited in terms of healing the individual on the deep unconscious and spiritual level. The journey to complete recovery, as described in this book, combines community-based therapy, (such as Twelve-Step, rehab center, therapeutic community, and other healing groups), spirituality (such as wisdom from indigenous cultures, Buddhism, and other ancient, open-hearted approaches to understanding our rightful place in the universe) and psychology in a way which optimally addresses the needs and interests of both the group and the individual. As a result, the individual learns to connect with the outside world in a multi-dimensional way.

Psychologically, APT borrows from many mainstream models, such as psychoanalytic, cognitive-behavioral, Freudian, existential, transpersonal, transformational, and experiential psychologies. People in the recovering community often encounter inherent limitations in traditional clinical theories. APT is an expanded view of the recovery process that can direct and nurture us to a more complete recovery. Based on my personal experience, as well as the results I've gathered from research studies with hundreds of individuals and groups over many years, I believe the Staged Recovery process now offers a viable, holistic approach for recovering individuals and groups.

As I stated in the introduction, APT is the "new psychotherapy" generated out of the maturing recovery movement and the sexually diverse community. It is a healing process grounded in building on our inherent strengths and talents, *not* on what is wrong with us. Our life challenges are placed in authentic cultural and historical contexts so that they make sense in a way that they can be appropriately addressed. This psychospiritual approach allows each individual to chart their own healing and plot their course to empowerment, either within the suggested framework or by expanding the framework to suit themselves.

Throughout the years other authors, particularly Ernie Larsen and John Bradshaw, have suggested an expanded model of recovery, and others have articulated the need for a more holistic approach. APT recognizes the need for an expanded approach and offers a living map through the wilderness. I began developing Stage Two of APT in 1984, when I became a professional addictions counselor. At that time I was six years into my own recovery and psychotherapeutic journey. Since then I have been guided and propelled by my own recovery and the plight of the recovering community.

During these years, I have heard enough stories with similar themes, and had enough experiences to formulate a theory, which is validated by my observations. I have come to believe that people benefit most direct-ly from community-based healing. This "community" is defined as two or more people who have shed their defensive "masks of composure" and agree to share wisdom, struggles, joys and sorrows with each other, making each other's condition their own. This is done in structured settings where there is the necessary "psychospiritual component," es-sential for healing.

Stage Two sojourners bring with them their deepest and most con-cealed wounds, fears, and defenses. As a facilitator, I share with them my own experiences, transforming them into a therapeutic mirror to clarify the meaning of such rites of passage so common to the human experience. This is where the deep healing begins.

Individuals in recovery share an unconscious tendency to blame themselves for what, on some other deeper level, they know are cultural faults. We recovering people represent a community. We share a com-mon culture that needs to be understood, respected and honored. When two or more people bring a sharing spirit and an open heart to the reso-lution of a common struggle, a spiritual bond results. This bonding can become the foundation for a safe journey into unconscious regions, to ward a new integration, and the fulfillment of lifelong needs. Each par-ticipant brings with them the intention to begin a process aimed at the fulfilling of complex needs. "Shared intentionality" means that individ-uals join in community with the express intention to heal. This is the beginning of the spiritual dimension in these healing relationships.

At the spiritual core of the healing community is the shared struggle to meet basic, life-long needs. Our internalized traumas usually cause disempowerment and disconnection from others. Recovery, therefore, must be based on our empowerment and the creation of new connec-tions. Recovery can take place only within the context of relationships and community; it cannot occur in isolation. This profound healing is always community centered.

The shared journey is key to Authentic Process and reveals how APT differs from conventional therapy. In conventional therapy, the therapist is more likely to observe and offer a clinical interpretation of the "pa-tient's" condition. In APT, the therapist — who certainly has addictions, as well as clinical and psychological training and experience — will shed the clinical composure for an authentic, interactive, and non-judgmental relationship. APT encourages the therapist to participate actively.

The relationship between the "patient" and the therapist is one example of how APT reapproaches — and redefines traditional therapies. In many cases, APT offers a new vocabulary and a new perspective on a traditional situation.

Under the Authentic Process approach, the "therapist-patient" relationship is redefined as the "practitioner-client" relationship. The distinction is more than mere semantics. The new vocabulary creates a co-creative, non-judgmental situation, and it empowers the client to make choices about the relationship rather than remain a passive participant. In many cases, APT redefines established approaches. In some cases the model merely shifts or reframes traditional ideas about psychotherapeutic approaches. In other cases APT relies on an entirely new vocabulary to describe the psychotherapeutic healing process.

In APT, the relationship between the practitioner and client maintains a consistent tone of helping, empowerment, clarity and freedom. Many traditional clinical settings foster unconscious transference, the substitution of the therapist for the object of repressed emotions and impulses, such as a parent or authority figure from childhood. The therapist often has been taught to use and manipulate the transference, usually with the best of intentions. Recovering people keep discovering that this type of relationship makes them feel manipulated, often clouding their continued growth with confusing power dynamics. In APT, therapists are encouraged to appropriately share their own experiences and life challenges with clients to establish a role-model relationship. This sharing by the therapist is done sparingly, and only when it skillfully eases the client's process, either by creating a natural and real relationship, reducing shame, or creating a larger framework in which to process feelings and ideas.

Psychoanalysis demands that the therapist submerge the "self" in order to create a "clinical" setting. Unfortunately, for recovering people, this clinical setting eliminates the spiritual nurturing that leads to healing. Furthermore, the therapist's removal of the "self" can create a painful re-enactment of dysfunctional, childhood deprivation. While this might be a treatment goal in psychoanalysis, it can be counterproductive for people in addictions recovery. Recovering people want empathic understanding from the therapist. When this is withheld, old wounds are triggered. This can be confounding when the client has limited understanding of complex feelings.

The Evolution of Stage Two

When I began to formulate ideas for a two-stage model of a complete recovery, I realized that new approaches would be needed. Fortunately, I did not have to look far. These "new" approaches have been evolving naturally and organically since 1935 out of conventional community healing groups such as Alcoholics Anonymous, and the many groups it inspired. In defining the second stage of the processes toward complete recovery, I needed an approach that would respond to the unique experience and needs of those already in recovery. It needed to respect-fully build on the profound Stage One healing experience.

As an addicted person emerges out of Stage One, they may realize that considerable emotional damage led to their addictive/compulsive behavior. At this juncture, a recovering person may find themselves "acting out" in other self-destructive ways. Involvement with abusive or emotionally unavailable people, financially disastrous behavior, eating disorders, sexual compulsivity and other obsessive behaviors are a few examples. This can also be a time when low self-esteem can become pronounced, leading to isolation, depression and hyper-vigilance. Deep, enduring friendships or a loving, sexually fulfilling relationship with a partner may seem impossible. It is at this point that one can see and experience the importance of engaging in Stage Two healing.

Saying "Yes" to Stage Two Recovery

These illuminating words from Eva Pierrakos' *The Pathwork of Self-Transformation* suggest the awareness and willingness that people may find useful in their evolution into Stage Two:

Through the gateway of feeling your weakness
  lies your strength.
Through the gateway of feeling your pain
  lies your pleasure and joy.
Through the gateway of feeling your fear
  lies your security and safety.
Through the gateway of feeling your loneliness
  lies your capacity to have fulfillment, love and companionship.
Through the gateway of feeling your hopelessness
  lies true and justified hope.
Through the gateway of accepting the lacks in your childhood
  lies your fulfillment now.

We enter Stage Two only when the timing is right for us, or if there is no other alternative available to deal with a current event or set of circumstances. Sometimes situations beyond our control compel us to feel and face complex emotional issues. A loved one leaves or dies, leaving us with an unresolved feeling of loss. A dating experience could bring to the surface a conflict between spiritual belief and sexual needs. In such cases, Stage Two offers a living map for beneficial process and resolution.

In order to reach a complete recovery, it's very important to complete Stage One before moving onto Stage Two. Some people in the Twelve-Step communities discount Stage Two, and may encourage others to limit their growth to Stage One. However well-intended these people may be, they are not considering the potential empowerment Stage Two can bring. When we in recovery are dissuaded from exploring Stage Two issues, we are being asked to promote the secrecy and repression all over again.

In saying "yes" to Stage Two, we take a bigger bite out of the commitment apple; we further commit to our "decision to recover." We are also making a choice to put a stop to hiding and secrecy (both conscious and unconscious — after all, Stage Two is primarily about examining the content in our unconscious). In a healing community, we can pierce the membrane of shame that fuels the secrecy. We can begin to experience a shame-free presentation of self. Once we are no longer ashamed of ourselves, we can present ourselves to the world without feeling like we must make excuses for who we are. We can learn to protect our inner selves and take full responsibility for our outer selves.

In many Twelve-Step programs such as AA, recovering people are taught that "feelings aren't facts." Although the slogan is useful during Stage One, by the time you are ready to explore Stage Two, the slogan can work against you. Feelings become important beacons. This awareness leads us into Stage Two and guides us through the darkness and into the holistic state of complete recovery.

What Do We Want From Our Recovery?

The first step toward regaining the sense of wholeness and happiness we seek is to name our most important desires. What do we really want from life other than to be able to survive in a dependency-free state from day to day? Most people will name several without hesitation.

Before I tell you what the eight most common aspirations and desires are for those well into Stage Two of recovery, why not put on paper your own eight foremost aspirations for this work. This way you can see how your current needs might fit in the "constellation of desires" as described by APT clients who were interviewed about what they hoped for from their recovery. Remember, there are no right or wrong answers, only insights.

Based on these interviews, I have found that there are many things that most people in recovery aspire to. In the next section we will look closely at the eight most common of these, but there are others as well that we should be aware of. When we recovering people present ourselves for help, we want tangible and specific results from our personal healing (whether that be individual or group therapy, workshops and/ or community processes). We want to establish more meaningful connections with others. We want to resolve our difficult relationship dynamic with authority figures. Many of us want a consistent, loving sexual relationship, and we want to have the skills to be able to sustain it. We want to feel more confident, so that when we express our feelings, intentions, desires or needs, we can do so securely and with a sense of entitlement. We want to know our purpose or mission in life so we can feel there is meaning to our existence. We want the ability to separate this purpose or mission from obsessive drives. We also want help in sorting out and identifying our own complex and appropriate feelings. Essentially, we want to realize who we are and clarify where we might be going and with whom we might be traveling. This is a very intuitive, sacred, and personal journey.

Clients I have worked with often have difficulty articulating their desires, but over the course of time, a whole constellation of desires will most certainly surface. It would be wise for therapists and educators to be aware of these needs from the very first therapy encounter. Once the professional community is aware of these needs, we can then better educate our clients about them (a great deal of Authentic Process includes psycho-education), and share what their intentions are (shared intention is also a key part of Authentic Process) and the therapeutic processes will become more fluid and purposeful.

We recovering people are often impatient in our attempts to attain our desires. Our quest for gratification, juxtaposed with an inability to clearly define inner needs and feelings, often results in self-flagellation. We have cause to be impatient, since we have often lacked emotional fulfillment for a very long time. Simultaneously, we intuitively knew something was missing — something that would make us feel whole. Recovery is the yearning for wholeness and the gradual fulfillment of this profound human experience.

Some who have been in recovery for many years feel disheartened that they were not informed about Stage Two recovery earlier. At one of the workshops that I facilitated last year, a construction worker with nineteen years of recovery approached me and cried, saying, "Why didn't you tell us this sooner? I could have done this work and not beaten myself up all these years."

I explained to him that the Stage Two concept is a very recent phenomenon. His face revealed a poignant, complex mixture of grief and relief. I understood and could identify with his feelings. I have come to know this expression well. I have now seen it on so many faces of individuals in long-term recovery, and I truly empathize with the complexity of their feelings. Those willing to engage in this second tier of the recovery process have an opportunity to move into experiences of deep personal fulfillment and self-understanding. This is a very exciting and rewarding journey.

The Constellation of Desires

Over the years, in workshops and in my private practice, my clients have struggled to articulate what it is that they truly want from the recovery process, other than the simple freedom from addiction and compulsion. I identified eight common desires for fulfillment that surface time and time again. The authentic yearnings which actually define the second stage of recovery can be linked to eight categories, which I have named "The Constellation of Desires."

If you are like most people, upon entering Stage Two, you will not yet have full clarity as to what your needs are, but over time, you will most likely have:

1. A desire for help in accepting, identifying and expressing complex feelings.
2. A desire to connect in more meaningful ways with others, and to be part of a community.
3. A desire to heal the internalized sexual-spiritual split.
4. A desire to grasp our role in power dynamics, thereby resolving our difficulty with authority figures and intimates.
5. A desire to sustain consistent, loving relationships, and experience real intimacy on all levels.
6. A desire to achieve a "shame-free presentation of self."
7. A desire to discover our individual "life purpose."
8. A yearning to "know who we are" in a real and spiritual sense.

These core issues may not be initially evident in everyone. We may cloak them in shame because we were unable to have our needs met in the first place. We may deny that we have needs at all or we may have difficulty articulating them.

Let's take a closer look at these desires and what is behind them.

1. A desire for help in accepting, identifying and expressing complex feelings. Many traumatic situations and subsequent reactions are not black and white but quite vague and complex in nature. There's often good news with the bad. We have a tendency to be overwhelmed by the mixed feelings they might cause. One of the most important things any therapy can do is provide help in sorting it all out. Once the situation is sorted, we can express our emotions more fully. We can express gratitude and joy for the desirable news and sorrow, grief, or even rage at the undesirable news. Authentic Process gives us an opportunity and a structure within which to do this.

2. A desire to connect in more meaningful ways with others, and to be part of a community. A growing number of people realize the lack of community in their lives and seek to either tap into existing ones or build a community of their own. This is yet another area where the recovery community is at the forefront of a major social trend. The healing community concept is therefore central to APT. We must join or create new additional communities as we grow and follow the intuition of our inner healer, the compass part of us that knows what needs to be healed next, or that *something* needs to be healed.

3. A desire to heal the internalized sexual-spiritual split. Many who enter therapy have no idea that they have such a schism within themselves, or that it is an issue, but a few appropriate questions often brings them to the surface. It is the landmark of the fundamental stations described in Chapter Six.

4. A desire to grasp our role in power dynamics, thereby resolving our difficulty with authority figures and intimates. A large number of people find themselves expressing a very painful frustration or difficulty with authority figures, or in handling authority. Similar dynamics occur in intimate relationships once bonding takes place. Stage Two healing disengages these power dynamics, enabling free expression in all relationships.

5. A desire to sustain consistent, loving relationships, and experience real intimacy on all levels. Authentic process and the healing of shame through community process work and healing the sexual-spiritual split play a significant part in fulfilling this desire.

6. A desire to achieve a "shame-free presentation of self." This is one of the Fruits of the Tree, and arises out of knowing who we are and that we belong here and have a right to exist. Again, Authentic Process, community healing, self-esteem work and healing the sexual-spiritual split play a part in fulfilling this desire.

7. A desire to discover our individual "life purpose." Also a Fruit of the Tree, this arises out of discovering our sense-of-self spirituality. Along with this comes the desire to achieve our own greatness, to contribute meaningfully to society, to give back to those we love, to help establish a better future, and to walk with strength and dignity.

8. A yearning to "know who we are" in a real and spiritual sense. This is the desire for returning to the holistic state of being "coworkers with the universe," to become part of the teeming whole of creation in this moment. This in a sense is the yearning which propels us through to complete recovery.

Though these needs might be blurred in early Stage Two, they are consistent and will emerge again and again. The expression of such needs, and the shared commitment to fulfilling them, leads to an energetic alliance. The practitioner, client and/or community agree upon the common goals of the healing. This new alliance helps us present issues in a more workable way while simultaneously bringing the spiritual power of shared intention and belief to the core issues. This is similar to the way primary addictions are healed.

How do you fulfill these desires? By going back to the barriers and blindspots, and dissolving them through Staged Two recovery, so that gradually a clearer vision and experience emerges. Then these needs begin to be met naturally as time passes.

Jason's Story

Jason is a single, 32-year-old, Irish-Catholic who had been in Cocaine Anonymous recovery for two years. Though he had adapted fairly well to his self-help group and remained abstinent from addictive substances, he entered Authentic Process Therapy in depression and with serious financial difficulties. He was an attorney at a medium-sized firm. He reported that he "hated" his job and his profession. Additionally, he shared with me that his cocaine use was directly related to his sexual activity, which became almost non-existent in recovery, and that he had never had a significant, intimate relationship in his life.

In our third session, Jason asked the question that signaled an opportunity for education, "What is wrong with me?" I answered his question, explaining that my response was drawn from personal experience and observations with recovering people. In attempting to respond and address his dilemma, I reminded myself to remain conscious of the required framework. Our dialogue follows.

Jason: What's wrong with me? I hate my work, I am underachieving and I don't know what I want to do. Other people seem to know what they want. I don't think I ever really wanted to be a lawyer. I am smart, reasonably attractive, and personable. Why am I so afraid? Why don't I know what I want? What is wrong with me?

M.P.: Many recovering people have lost touch with their deepest sense of "self." This, among other things, is the part that gives us a sense of wonder and interest. When our wonder and interest are ignited, we anticipate exploring with energy and enthusiasm.

Jason (after intensely listening in a trance-like state): What do you mean, I have no self? I hear what you are saying, and it rings true for me, but I don't understand it.

M.P.: Let me try to explain. As you probably have already figured out, drugs served as an escape for you; an escape from having to deal with internal feelings, conflicts and perhaps inadequacies. Additionally, your cocaine served as a defense. Not only did it defend you from your own inner turmoil, but more importantly, it prevented others from seeing these hidden conflicts as well. People often report in their therapy that they are only somewhat aware of this escape mechanism at first. Little by little they realize what it was doing to them and that it was all concealed under a membrane of shame; a shame which perhaps existed because they, or you, felt inadequate to resolve the conflicting feelings and double binds.

Jason: What you are saying seems to make sense. In a strange way, I like hearing it. I'm just not sure that I'm getting it all.

M.P.: You don't have to. With the level of intention for healing and resolution that you are bringing to this therapy, my words will probably resonate in deeper levels of your consciousness. This is good, as they will be able to permeate your psyche, eventually resurfacing in a way that may be even more meaningful for you.

Jason: Okay, if what you are saying is true, how do I find this deeper sense of self?

M.P.: You have already begun the process. Your recovery from drug addiction was the beginning. You've removed the first layer of defense. That took a lot of courage, yet you persevered, accepted help, and you have gained self-respect because of it. The dissolving of, or developing management over, other debilitating defenses will also take courage, help and commitment. Of course, I think you intuitively knew that. My guess is that you have come to therapy for this purpose. To me, it means that you are ready to do the next stage of this work, and I will gladly bring whatever experience and knowledge that I have to help you.

Jason: What is it that I need to do? How will I know?

M.P.: Before you leave today, I will give you a graphic illustration of a model for working through Stage Two of your recovery. You can take it home with you, think about it, and we can discuss any questions you may have at your next session.

Jason: Okay, I'd like that.

M.P.: In preparing for the model, I want to take a few minutes to discuss that membrane of shame I referred to earlier. Does that resonate with you at all? When you're around others, or even with yourself, do you feel like something amorphous is holding you back?

Jason: Well, I certainly feel held back in all areas of my life, but I'm not sure if that's shame. I don't even know what I should be shameful about. Sometimes I feel embarrassed for no reason, just for being me.

M.P.: Shame is an interesting emotion. When it is internalized and masked in childhood and adolescence, it sort of takes on a life of its own. From that point on it surfaces like a wall or barrier. On an unconscious level, it makes you feel that self-exposure is dangerous and it sends up powerful signals, sometimes feeling like brick walls, to hold you back. On an adult, conscious level you may want to move forward and engage yourself, while this unconscious force keeps you locked in conflict. That is the way shame tends to manifest in recovering people. After allowing shame to surface, and then non-judgmentally accepting it, a natural dispersement takes place, like clouds dispersing in the wind. It no longer has a reason to be; repression and judgment can no longer hold the shame in place, and so the energy disintegrates and blows to the four directions. With the acknowledgment and recognition of this shame, more options and deeper self-understanding become available.

Jason: Well, I certainly have the barriers, the walls, especially with sex. What do I do with these walls, or shame, and how can I get beyond it all?

M.P.: You only need to become aware of the barriers and shame. As you study the tree diagram I am giving you, particularly Stage Two, be aware that you may have barriers that will prevent you from engaging in it. These barriers may cause you to resist the entire stage or aspects of it. I suggest that you study it in a relaxed state and with an open mind. While you read, note if any thoughts or feelings pop through "cracks" in the metaphorical wall. As you relax and open your mind, long-forgotten memories may be revealed to you. Also, watch your dreams if you have them; often they are insightful. This will all be very helpful to your process.

Jason: One last question. If I do have internalized shame, and if it's in the walls and conflicts, will I know what I am shameful about and will I be able to free myself of it?

M.P.: There are a few things I feel comfortable assuring you of: If you bring the same determination and will to live to this work as you brought to your primary addiction recovery, you will resolve these painful and frustrating barriers. By the time the process nears completion, you will have not only identified the varied aspects of your shame, but you will have transformed them into substantive, important parts of your personal history. You will have created a stronger, more integrated foundation and you will feel more empowered and free. With this new integration emerges the useful sense of self we spoke about earlier.

Jason came to his next session with a few insights and questions. Gradually he went on to resolve his conflicts, cultural pain, and shame-based sexuality issues. He discovered how his shame fueled a repetition compulsion that kept him blindly in a work and debt situation that re-created energetic feeling dynamics from his childhood and family-of-origin double-binds. These are the opposing forces within us: on the one hand we pay homage to old family values that we don't subscribe to and on the other hand, we recognize our own real desires based on our current adult experience. There can be quite a deep pull to each of these conflicting directions.

4

The Four Powers
Dissolving Barriers
to Complete Recovery

The process of dissolving the barriers to complete recovery usually requires support from a community as well as from a therapist. It is important to choose the right support, either in a structured setting or in your daily life. These barriers will not necessarily resolve themselves in any particular order, but in relationship to each other. It is important to remember the vision of holism (as described in Chapter One), as patterns of self-defeating behavior slowly start to emerge. As we begin to experience the Twelve Stations of Stage Two Recovery as described later, these barriers will emerge more clearly and will dissolve in Authentic Process and through individual soul-searching.

In APT we discern four "powers" that assist us in the process of dissolving the barriers to complete recovery. They are:

1. The Power of Community-Based Healing
2. The Power of Shared Intentionality
3. The Power of Shared Belief
4. The Power of Authentic Process

1. The Power of Community-Based Healing

There is an unexplainable magic that occurs when people join together with a shared intention to heal. When they let down their masks of composure and nonjudgmentally share struggles, joys and sorrows, in a ritualized format, an indescribable healing takes place.

I have discovered that in dealing with emotional and psychological limitations, the true healing takes place in community. We have seen this within the powerful Twelve-Step movement, as well as with workshops and retreats that incorporate experiential processes to help people turn inward. In Stage Two Recovery, community is considered to be two or more people with common struggles who are willing to shed their masks of composure in a structured setting. In an Authentic Process community we intentionally bring the complexity of such challenges out in the open. In such safe places, framed with psychological and cultural education provided by a skilled facilitator, individuals resolve their own unconscious barriers to emotional intimacy.

Different types of community settings for Stage Two Recovery that are currently available: one-on-one individual process with a practitioner and client; group sessions with several recovering people and a practitioner; and special in-depth, focused community workshops. Typically, group or individual sessions are on-going, whereas the focused workshops are time-limited and can be organized on a weekly basis, as a weekend retreat or as a series of day-long Saturday sessions. Many therapists encourage clients to participate in community healing as an adjunct to individual therapy. Other therapists will also create a community milieu within the individual therapy setting.

The following is a description of "community" as defined by M. Scott Peck in his book, *A Different Drum*:

> Community is a group of individuals who have learned how to communicate honestly with each other, whose relationships go deeper than their masks of composure, and who have developed some significant commitment to rejoice together, mourn together, and to delight in each other, make others' conditions our own.

The author goes on to explain that when we meet in clearly defined community, "something more" takes place, something quite mystical. There are no words to explain these experiences. According to Dr. Peck,

> Community, like a gem, is multi-faceted, each facet a mere aspect of a whole that defies description... The gem of community is so exquisitely beautiful it may seem unreal to you, like a dream you once had when you were a child, so beautiful it may seem unattainable.

Within the context of APT, as we said before, we define "community" as being two or more people. It becomes a *healing* community when we add the focus of committing ourselves to a common purpose, such as the constellation of desires, or any other common healing nucleus.

2. The Power of Shared Intentionality

When two or more people consciously bring their intention to healing in a specific, often structured way, this is shared intentionality. This is very effective in bringing the therapist and client into alignment with each other, creating a conscious bonding between them. It creates a solution orientation rather than a problem orientation.

The method that provides the most efficient access to our emotional center is the delicate (or compassionate) intention to do so. Barry Walker, a therapist and long-time educator in unconscious energy defense patterns, believes that "intention" is the fueling energy that coalesces our personal and community growth. This journey to complete recovery is driven by the individual's intention to experience holism and the shame-free presentation of self. In ATP we define ten specific intentions that can be shared in the community healing process. They are:

1. To create and commit to a "healing community"
2. To identify and acknowledge needs
3. To pierce through personal isolation
4. To acknowledge resistance
5. To disarm primary defenses in the community setting
6. To create group rituals and projects
7. To "mirror" with peers
8. To identify and acknowledge transference
9. To learn about "reality checks" and "checking in"
10. To experiment with "community" support and participation outside the group setting

1. To create and commit to a "healing community." In Stage Two, recovering people have an opportunity to reframe their histories. Their previous experiences of family and culture take on new meaning after they have a chance to explore these issues in structured community. Many people believe (consciously and unconsciously) that they are forever limited in their "needs fulfillment" because they feel hopelessly conjoined to the limitations of their "culture-of-origin" and "family-of-origin." They may believe that they must live up to the expectations — or remain within the limitations — established by their family or culture. By reframing this belief, in community, we can gradually emerge out of our psychic prisons to consciously explore fulfilling relationships. Commitment to the community comes first; passion, and healing will follow.

2. To identify and acknowledge needs. Most recovering individuals have extreme difficulty expressing personal and emotional needs in a straightforward manner. In the workshop setting they are supported in a structured format to begin risking this fragile exposure — whether they need to be acknowledged for a work promotion or a personal breakthrough, to share a joy or a painful conflict, or to ask for peer feedback on an issue involving recovery or relationships. While many participants are extremely reluctant to share, the group helps them work through their resistance by providing a structure, an alternative, a core experience and a new frame of reference. Group members who have rigid components to their defense structures may have a heightened resistance to the experience of "need exposure." As with all defenses, this must be respected. As the trust level in the group grows, and appropriate compassion and understanding are brought to these defenses, they will gradually relax.

3. To pierce through personal isolation. By coming to community and sharing in structured and unstructured ways, we can begin to humbly break down our deep isolation through the experience of deeper connectedness with others. These experiential moments provide more than hope for establishing deeper emotionally-connected relationships. They actually give us the bodily feeling of this experience, so that the body and psyche can organically grow in this healthier, wholer direction. When we connect in this deeper way with others, we are also doing so with ourselves and the universe.

4. To acknowledge resistance. There should be enough psycho-education in and around the community experience to make individuals highly aware of their defenses and resistance. In order for resistances and defenses to relax, it is vital that a person respectfully acknowledge that they exist. The community becomes intuitively skilled in emphatically supporting one another through resistance, while exhibiting heartfelt identification and compassion.

5. To disarm primary defenses in the community setting. Primary defenses are the ways we learned to stay safe in childhood. In adulthood they often become involuntary barriers to getting our most basic needs fulfilled. Primary defenses become glaringly apparent for many during their first group experiences. While participation alone is usually enough to bring forth defenses, the community can accelerate the process. As people's defenses are gracefully (or awkwardly) exposed, they and the group begin to understand how people unconsciously distance themselves from others. While the initial exposure and recognition of our defenses can be jarring and disarming, this experience quickly transforms into more adaptive, integrated and useful behavior. Awareness and the intention to heal create an organic reorganization of defense reflexes that is more appropriate to current needs and desires.

6. To create group rituals and projects. Rituals help relax resistances and create the opportunity to accept human awkwardness as relationships deepen and people work through their unconscious personal barriers. They are sometimes in the form of community structure or exercises, perhaps in the way we begin a community meeting and the way we close, or the way that sharing is conducted. Perhaps a lit candle or dimmed lights helps create the moment. We can be very co-creative in the use of rituals once we all understand that they are intended to help us relax involuntary defense reflexes so that we can be more authentic with our own experience. Structure and respectful ritual are powerful ways to safely relax our defenses so that we can see what is under them, what they are made of, and what they may be depriving us of.

7. To "mirror" with peers. "Mirroring" refers to the personal identification that comes from witnessing others struggle through fears, defenses and delight in liberation and creativity. As group participants begin to reframe their self-image, other members can identify with them. Once we witness the strong survival skills in a co-member, we begin perceiving ourselves as survivors. Once we experience courage, we become more courageous. Once we witness someone else's grief, we can find our own. This conscious mirroring becomes transforming and appears to be the best grounding mythology available in our fast-changing times. While it is hard to describe in intellectual terms, mirroring is an extraordinarily powerful tool.

8. To identify and acknowledge transference. Again, transference is substitution of another person (such as the therapist or partner) for the object of the repressed impulses. Through psychological and cultural education, the group is taught about the varied manifestations of transference in relationships and in community dynamics. Participants are encouraged, in the group, to embark on a process of identifying past instances of transference onto the facilitator, onto individual members, or onto the group as a whole. Often by understanding and acknowledging this transference, whether it be distancing or seductive, they are able to move beyond it and form more meaningful relationships based on authenticity, directness and honesty. This facet of group participation is instrumental in resolving personality conflicts within the group and with authority figures.

9. To learn about "reality checks" and "checking in." Because the recovering person is consciously and unconsciously laden with transference, paranoia, denial, and self-delusion, it is important to develop new skills to realistically anchor experience. Reality checks are used in the community to help us explore perceptions about ourselves and our world, turning to other members for feedback. The feedback is important in two ways. When a participant's feelings are hurt because of another's remarks, checking in allows them to share the impact of the remarks. They can also use the feedback to help interpret the remarks. Checking in with others on their experience helps participants learn communication skills, resolve conflicts, expose sensitive areas and experience a deeper, shared sense of reality.

10. To experiment with community support and participation outside the group setting. The Authentic Process Therapy community supports and encourages members to engage with each other outside of the group setting. In the first meetings, this often causes some confusion in terms of members' fears and expectations. Experience has shown that this outside participation comes very slowly for many and is met with personal barriers and considerable resistance. It is difficult to bring the level of intimacy and honesty shared in the safety of the structured community setting to the outside world without awkward defenses surfacing.

Once our defenses surface and are respectfully acknowledged; however, there tends naturally to be more experimentation with outside participation. Out of these encounters can grow mature, respectful relationships that benefit individuals and the community.

The desire to connect with others outside the community may not in fact be possible for many of us. This is because defenses that can relax in the safety of structured community are not yet ready to do so outside. Structured community is a non-ordinary environment. Transferring this ability to the ordinary outside world can take time. The body must take its own time to trust when and where it is safe to do so. *It is important that one does not invalidate their community healing because they cannot yet bring it to the everyday world.* For some, this happens slowly and organically in the everyday ebb and flow of their lives. Trust and belief will make it so. While outside participation is supported, it is not necessary. We come to community as a personal, self-healing experience.

3. The Power of Shared Belief

Belief creates experience: experience shapes belief — it's an equal partnership between you and the rest of the world. Bond with others who share your heartfelt beliefs and those beliefs will affect your experience to a much greater degree, and this will alter your belief forever after. On the other hand, if you believe you are a victim and powerless, you are right — just because you believe it! Experience will prove it. Healing of any kind requires some belief in the methods used, and this is especially crucial in psychological healing when we become aware that our environment always reflects our deep beliefs back to us.

I had the good fortune of learning from and reading all the works of Gerald Epstein, M.D., an authority on mind medicine, or spiritual medicine. They are early healing traditions that can be traced back to ancient Egypt that are presently being carried forward by Epstein's teacher, Colette Aboulker-Muscat in Israel. As Epstein said in his book *Healing Into Immortality*, "The New Age is reaching out to touch the 'Old Age' — the living tradition of the ancient spiritual doctrines..."

In mind medicine we learn of an invisible reality that is synonymous with what we sometimes call a spiritual reality. According to Epstein, "It lies behind our everyday sensory reality, the visible, objective, physical reality. You discover and experience invisible reality by turning your senses inward, when you use your imagination and its functional process of mental imagery... mind medicine... moves us in the direction of spirit, of the invisible reality. It is a medicine of truth and love... [where we] experience vertical reality... a timeless realm, the experience of the eternal moment or instant."

The concept that *belief creates experience* is critical to spiritual medicine. In dealing with a vertical reality we allow our inner most needs and desires to create actions by first creating images. As I share below, we all have some experience of this if we look at our history. As Epstein says, "The invisible gives rise to the visible, the inner creates the outer, and thoughts create action by means of images... The fact that our beliefs create our experience means that the experiential world is the effect of our beliefs rather than the cause. And because we are the creators of our beliefs and, thereby, of the experiences that flow from them, we are the active source of experiences and not the passive recipients of them... Our power to control our own creations can shape a new course in life for each of us."

The empowerment that comes with acknowledging that *belief creates experience* is in the ability to consciously apply this new power. To do so in a healing community context, where the beliefs are consciously agreed upon with shared intention, amplifies the true magic and mystery of creation. However, this could happen anywhere, at a church, a sports event, a hospital, or at a town meeting. We see, feel, sense, and experience this truth in the eternal moment of its happening. It is a powerful truth.

An example of this power of shared belief occurred when I first consciously faced my drug and alcohol addiction. At the time, I did not believe I could live without these substances. They had been my constant companions and refuge for 18 years. When I first went to a Twelve-Step meeting at 32 years old, I met people who were sharing a belief. They held in common the belief that one could live and be happy without alcohol and drugs. Although I first resisted entering their *circle of energy* centered in this belief, I was impressed by the group's demonstration of it and their loving willingness to share it. I came around and gradually began to internalize the idea that I too could remain sober. That belief, and watching others demonstrating it, afforded me the gift of living and growing for more than twenty years without an addiction to drugs and alcohol. This is something I could not have conceived of prior to my experience of seeing other recovering people accomplish it. For me, this was and still is a miracle.

Miracles for me have become everyday occurrences. I watch people, and sometimes myself, change old patterns in the blink of an eye. This is dramatically true in Authentic Process Therapy healing community. By believing one can achieve a state of "enlightenment" and find one's rightful place in the universe, and seeing others make spiritual breakthroughs within the healing community, they too find they can experience it. Just imagine for a moment: We expand the healing *power of shared belief* used by the Twelve-Step programs, we incorporate grounded psychospiritual techniques for healing unconscious drawbacks — then we add to this a shared constellation of desires. How could we possibly fail?

Whenever I facilitate a community healing experience, I share my intentions for our coming together at our first meeting. For example, if I am leading a workshop on "healing the sexual-spiritual split," I will make it clear that *this* is what we are here to do. I lead discussions with the group until we get a sense that we are all aligned, that this healing is what they want, and that they believe that it can occur. This *belief* is fundamental to the healing process. For those who are afraid to believe, for fear of disappointment, the desire for belief is usually enough to allow healing to occur.

Before long, we are enraptured in a self-organizing, co-created process where we are learning from and healing each other with extraordinary compassion, love, and understanding. Authentically facing common challenges together bonds us in a unique experience of triumphant love. Healing and spiritual awakening occur out of our belief.

4. The Power of Authentic Process

At the heart of Authentic Process Therapy is "Authentic Process," a therapeutic approach which gives a new twist to what we generally call psychotherapy. To do Stage Two recovery work we will need to reconstruct the terms for what we are doing. We will need to shift the energetic relationship between the helper and the one being helped and how it is perceived.

The word "therapy," in our culture, has come to signify "pathology." If you believe that something is wrong with you, you go to the therapist to get "fixed" or to adjust yourself to the perceived "normal" society. Both the therapist and the patient culturally subscribe to these dynamic roles. In this dynamic, and in traditional psychotherapy, there is a "removal of self" on the part of the therapist. In Authentic Process the therapist, or facilitator, coaches individuals and groups to bring their own life experiences to the Stage Two structure for healing. The facilitator remains authentic in this process and shares experiences, hence becoming a role model in authentic processing.

This will prepare us to integrate our complex natures into society, thereby transforming society, rather than shaping ourselves to it. Because of the dynamic shift in the therapist-client relationship in Authentic Process, all processes become community-driven rather than clinically, or pathologically driven. The shared intention to heal fuels the process rather than a desire to be fixed or to fit in. Speaking from the heart within a circle of friends is so necessary and so rare in conventional society, that people all over the world are creating their own circles for authentic process, or "wisdom circles" as reported by Charles Garfield, Cindy Spring, and Sedona Cahil in their book *Wisdom Circles*.

"Being real" is the keynote of Authentic Process. The desire to be authentic — to express true inner feelings rather than to present a false front — is an absolute minimum requirement for participation. When we express our "real" selves, we allow our true inner "authentic" feelings to surface, and we present them as-is, unedited, and without judgement. Certain African tribal ceremonies refer to this as "speaking from the pit of the belly." While it seems easy enough, it means more than merely speaking what is on your mind, because "what is on your mind" usually refers to surface issues that have been filtered through society's value system. "Authentic Process" reaches down, past the surface into the deep regions of our consciousness, to summon feelings that have long been suppressed. This is the goal of Authentic Process.

Community participation in an open, authentic atmosphere of sharing exposes us to experiences which can trigger inner conflicts and defenses that might be overlooked in a traditional individual therapy setting. This means we feel and connect spontaneously to our experience, in an almost zen-like manner, unexpectedly, rather than merely rehashing old thoughts and chatter about safe, filtered, edited memories of old experiences. For this reason, I encourage participation in groups of this nature for most recovering people. Recovering people who come to the community with an intention to work through sensitive dynamics will learn that power, wisdom and other rewards come from the challenge to be authentic in speech and action. This power will ripple out from the group and begin to influence other aspects of our life. Once we begin to disarm our defense reflexes in the group, we will find a greater variety of choices begin to present themselves in our daily lives.

Authentic Process is an experiential therapy that affects both the practitioner and the client. Both are experiencing anew and learning in the very moment of the therapeutic experience. It is more about feelings and sensations in the body than about thoughts in our head, though both are important. The experiential, here and now nature of these encounters often help people reconnect with their feelings and their histories. For many who feel cut off from feelings and histories, Authentic Process workshops are often an emotional jump start. These community healing events use a variety of appropriately designed exercises from many experiential therapy techniques. The process, by its very nature, weaves in and enfolds all that authentically occurs into the experience. Like jazz, there is structure; but within that framework, participants are encouraged to create their own *music* of magic, messiness, and bliss. They improvise!

The following excerpts from workshop evaluations and letters received weeks and months later from delighted participants, are representative of people's experiences of doing Authentic Process community healing:

- "I discovered feelings that I didn't know I had. I have a new world to explore."
- "I feel more comfortable in my body."
- "The room was so safe, I could never have done this on my own."
- "It has propelled my recovery into a higher plane in a very short time."
- "I feel like my heart has been opened, what a relief!"
- "This workshop was a tremendously powerful and emotional occurrence. I felt in touch with all aspects of my life for the first time."
- "I feel that what we experienced should be packaged and made available to all recovering people."
- "It's like a high. I don't feel ashamed of myself and I feel spiritually connected to the rest of humanity."

One therapist in recovery who participated in a weekend workshop in Minnesota wrote, "I feel changed, and I feel privileged for the opportunity to engage in that process with such exceptional people." This colleague has since been trained in Authentic Process Therapy and has become a workshop facilitator.

Choosing A Practitioner For Deeper Authentic Process

Since recovery takes place in a relationship between two or more people, it's extremely important to choose your practitioner and/or group settings with care. It's especially important to choose a psychotherapist who has a humanistic approach. Some earnest self-disclosure on the part of the practitioner (at appropriate times) can go a long way in fostering a supportive environment. It is essential to anchor the client-practitioner relationship in a more heart-to-heart and person-to-person orientation. An effective Stage Two practitioner administers grace. The practitioner must be generous of spirit, helpful, protective and sanctifying. These qualities will help foster a trust that leads to a safe healing environment.

As a practitioner, when I share experiences with my client, my intention is always centered in the client's growth and well-being. For example, if a client shares with me that he or she has uncovered a sexual-spiritual split in the psyche, and is saddened, frustrated and hopeless, I might respond by telling that person, "I understand. I remember when I first uncovered my own." I might also share a healing or humorous vignette from my own related journey. This is what Authentic Process for two looks like in community healing.

Thus, a here-and-now relationship is created in community. We discover our uniqueness in relationship with each other. The human-to-human encounter, the presence of community spirit, and the authenticity of the here-and-now are crucial to healing. By continuing to come back to the here-and-now of the personal experience, we anchor ourselves in its emotional center. This is where the healing takes place.

We as practitioners must be on our own journey of personal recovery from whatever addictions or unworkable emotional constructs we may have created, inherited or absorbed. We must be ever cognizant of our own recognized and yet-to-be-overcome psychological and emotional limitations and difficulties. The practitioner-client dynamic must never imply that the practitioner is perfect and that the client is sick. Rather, the community dynamic requires that the client view the practitioner as an advanced traveler or someone who is specially educated in this adventure of life. The old dynamic that evokes approval-seeking from an authority figure instead becomes a shared drive toward empowerment. This takes an ever-growing courage and confidence on the part of the practitioner. We therapists learn to trust our own experience and our intuition as we develop skills to separate our needs from our clients' needs. As healers we learn to create additional communities for our own needs as they present themselves.

Authentic Process requires the practitioner to come from a place of intuition and flexibility as well as one of structure and understanding — to come from a heart-centered place as well as a clear-minded one. A good practitioner will strive to integrate both approaches. It is from this place of centered, affirmed individual freedom and responsibility that the Stage Two Authentic Process can unfold.

In 1993, I surveyed 130 Stage Two clients and workshop participants as to what their specific needs from a practitioner were. Based on that research, these are a few of the most prominent expectations that recovering people have of their therapists:

- To encourage the client to take healthy risks
- To give feedback, without which therapy would be frustrating
- To provide a role model of what a fuller recovery might look and feel like
- To be interactive and help illuminate dynamics that are debilitating
- To compassionately include and have understanding of the "shadow self"

- To understand that therapy is ineffective if a client is suffering an active substance addiction
- To recognize that a new approach/strategy is required if the process becomes stagnant
- To be confrontational in a respectful manner and in the spirit of illumination

I consider my office a place of community healing, a holy ground on which dedicated individuals have inspired conversations. Together we birth a whole and more spirited sense of self. Stage Two recovery is nothing less than a re-birthing process. We must set the tone, gently guide the process, and sometimes even help each other with the breathing. The word breath in Latin means spirit; we see and feel the spiritual connection in this process. It is the living, breathing birth of a whole, new person.

The story of Christine, who joined an on-going group, illustrates one of these occurrences, giving us a peek into the authentic group process.

Chris' Story

Christine is a 40-year-old Asian-American mother of two teenage girls. She was divorced for several years before she began her recovery process. She is a high ranking executive for a major corporation and found her way into treatment, at a prestigious 30-day rehab, through her Employee Assistance Program. She was poly-addicted to alcohol, cocaine, and marijuana. Upon leaving treatment, she was referred to my office for family counseling and to an aftercare group, sponsored by the treatment facility. She began going to AA regularly, her family counseling helped to normalize the home environment, and she was fully engaged in her aftercare group.

One year into recovery, Christine came to see me for a consultation. She explained that her one-year commitment to the aftercare group was coming to an end and she wanted to join one of my groups. She explained how group work was important to her and that she liked the work we did together. I explained to her the difference in the advanced group and I told her I was uncertain about her preparedness for Stage Two group work at that time. Because of her strong motivation, her excellent recovery work, and my inability to suggest an alternative group experience, Chris was invited to join a new group in formation. Much of the first year in the group was difficult for her and the other seven group members. While they were uncovering and getting perspective on

their early wounds and defense structures, Chris was looking exclusively for behavioral support. She wanted help and suggestions to make
things better now, and she remained very protective of her past. During
group projects, particularly ones regarding family history, Chris would
avoid meaningful participation and present a defensive, armored position. Although she attempted to participate, she really did not have a
good fit in the group for a long time.

After a while, there was a shift in Chris's energy and presence. She
seemed more secure and more trusting. It was as if the group had
passed some litmus test. Intuitively, members felt her defensiveness
relax. Shortly afterward, Christine took a full evening session to share
her early family history with us. She admitted that, after watching other
group members present their histories, she had been secretly preparing
for a very long time. Her presentation melted all defenses in the room.
In listening to Chris stoically tell her story of constant humiliation and
horrific abuse by her alcoholic mother and three step-fathers, the group
members could see their own innocence reflected in her. They looked at
photographs of her childhood and were stunned by what she called
home. They all identified with her repressed trauma and confusion. One
member, Bill, said to Chris, "I can't believe how brave and strong you
are. I understand why you had to wait so long. I couldn't stop my tears
during your presentation, and I haven't been able to cry before this in
my recovery. It may sound weird, but I truly thank you for that." Bill
continued, "Chris, there's one thing I don't understand. Why were you
protecting those rotten bastards? They were maliciously and despicably
cruel to you."

Chris, now wiping one quiet, single tear, responded, "I was never
protecting them; it was me I was protecting. I was afraid that if the
words ever came out I would lose all control, and that continues to terri-
fy me." After each member was able to give Chris feedback, I asked her
how she was feeling, and if she was still terrified of losing control. She
replied, "I feel good, I am so glad it has come out. No one in my adult
life knows about all of this. It has been such a burden. I am feeling a
little light-headed and vulnerable right now, but I am so glad that I
shared it with you."

From that day on, Chris blended more smoothly into the group. Currently, I would encourage someone like Chris to participate in the type
of workshop we do at the Institute called "Getting Where You Want To
Go." It is a 35-hour process (over the course of nine weeks) that experientially leads participants through Chapters Six and Seven of this book.

This core learning opportunity builds the groundwork and vocabulary for Stage Two healing. The depth of personal healing that takes place in this created community is profound — far beyond what I have been able to consistently facilitate in individual settings. In these workshops, we reclaim and integrate our unique, authentic histories. We then use these histories as foundations for our wholeness and fulfillment, rather than for our own victimization. We are no longer victims, and move into powerful feelings of aliveness.

Other examples of healing community are one-day or weekend workshops where we come together with a common focus. Some examples of the topics applied in these focus workshops are: "The Journey Toward Complete Recovery," "Healing the Wounds of Sexual Abuse," "Soaring Relationships For Couples," "Spirituality for Singles," "Sexual Diversity in Recovery," "Healthy Rage Expression," "On Loss and Grieving," "HIV/AIDS in Recovery," "Men's Issues," "Women's Concerns," or issues related to esteem for lesbians, gay men, bisexual and/or transgender people. A workshop can be created on any number of subjects as long as there is a common focus, a healing intention, and a facilitator who possesses experience and wisdom in the central community theme. When such workshops include a Stage Two awareness and use the concise vocabulary of Authentic Process Therapy, they provide the dynamic healing quality that I refer to as Authentic Process in Community.

5

Getting Through the Hard Part

The work involved in complete recovery is not always easy. At some point you have to bridge the authenticity gap. This is the discrepancy between who we present ourselves to be and who we really are. There are at least five areas which pose special challenges for different people at different times. They are:

1. Breaking Down the Mask of Composure
2. Getting Through Cultural Pain
3. Overcoming Feelings of Isolation
4. Looking at Original Pain and Trauma
5. Getting Through Severe Depression/Anxiety

Fortunately, there are five specific remedies and procedures in Stage Two healing which address each of these "dark alleys of the soul." Some might think of them as bridges over troubled waters. Others may see them as tunnels through a mountain of unreality which they must dig themselves. Either way, the land of "milk and honey," psychologically speaking, is on the other side, and the only way out is in. It's a question of when. The five remedies are:

1. Finding One's Authentic Self: Getting Through the Mask of Composure
2. Cultural Education: Getting Through Cultural Pain
3. Psycho-education: Getting Through Isolation
4. Grief and Rage: Getting Through Original Pain and Trauma
5. Medication: Getting Through Severe Depression/Anxiety

Together, these five challenge areas and their remedies are five bridges to the authentic self. Let us take a look at each of them in turn.

1. Finding One's Authentic Self: Getting Through the Mask of Composure

Finding our "wholeness of self" sounds very nice, but in actuality it usually involves an examination of the pain or trauma that keeps us from experiencing that wholeness. Stage Two Recovery can help us "get through" this "dark alley of the soul."

At some point, we all begin to acknowledge that we need to find a more emotionally connected existence. In order to find our authentic self and loosen the habitual mask of composure we wear to hide our rage and pain, we must begin the gradual process of uncovering wounds from the past. I say "uncover," rather than "discover" or "recover," for a reason. When we uncover our repressed feelings, we allow them to surface by removing the layer of shame that keeps them repressed. We don't necessarily go actively searching, tearing through the layers of our unconscious. Instead we consciously permit, or "permission" the material to surface on its own accord. Once we make a conscious decision to allow this process to unfold, the material will surface naturally, in its own mysterious order.

The process only works when we are ready to accept the material and only if we are in a safe environment, such as with a trusted practitioner or with a community group that supports our intentions. It also occurs during meditation, contemplation or personal crisis. When all these components are in place, deep healing can begin. When we awaken to our own hidden and repressed conflicts while receiving compassion and support, we become more alive. This aliveness brings with it a sense of self-respect, self-love and a genuine feeling of entitlement.

Many in recovery do not feel entitled, on conscious and unconscious levels, to be successful. They fear that they don't deserve to be loved or they don't deserve to feel pleasure or they can't have deep needs fulfilled. In the words of author Stephen Levine, who has made significant contributions in our understanding of this profound human phenomena, "Healing is to enter, with understanding and compassion, that which we have withdrawn from, in fear, anger or judgement." In my own recovery and in my experience as a practitioner of Stage Two Authentic Process Therapy, I have learned that the job of the practitioner and/or facilitator is to provide fair witness to this awakening / sorting out process, and to coach the birthing of a new way of life for the one in recovery.

During this deep healing, we begin to discover our "inner child," and the unconcious and higher self behind it. This process unleashes a powerful energy. As the inner child surfaces, we awaken to new sensations, and may even experience waves of energetic currents. There will be periods when we make an empowering breakthrough and discover a fuller and richer capacity for getting our human needs met.

Along with transformation we may experience passing, bittersweet waves of joy, grief and sadness. This is the grieving for the long, lost years that we had lived in the ache of deprivation, glaringly apparent during these times of revelation. We reconnect with, and in some cases, re-experience or re-enact unresolved original pain, deprivation and trauma. We rediscover long-forgotten losses, whose grief never had full articulation or witness. Periods of grief, while painful, offer an opportunity for personal integration. It is from the depths of this grief and reintegration that we become extraordinarily open to corrective experience; to ways that we can proactively prevent more suffering in our life, and also take steps to insure a more meaningful and fuller life. In the end, we find that, as we relax our defenses, the mask of composure, which once served us, no longer fits our face and must be dropped.

2. Cultural Education: Getting Through Cultural Pain

An important aspect of healing into wholeness that is often overlooked is cultural pain. It refers to healing the damages, traumas, and deprivations that were culturally induced. During our cultural education we put all learning and information in a context that respects the cultures that both we and the learning come from. We see how many of our challenges are rooted in cultural ambiguity, bigotry, and ignorance. This reduces our shame and sense of isolation and facilitates healing.

"Cultural pain" is a phrase I learned from Peter Bell, a psychologist who has worked extensively with African-Americans in recovery. A relatively new area of therapeutic healing, cultural pain is pain that has its roots in cultural dimensions. Full recovery cannot take place without its due process. To accomplish the delicate work required here, we must be highly sensitive to the struggles of all oppressed minorities in our society. This includes all racial, ethnic, and sexual minorities and the prejudicial subsets that lie within. It includes the internalized effects of sexism, homophobia, racism, classism and other forms of underprivilege and being privileged. Many people are in denial about their lack of resolution, thinking that they have already come to terms with these prejudices. Even though they believe this to be the case, it is often untrue. This illusion covers up the real pain, confusion and complexity that lies for many years beneath our defenses. Remember that recovering people under the trance of their addiction have been unable to process these complexities in an integrated fashion.

As we begin to examine how culture has affected our perceptions, there may be many new insights. We may realize that much of our suffering comes from living in a dominator society (rather than a partnership society) that has, at its core, dualistic thinking and patriarchy. We then may realize that *there is really nothing wrong with us,* that we are not uniquely flawed. As we come into complete recovery we begin to have societal relationships where we *link* our authority and power with others in unique creative partnerships rather than engage in draining one-up/one-down dynamics. To better understand these cultural dynamics and their cultural manifestations, I recommend Riane Eisler's book, *The Chalice and the Blade.*

"But if there is nothing really wrong with me," you are probably asking, "then why do I *feel* so bad?" From a certain point of view, the cause of our suffering and illnesses are culturally imposed. They are products of our dualistic thinking by which external standards of acceptable and unacceptable, good and bad, right and wrong, are applied to everyone, regardless of their complex and specific needs and natures. Implicit in this system is an ideal of perfection, an ideal that embodies everything good. Interesting, however, this ideal of good that is set with such fierce certainty does differ from one nation or community to another. And where it differs, conflict ensues, for, within the context of our own culture, someone's ideal has to be right and the other wrong.

To be wrong in our culture is to feel shame, and nothing cripples faster or better than shame. To feel crippling shame is to feel our *being* is bad. Crippling shame flourishes in a culture like ours that grants its members no inherent worth, that values only products and deeds, and only of certain kinds. It is no surprise that most of us go to extravagant lengths not to be caught in the wrong: like the politicians who run the system, we lie, we make ourselves deaf and blind to the struggles around us, and sometimes betray our family and friends. Because of this cultural phenomenon, we are sometimes hardened into defensive machines like army tanks, while beneath the armor, we cower and quiver in terror, feeling totally isolated. One unfortunate catch in a dualistic system is that if we are right about one thing, we are sure to be wrong about something else; one way or another we will eventually feel ashamed.

When you think about it, ours is far from being a flexible, imaginative system, and it is not surprising that most of us at one time or another have run headlong into its walls. At an earlier stage in the evolution of consciousness, this system must have worked, to the extent that it supported life. Now it does not. We have only to check out our psyches and poor Mother Earth to assure ourselves of that. Without blaming ourselves or anyone else, we must recognize the need for a change. To heal ourselves and our world we must begin to transcend the dualistic thinking that blocks our perception of the holistic state and causes so much cultural pain. This process involves re-educating ourselves about history, evolution, class, status, economics, "success," power, and a great many other things. This is cultural education on a grand scale, but its a choice we can make when we're ready.

3. Psycho–education: Getting Through Isolation

In APT, the idea of psycho-education is paramount. The more education and awareness we can bring into the therapeutic process the greater the opportunity we will have to grow. Let's face it: Ignorance is not bliss. It can cause a lot of pain. In APT, this education focuses on the "constellation of desires" and the unconscious defense reflexes that prevent their fulfillment. Through education, we bring these defenses to the surface so we can explore their energetic underpinnings and begin relaxing them. In a sense, it is a lifetime study. Once we get a sense of the psychological principles underlying our own behavior and defenses, we can take it from there to a greater extent, and our whole life becomes a healing workshop, an experiment in transformational psychology.

Psycho-education is nothing like lecturing. It is introduced skillfully by the practitioner at opportune moments in response to questions or struggles presented. For this psycho-education to work, it is important that the authentic therapeutic relationship is solid. The client and the practitioner must have an interactive, cohesive relationship. In Authentic Process of this nature, this education has a hypnotic quality to it. This cohesion creates a shared, interactive, mild trance-like state, while the simultaneous, appropriately framed education imparts a suggestion for moving through the process. As hypnosis trainer Stephen Gilligan suggests, "Trance unfolds from an experiential, interpersonal encounter in which practitioner aligns with client, thereby enabling both parties to become increasingly receptive to each other."

I have found that education of this style is crucial for recovering people, who otherwise may continually live painfully ensconced in shame and confusion.

4. Grief and Rage: Getting Through Original Pain and Trauma

In healing through Stage Two into complete recovery, we can no longer either consciously or unconsciously shy away from our grief or rage. In reality, it is not the grief and rage that we are blocked from (or acting out), but the fear of their healthy expression. As you will clearly see in forthcoming chapters, we all have repressed hurts, losses, sorrows, abuses, neglects, loves, and joys that are not part of the whole that we express. Therefore, we are not expressing an energetic whole, but a contorted piece of ourselves that feels safe enough for the present.

You will discover that when you enter healing community, committed to Stage Two recovery, that the fear around our repressed feelings and experiences will relax. The safety of the sharing and shared intention organically create this relaxation. The psycho-education process corrects our learning deficiencies and teaches us the healthy expression of feelings and also how to reframe our earlier experiences to our advantage. We learn to accept that in order to experience the fullness of who we are, our histories, pleasant or unpleasant, are our only true foundation. To the degree that we truncate or dissociate from parts of ourselves, we experience less of our potential for full expression. When we think of this from a body energy and repression perspective it all becomes abundantly clear.

While the idea of engaging with grief and rage and original pain and trauma seems daunting, the experience need not be. It can simply be part of our present day life, an informed and empowering flanking of whatever else life is bringing us in the moment. Often there is a synchronistic, mysterious interweaving of the inner and outer experiences. There will be times when feelings surface that bewilder us or throw us off balance, but isn't that just the nature of things? At least in doing this healing work we are consciously hosting and prepared for whatever comes through us, so that we can own it and use it to our advantage.

The key to managing our inner anger is in learning the difference between acting on a feeling and expressing a feeling. Most of us learned that it was not okay to express anger, so we found our own ways of acting out or holding it in. We become angry for a reason. When we act out on a feeling such as anger, we project it at someone or the world around us. Sometimes when we act out on the anger we malign ourselves and cause depression and isolation. Instead of acting anger out or acting it in, we can simply express it where it is safe to do so. Remember that feelings want to be expressed — they live themselves out through expression. If we do not find an appropriate channel to express the anger, it will go elsewhere within our internal systems and cause disease and stress. Either way the damage comes back to us.

Learning safe ways to express anger and rage is an important part of Stage Two. I occasionally conduct rage workshops to assist people in "permissioning" these feelings and experientially learning what it feels like to process the feelings in a rewarding manner. As you will read in the following chapters there are many very safe ways to express rage and grief. While some may look messy, others are quite elegant. Although I have personally enjoyed some really messy rage work, some of the most efficient and eloquent was through the use of poetry. Vile poetry it was, but it had a healing sweetness to it. Ten years later, when I read those poems, I gently weep. Far from being a poet, my crude efforts have been nonetheless greatly rewarded by the healing graces. This work is important because experiencing these feelings develops our personal power and fuels us to get our needs met.

5. Medication: Getting Through Severe Depression and/or Anxiety

Sometimes in Stage Two healing, a masked depression or anxiety problem will become uncovered, resulting in a trauma reaction. Inversely, a repressed trauma may be uncovered, causing a temporary reaction of severe depression or anxiety. It works both ways. Either can throw us off balance, making us very uncomfortable. This can confuse or interrupt the healing process. Medication can help at these times, allowing us to function more comfortably and give us the courage to continue the healing process.

Using medication to support a more expansive recovery can seem like a paradox to those of us who have been addicted to alcohol and other substances. Yet many of us have been significantly helped by medication at some point in our recovery.

There have been revolutionary advances in non-addictive psychotherapeutic medications in the past ten years, just as there has been unprecedented progress and acceptance in psychospiritual healing. When necessary, we bring the two together. In a holistic universe, everything is here for a reason. I believe that many of these newer medications are here to facilitate healing for many of us into a more complete recovery. If our world had a calmer, more natural and less hectic pace, medications might not be necessary. However, for the present we must use whatever is available to us to create equilibrium in our sometimes chaotic healing journey. Chapter Ten will further address these issues and what I refer to as "applied psychopharmacology" for recovering people.

To elaborate on these dark alleys of the soul, I'll share with you a part of Edward's story.

Edward's Story

Edward is a 40-year-old African-American gay man. When he came to see me, he had been sober in Twelve Step recovery for eight years and was experiencing both a health crisis and a job crisis. Additionally, Ed reported that throughout his recovery he had been depressed, with a tendency to isolate himself from people. Even though he had a life partner, he felt alone and dissatisfied.

After several months of therapy, Ed came to a resolution with his job situation and his health crisis became manageable. We began to explore the deeper issues surrounding his depression. It was apparent to me, having worked with many lesbians and gay men in recovery as well as with racial minorities, that Ed had ignored his sexual orientation and race as sources of consternation. On being probed about both of these cultural aspects, Ed quickly responded that he "never liked the idea that he was gay and that most blacks deserve the treatment that they get."

As part of a deeper exploration of these subjects, I shared with Ed a concern I had. I was concerned that in childhood, for whatever reasons, he may have internalized negative and/or shameful feelings pertaining to sexual orientation or being a person of color. I wondered if these feelings may still be unconsciously contaminating his relationship and his overall outlook on life. I then suggested, as a way to address and explore these concerns, that Ed write or outline an autobiography that focused on his childhood, his race and his sexuality. I suggested that he probe his memory and honestly delineate what his early exposures were and what impressions shaped his thinking and feeling in these areas.

When Ed shared the discoveries from his writing with me, I saw a whole different aspect of his nature: he was deeply saddened and vulnerable. He said, "I can't believe all this happened to me. I can't believe I absorbed so much small-minded ignorance about who I am. Some of it was downright evil and untrue. But I began to believe prejudicial remarks and I used them to define myself. I never questioned my beliefs before. I can't believe that my opinion of myself has come out of such ignorance and stupidity. What am I going to do with all this? It just makes me feel sick."

Previously, Ed had not been able to express himself authentically because his feelings had been buried under a layer of self-rejection based on cultural ignorance and shame. His feelings of isolation, grief and rage were the result of this, exaggerated by his need for psycho-education.

I suggested to Ed that his present vulnerable state was a good time for learning new behavior patterns. I suggested he bring his new consciousness about these subjects into new settings, where he could identify with others who had similar struggles.

After exploring his options, Ed was able to find several social, political and recovery organizations that addressed sexual diversity and people of color issues in affirmative and empowering ways. These groups, combined with his therapy, have helped Ed expose the repressed shadow aspects of his psyche, take proactive steps in transforming them, and begin a new compassionate journey of self-understanding and healing. Thus, for him, cultural education and psycho-education were closely linked. Together, they helped him begin to process his own grief and anger without medication.

It seems that, as with Edward, if we do not probe for cultural pain issues, they may never surface. These issues are prevalent today, and integration and fuller healing may not occur without addressing them. Although it may take some dedicated exploration, once we understand the larger process, how the suffering we went through relates to the suffering our parents and neighbors went through, and how that relates to the community and culture as a whole, we can begin to see ourselves and others in a more compassionate light. We accept ourselves for who we are. From that point onward, no one can make us into who we are not. We "won't go there" any more.

The
Twelve
Stations

Clouds are flowing in the river, leaves are flying in the sky.
Life is laughing in a pebble. Does a pebble ever die?

Flowers grow out of the garbage, such a miricle to see.
What seems dead and what seems dying makes for butterflies
to be.

Life is laughing in a pebble, flowers bathe in morning dew.
Dust is dancing in my footsteps and I wonder who is who.

Clouds are flowing in the river, clouds are drifting in my tea.
On a never-ending journey, what a miracle to be!

EVELINE BEUMKES
Earth Prayers From Around The World

P art Two represents the crux of what Authentic Process Therapy is all about. In this section, comprising approximately half the book's contents, we'll discuss what the twelve stations of the journey are like, plus what the rewards will be once we've tapped into the holistic state.

In Chapter Six you will discover the first six "fundamental" stations of the deep inner process of APT. They provide important healing and put your personal history in an updated perspective that gives you a new, personal foundation for the six "emergent" stations in Chapter Seven. It is in the later stations that you can more fully transform your life and way of being to bring them into harmony with the experience of holism and of knowing your rightful place in the universe. In Chapter Eight you ride the wave of complete recovery as you taste the Fruits of the Tree and discover how delicious they are.

The twelve stations of Stage Two, like the eleven in Stage One, have a transitional nature. Though they are foundations, they represent a significant personal experience that becomes a platform for richer, more expansive future experiences. I call them stations, rather than steps or stages, because they are not necessarily progressive. You can move among the stations and return to one or another again and again as you continue your transformation. The stations are not two-dimensional, as they are portrayed in the Tree Diagram. They have a depth that can only be appreciated as you earnestly engage in them. Once you use the model in action and in community, the stations begin to come to life and yield rich results.

Although the stations are numbered and listed in a linear fashion, your movement through them will not necessarily follow the numbered order. Real growth does not take place in such a structured way. These processes are far more fluid and highly individualized than can be depicted in a book. Some of these stations are more challenging than others, and will require more time than others, depending on your particular circumstances. You may have to return to some of them many times in your recovery. I have numbered them to aid our discussion.

The Twelve Stations of Stage Two Recovery:
1. Finding the Unconscious Through the "Inner Child"
2. Awakening Your Body: Finding Your Grounding
3. Exploring the Sexual-Spiritual Split: The Cornerstone of Self-Recognition
4. Revisiting "Adolescent Awkwardness"
5. Re-experiencing Original Pain and Trauma
6. Grieving Unresolved Losses
7. Letting Go: The Authentic Presentation of Self
8. Corrective Experience: Learning More Effective Behavior
9. Separating Adult Needs From Childhood Needs
10. Integrating the Shadow Self
11. Updating and Re-tuning the Unconscious
12. Experiencing Self-love and Self-assertion

6

The Six Fundamental Stations

The six fundamental stations of Stage Two presented in this section are the heart and soul of advanced recovery work. Each represents a kind of healing crisis in which you recognize specific points in your biographical history and in your psyche where you have lost touch with your holism, your rightful place in the universe, and begin to heal that point. These stages provide the insight, depth and foundation for the Six Emergent Stations, which are outlined in the next chapter.

At first, Stage Two may appear overwhelming. Remember to be compassionate towards yourself and take a process-oriented view of this material. It is intended to provide enrichment and illumination, *not* pressure. Despite appearances, this is a non-linear, sometimes chaotic, dynamic process. I have found that it is also self-organizing. By this I mean that once a recovering person consciously commits to and begins to trust this Stage Two "program," and believes that clarity will surface out of the inherent confusion, the process will self-organize to fulfill needs as they arise. This is nature's way.

Commitment is the key ingredient. You must complete the work in your own time, but be committed to returning to it again and again, especially in hours of need. These concepts have been developed to provide comfort, grounding and expanded community opportunities.

As always, earnest commitment is followed by passion and reward. There is a paradox in this so-called *hard work*. Once people commit themselves to this healing process in community, it often becomes fun. Unveiling repressed feelings sounds like anything but fun, but with the special chemistry and adventure of the process it *is* fun because there is a shared sense, an ongoing anticipation, of aliveness. Healing can be pleasurable and painful. Most importantly, in community you'll discover that you are *so much more than* your conditions or feelings. People often look forward to coming together to be able to safely share and discover and nurture whatever organically needs to be healed next.

All twelve stations of Stage Two are designed to help you further reach into and take responsibility for your core energy, or essence. This is a God-like energy which begins to awaken your succinct role in the collective consciousness. It offers glimpses of a collective coming-together of all the myriad fragments of your world into a resonant personal whole. This is the holism within yourself that reflects your divine nature and the nature of the cosmos.

In clarifying a path through these stations, I respect the fact *that most of us will have unconscious resistance at various points in the journey.* Stage Two is a focused searchlight into our unconscious (previously rejected) material. Since this material was rejected or compartmentalized when we did not have the maturity or equilibrium to fully integrate the complexities, *the resistance is natural.* The fear of an inability to deal with this material was psychologically encoded into our repression. This also was the appropriate natural phenomena at that time. It is exactly this unconscious resistance that makes the work confusing and painful at times. In doing Authentic Process Therapy, it is always our intention to respect and honor this reality and greet the resistance with support, compassion and understanding. Resistance is always the first emergent barrier to the process of resolution and further empowerment.

I welcome the newcomer to these concepts and to community, as well as those who are adult children of alcoholics or other troubled families. You may find a home here and grounding for your personal journey. Since engaging in and developing APT has made my own life one of wonderment and grace, I am blessed to be able to share these stations in community. This process reminds me of *Ano Ano: the Seed*, a book about Native Hawaiians. The author, Kristen Zambucka, traces the group's journey out of 158 years of imposed Christianity back "full circle" to their spiritual Polynesian roots. She writes:

We are all on a spiral path.
No growth takes place in a straight line.
There will be setbacks along the way...
There will be shadows, but they will be balanced by patches
   of light and fountains of joy as we grow and progress.
Awareness of the pattern is all you need
   to sustain you along the way...

Station 1: Finding the Unconscious Through the "Inner Child"

The Unconscious and the "Inner Child"

As we touch the past and reconnect with our grieving and loss, we may begin to discover our "unconscious self." For most people, the "inner child," which Bradshaw has written about so extensively, is the most direct roadway to the unconscious self. If we continue in this direction and begin to touch holism, we emerge into yet another related area called "the higher self." Developing inroads to these three areas helps empower "the inner healer," which we will talk about more later.

In acknowledging the emotional twists and turns that are fundamental to our Stage Two healing, I am again drawn to the writings of Kristen Zambucka about the Hawaiian seekers:

Long had they searched and far, in seemingly endless circles outside themselves for a meaning to their existence. The time had come for answers as their journey took a new turn... inward....

Upon listening to the older ones, they were told:
It is then that you will hear a voice within yourself. It was there all the time, but you never listened before. Faintly it will speak to you at first, but it will gradually grow louder and clearer the more you take heed of its message until one day it thunders inside you and you will have come home.

Having heard this message they began to listen:
And listening... listening they came to rely on its judgment. They made fewer mistakes as closing their eyes, ignoring appearances, they "saw" with that voice within and learned to trust it, as it was the nearest they came to hearing the voice of God.

Similar to the experience of Zambucka's Hawaiian seekers, self-affirmative messages and the external healing community can transform consciousness with supportive images and voices that are in tune with a thoughtful, self-respecting, adult mind.

Though this may seem like another long journey, each accomplishment in a "station" results in a greater sense of empowerment and will bring with it an expanded repertoire of personal choices and relationships. It is a continuing, walk-through diorama depicting the journey toward holism. With this fresh perspective, you will begin to experience what it means to be truly recovered. Eventually you will be able to emerge from the Stage Two recovery process, maintaining its useful tools, lessons and processes. Those who do will finally make peace with the "ancient ache within," and become less limited, holistic beings.

To most of us, the unconscious is a very elusive concept. Our conscious awareness is what we know: the information and ideas that we have access to. But what is the unconscious? It is more difficult to define, since it encompasses all the complex forces that we do not readily have access to. How can we understand a force we don't have regular access to? The first step to unlocking its secrets is the willingness to see, feel and experience our unconscious.

I discovered in the course of my own recovery that the resistance to the unconscious keeps us addicted to fruitless behaviors such as habits and addictions. Our habits fend off intrusions from haunting thoughts that live in the dark of our internal basement.

In this simplified view, the top layer of the unconscious contains what is called "rejected material." Rejected material includes any event from our childhood that made us feel wounded, ashamed, inept, overwhelmed, or confused. A child's sexual urges are a good example. Since society judges children's sexual urges as bad, the child considers them bad. The child is confused and ashamed of these urges and relegates them to the unconscious, where they are covered up and "forgotten." These feelings will stay in our unconscious, mostly forgotten, while we busily present our more acceptable false mask of composure to the world. This is a coping mechanism, and without it we would be overwhelmed by uncontrolled psychic material. Our survival mechanism uses the unconscious to create balance and homeostasis in our organic system.

In order to understand this hidden material, you must gradually allow it to surface. Since much of the repressed material consists of wounds, it is extremely important to create an empathetic community environment in which to explore the unconscious. I call it creating a host environment.

The safety, empathy and intention present in the host environment causes a rebalancing of the homeostasis. This allows the previously rejected material to surface. Appropriate community environments include individual therapy, group therapy or healing community settings with other recovering people who will understand our feelings and help us put them in perspective.

The surfacing of this material in a safe setting creates what we referred to earlier as "transcendent function." This occurs when new energy is released as a result of resolving the inner conflict that was keeping unconscious material suppressed.

Your unconscious is under pressure to hold back years of repressed material, and when you finally release it, the pressure bursts out with a physical force. This energy in turn fuels recovery work, allowing for attitudinal shifts that previously seemed unattainable. These personal shifts, such as deciding it is okay to ask for what you need, enhances your life.

When unconscious material becomes conscious, a new energy is freed up, the energy that held it in place. With that new energy, a clarity comes, and we are in a "transcendent state," and are able to make changes and shifts that we were not previously able to handle.

Sometimes the unconscious material will surface when you least expect it, for instance, when it is "triggered" by an event. To visualize this triggering action, think of the way an old juke box works. A selection button triggers an underlying mechanism to search for a record.

In the unconscious, the "record" is the stored material. The selection button that triggers the material can be a visual, energetic, or emotional stimulus. For example, seeing a person or place from our past might trigger unconscious material to surface; likewise a person's action or style might evoke a reference to an earlier incident, person or event. This is why you might sometimes experience confusing responses to events, places, people and the way that people present themselves. Often these involuntary responses are signals that both a fearful defense and subterranean material is being evoked. In Authentic Process Therapy, we create the time and safety to respect these emergences and allow them to more fully develop.

The Higher Self

The "higher self," is the energy that radiates out of your core life force. We have all had at least fleeting experiences of connection with our higher self. When you connect, "everything feels right" and integrated for a moment. It could be called your place of wisdom or creativity. It is also your "inner healer."

The inner healer is an expression I first heard used by Stanislav Grof to help people become comfortable with the intuitive part of themselves which knows what needs to be healed next. We all have an inner healer; the more you trust it, the better it works. In other words, don't bring any preconceived ideas into the process. Let yourself be surprised.

The higher self experience transcends or goes beyond personal individual identity and meaning; it includes purpose, meaning, values, and unification with universal principles. When you experience your higher self, your sense of self expands. This is when you know that you are larger than your feelings and present conditions.

Scientist, educator and healer Barbara Ann Brennan illuminates this view of the higher self in her text, *Light Emerging*. "Wherever there is peace, joy, and fulfillment in your life, that is where your higher self has expressed itself through the creative principal. If you wonder what is meant by 'who you really are' or your 'true self' look to these areas of your life. They are an expression of your true self."

Your higher self, your true self, your core energy, your essence, or divinity: all are synonymous. What many of us are recovering from, in the larger view, are blockages and unconscious defense reflexes that inhibit our access to this core or higher self.

As you look inward, without judgement, your higher self or essence will open to you. As the inspiring author A.H. Almaas writes, "This is the basic law of the heart." It is the nature of the higher self to want to be known. Once it has been recognized it will lead you to other ways in which you can know it and be it. From this point on, your progress on the path seems to quicken, and the hurdles that lie before you are less riddled with the thorns and barbed wire of your resistance. From your higher self, you begin to accept the lessons that present themselves, and to understand the ways in which each of us creates our own curriculum. To put it another way, once you have drunk from the well of higher self, or essence, you know the drink that will quench you. Not only do you become more willing to do what you must to find that hidden essence, it is more willing to be found.

From identifying my "observer self," that part of me that is the perceiver of all that I am, do, think, and feel, I have begun to recognize *the location* of my higher self. When I realized that I cannot *be* what I perceive, then I realized that I must *be* the perceiver, or observer self. Emotionally flat at first, this observer-self gradually became more and more infused with energy and pristine awareness. It has since demonstrated itself to be my higher self.

The Inner Child

One of the simplest ways to reach into the unconscious and the higher self is to bring out the inner child. When we learn to extend compassion and understanding to this neglected inner child, we will begin to feel self-love and self-confidence. As we work through Stage Two, our inner child and our adult intellect come together in a joyous union, and we see life in a newly receptive way. What is the inner child?

When we were infants and children, it made sense to hide certain parts of ourselves. When these parts became overly dependent/independent, rageful/playful, willful/free, curious/spiritually knowing, or even imaginative, they were rejected by those upon whom we relied to feed, clothe, and protect us. What else could we do but push them downstairs? At the time, they were threatening to bring more pain and fear than we could have possibly borne. In some cases they could even have cost us our lives, so we kept them downstairs, as we still do. But somewhere along the line we forgot they were living down there.

Kept away from the light, most things do not grow. Likewise, as long as these parts stay in the dark of the basement, they also stay frozen in time, in a state of arrested emotional development. Thus they are usually not so much evil as underdeveloped, awkward, primitive, and unadapted. These parts gather to themselves their old unexpressed energies along with the stagnating forces of other dark-dwelling things that have been lurking in the basement, and the energy builds and builds.

As you can imagine, sooner or later one or another of these energies is going to explode. Bursting up the stairs, it will knock down any door in its way, not stopping until it sees the light. Such is the nature of the unconscious: it does not want to stay unconscious forever. Eventually, it demands to be known. In this station of healing we begin to host the unconscious and lead it into the light before all that knocking down of doors becomes necessary. It is a more graceful and efficient process that way, and less expensive emotionally.

"Every child is born a genius," said the inventor R. Buckminster Fuller. Taking a similar view, the German author J.W. Von Goethe suggested, "If children grew up according to early indications, we should have nothing but geniuses." The French poet Charles Baudelaire exclaimed, "Genius is childhood recaptured at will!"

The merging of the inner child concept with the idea of the unconscious was, let's say, my own personal stroke of "genius." It came from that unconscious child part of me, my assimilation of input and my inward struggles in my own recovery. Bradshaw calls it the "free child" and "the magical child." Emmet Fox, a theologian who wrote extensively on metaphysics, refers to both "the magical child" and the "wonder child."

In 1978 I was new to recovery and quite depressed and confused. My psychotherapist at the time, a very gifted woman, suggested that I seek relief from inner turmoil by comforting the "wounded little boy" that I carried within. My first reaction was cynical; I felt that I was being patronized. However, being in the midst of true psychic anguish and having nowhere else to turn, I began this inward nurturing.

I did as she suggested. When the suffering began to overtake me I would have a private dialogue with the wounded little boy inside. I would tell him "It is going to be okay... we can get through this... I will take care of you... I've gotten this far... you can trust me." There were many similar variations of these words — all intended to build a new caring and trusting relationship.

At first I felt silly talking to myself like this and the results were not exactly immediate. However, there was, even early on, a whisper of gentle comfort that softened the pain's edge. Accompanying this delicate impact was a slight hint of the possibility for empowerment. A possibility began to exist that I could, maybe, build a loving, compassionate relationship with a part of myself, a forgotten or abandoned part, and through that relationship locate an inner peace, calm and sense of wonder.

One of the difficult aspects of beginning to accept or "own" this inner child was the coinciding acknowledgment that to do so was an admission of imperfection. I began to realize that it takes courage to be imperfectly human. I started to understand that trying to maintain a "perfect image" was causing me shame and costing me my self-esteem. The parts of me that felt the best often did not fit society's "perfect" images. I understand Bradshaw's correlation between our perfectionist systems and our shame-based personalities.

His words help to articulate my feelings:

Fear of exposure lies at the heart of shame. As we allow our shame to be exposed to others we are exposed to ourselves. In this sense, the healing of the shame that binds you is a revelatory experience. Because your shame exists at the very core of your being, when you embrace your shame, you begin to discover who you really are. Shame both hides and reveals our truest self. Healing toxic shame is also revolutionary. As you truly feel your toxic shame, you are moved to change it. This can only happen by being willing to come out of hiding. We have to move from our misery and embrace our pain. We have to feel as bad as we really feel. Such a feeling moves us to change ourselves. It is revolutionary.

Shame is the nemesis that plagues recovering people in their crusade toward wholeness. When we encounter shame during childhood, we are extremely vulnerable, and cannot endure agony for long. We quickly begin to develop what some therapies call our primary ego defenses, which serve as automatic cover-ups for our protection. We begin to separate or split off parts of ourselves, (called dissociation) including parts of our own inner child. Until we find this inner child and become it, until our core powers are made conscious and free, we are hungry ghosts roaming the earth haunted by our own emptiness, we are cars in the dark on the highway without any headlights or horns. We are lonely, we are often miserable, we are dangerous to others and ourselves. We are so much without a sense of authentic *self*, so shrouded from the source of our being, from that mystery within that gives us life, that all we can think of is our *selves*. Whatever the picture, we are the biggest things in it and everyone else is just furniture. What could be more lonely than that!

How To Heal The Inner Child — Externalization

In order to understand how this repressed material is affecting your daily life, you must immerse yourself in what John Bradshaw calls, "The Externalization Process." At least for a time, consciously make contact with this inner child and with the shame that impedes its further integration. It is essential to share this reconnection with a "safe" person, community, or therapist who respects your pursuit.

People at the portal of Stage Two frequently ask many questions: How do I find this connection? How do I re-own my inner child? In Authentic Process settings, I hear time and again that clients cannot find their inner child or would rather not. They assert that they do not remember their childhood. Sometimes they just look at me strangely, as if to say, "Is this guy for real?"

I've heard a workshop participant say: "My inner child is a brat, I want to leave him right where he is."

Whatever the barrier is, some psycho-education goes a long way toward increasing your willingness to embark on a journey to your core. No one yet, to my knowledge, has been able to work through to full self-actualization without discovering his or her inner child.

At this stage of interaction, individuals will often ask for help in reconnecting with this more vulnerable, split-off experience of self. I suggest that it may be easier than they realize. I ask them to simply recall one incident from childhood, preferably before age ten. (Many recovering people initially have great difficulty remembering earlier years). I ask them to share that recollection, or image, with me. As they do so we engage in a dialogue about their image as we let it develop with colors, clothes, feelings, locations and body sensations.

When doing this exercise in group or workshop settings, I often incorporate visualization with music to provide closure and to facilitate the transition to more interactive participation. For some people in the group, this visualization is the first experience of physical tenderness towards the self. I ask participants to close their eyes and assume a relaxed posture with easy, conscious breathing. I instruct them to cross their arms and place their hands on their opposite shoulders (right hand to left shoulder, etc.) and gently rock themselves as if they were holding and rocking a child who is speaking to them. We acknowledge the awkwardness of doing this, which lightens the process and helps remove resistance. This gentle self-touch and rocking might be accompanied by a song.

Deep inside, most people feel isolated and alone most of the time. It is a tragedy. That is the wounded inner child calling for help. It is surrounded by countless other lonely "children," but often never reaches the point of finding out. These workshops have a way of proving to that child that he or she is not alone. Later on, as the layers of bandages and armors are peeled away like skins of an onion, we approach the holistic state of interconnection with the universe, and at some point realize we aren't alone at all. We are all part of one human race which is part of all life. We were never alone to begin with.

In workshops, after several people explore the inner child process, all or most of the participants have made their own inner child connection. In closing, I usually suggest that this experience is only a beginning, a first step, and that in order to progress towards the state of holism, it is up to them to engage in ongoing inner dialogues and sensory recall which can enhance the experience. This will lead to a vast and rich inner life.

This type of exercise is one example of how you can begin to tap your inner spiritual resources, your inner child, to make Stage Two work viable. It is an excellent way for therapists or facilitators to initiate the multi-faceted Stage Two uncovery process.

Because this facet of work is so important, and because it is so often overshadowed by more cognitive issues, I want to share the enthusiastic spirit that Dr. Emmet Fox brings to this idea:

Your ability to contact the mystic power within yourself, frail and feeble at first, will gradually develop until you find yourself permitting that power to take your whole life into its care. The conscious discovery by you that you have this power within you, and your determination to make use of it, is the birth of the child. The whole point is that the Wonder Child can lift you out of those very circumstances, and set you down in different circumstances. The Wonder Child is the Miracle Child. The Wonder Child will be your counselor, and the Wonder Child is never mistaken. It is because he is God, that the work of the child is independent of all conditions.

Once we assimilate this, there is little confusion as to why the "inner child" is a sublime metaphor for the unconscious — and why I join Fox and Peck in their assertion that embracing this unconscious region is nothing less than a spiritual awakening, a union with God or with the loving creative spirit.

Station 2: Awakening Your Body, Finding Your Grounding

During the deep healing part of my own second stage of recovery, I became aware of the importance of body energetics and sensations. With this discovery came a thirst for a deeper understanding and a sense of "grounding."

Grounding can literally mean connecting with the ground energetically. It is the feeling of "having both feet on the ground," or of "owning the ground you walk on," and all that comes with it.

The grounding was essential because the new awareness I was developing was quite overwhelming. I needed to know that my perceptions were not "crazy." (At that time, "crazy" for me was the unconscious fear that surfaced whenever I experienced something that did not fit with our cultural, mainstream, linear thinking.) By educating myself, and exchanging notes with those who embodied more complex, authentic realities, I was able to neutralize this unconscious, culturally induced fear which was stirring up my energies, calm myself, and become grounded.

In order to understand body energetics, I began a research project that started with my own personal and clinical experiences and moved back in history to include scholarly sources, including Wilhelm Reich's break from Freud. Reich believed that repressed traumas continue to express themselves in breathing and in gestures. By bringing attention to these sensitivities and awareness, he felt he could help people release and heal their repressed wounds. From Reich's work, psychiatrists Alexander Lowen and John Pierrakos went on to further develop understandings of energetic character defense systems. They created a program called Bioenergetics. Later, Pierrakos further developed his theories in a system called Core Energetics.

Practitioner and body energetics educator Barry Walker, who trained with Dr. Pierrakos for many years, showed me how to appreciate and use various body energetic approaches. Below is his simple explanation of how we construct our unconscious defense structures:

In the first several years of life, there are discrete and observable "developmental phases" which every human traverses. During these trips, "things" happen to the growing child which cause the child to feel wounded, limited, restrained, humiliated, controlled and betrayed. The child must go on, even though these events have happened. As the child "goes on," she or he adapts to the world in ways which take into account the "lessons" learned so far. Where these lessons have been painful, the organism and ego of the child learn behavior whose intent is to minimize the possibility of more pain, and/or to avoid the occasions when these pains might occur. So as the child grows, it modifies itself to create safety (less pain), and the personality it develops reflects these safety devices. These "devices," and their relationship to the developmental phases of that person, form the attitudes toward life called "Character Defense Systems." These "character defenses" become part of the fabric of consciousness for each of us, leaving their mark on the emotional, mental, physical and spiritual layers of consciousness.

Awareness of body energetics, physical defenses and inner sensations directs you to a more "hands on" approach, and can help side-step too much cerebral lingering. Body energetics and sensations can point you to the crux of the matter. Some of the composite stories in this text highlight examples of energetic forces at work.

There are at least two simple and basic energetic defenses that are restrictive and common to most recovering people. Many recovering people lack "grounding," while others suffer from too much grounding. The first type — let's call them Type A — are people who lack grounding and have most of their energy displaced in their upper body. Type B, those with too much grounding, have an opposite energy displacement.

Type A: Too Ungrounded

Those who lack grounding do not feel secure; with their energy displaced to their upper body they feel unstable, not firmly held up by the ground. They "live above and in front of" themselves. They have limited energetic contact between their feet and the ground. Along with this lack of grounding there is also a deadened, or less aggressive, feeling in the sexual region, resulting in the need for highly intense scenarios to provide ample arousal and (at least temporary) fulfillment. If you identify yourself as having these attributes, it is important to increase your sensory contact with the environment. It is crucial in Stage Two to build your sense of stability or grounding in the world. This means developing a feeling that your feet are firmly planted on the ground. This is particularly important in circumstances that may feel threatening. This sense of grounding will affect your homeostasis and allow more of your complex authentic self to surface.

Once aware of a lack of grounding, you can work to remedy it with a few exercises that can be built into your daily routine with very little effort:

EXERCISE # 1: THE GROUNDING DEVICE

Stand up, with your feet about shoulder width apart and your knees slightly bent (not locked). While maintaining this stance, focus on your breathing and remain aware of the energy between your feet and the ground. Visualize roots growing out of your feet and into the ground. Do this exercise as routinely as possible: while you brush your teeth, when you wash dishes, when you stand in line at the bank or any other time you think of it. The important thing is to consciously bring awareness to, and awaken the energy in, the lower body. I have found this exercise to be highly valuable in improving sensory self- confidence.

Another counterbalancing technique to offset the effects of being too ungrounded is the "opening of the chest," which is useful in facing up to the many challenges on your path. In recovery circles it is not uncommon to hear talk of "low self-esteem and its dualistic counterpart, *grandiosity*. The book, *Alcoholics Anonymous* recognizes these character traits.

Low self-esteem is a feeling of not being competent or deserving. With this come feelings of fear and weakness.

In body energetics terms, the body language (or behavior) which express these same characteristics are referred to as "collapse and compensation." Collapse expresses low self-esteem and compensation expresses grandiosity. I find these terms useful because they begin to illustrate the body defenses and energetic patterns that are at the root of those feelings and subsequent actions. Feelings of weakness and fear are represented by a weakness or emptiness in the chest cavity. When people feel threatened, their fear causes them to experience a kind of collapse in the chest. It is as if their body is literally protecting their heart. When our defenses are overwhelmed by conscious and unconscious fears they trigger repressed terror, which collapses the defenses into paralysis, depression, loneliness, despair, helplessness and withdrawal.

I have developed a simple exercise that relaxes the inner dualistic conflict while simultaneously allowing for an integrative, corrective experience. This exercise can also be used to prepare a person for a fearful situation that might elicit collapse. For example, when it comes time to ask the boss for that long overdue raise, or when you fear being confronted on a sensitive issue, turn to this exercise to help prepare you to manage the situation.

EXERCISE #2: THE ANTI-COLLAPSE DEVICE OR "OPENING THE CHEST"

Assume the grounding position, do conscious breathing (meaning bring significant attention to your in and out breathing), and then spend a minute or so rubbing your hands together to create friction and energy. When you can feel the heat and energy in your hands, put them on your chest, over your heart. With the flow of the conscious breathing you will begin to feel an energetic connection between your hands and your inner chest cavity and heart. The energy will saturate the inner hollowness, and will release a feeling of strength and mild elation. While at first these experiences will be temporary, the awareness they provide is transforming.

Type B: Too Grounded

Those who feel "too grounded" experience a different set of obstacles. When energy becomes displaced in the lower body, we tend to feel almost too grounded. When this is the case, we will feel an intense, often unconscious fear of moving ahead. People who are too grounded tend to

be highly independent, and in denial of their own emotional needs. They tend to approach life more visually than kinesthetically. If you have a naturally strong grounded sense, focus more attention on your upper body. To relax these defenses, you may need to relax your perfectionism. Meditation is the key to relaxing and raising our energy. Stretching exercises and gentle movements will help disorient the defenses and allow insights and tenderness to come forth from your core energy. The anti-collapse device, done while sitting, can be helpful for over-grounded people as well.

One of the problems for very grounded people is that they have difficulty inspiring themselves, finding the energy within that will lead in new directions. An exercise that I recommend for freeing up this potency is to consciously and intentionally do something *out of the ordinary.*

The Anti-Collapse Exercise

EXERCISE #3

Break out, even for an hour, of rigid routines and ways. For example, take a walk to *nowhere* without a time limit in an unfamiliar area. Whenever you encounter an instinct to go in a particular direction, go the opposite way. At the end of your walk, you will be amazed at your outer and inner personal discoveries and the motivated aliveness that you feel *in your body.* Use this energy to reassess your current life directions and help plot your course. Your energy will free up when you deliberately unbalance your rigid involuntary defense reflexes. Find out-of-the-ordinary experiences whenever you want to offset your regular energy flow. Enjoy them, and let them lead you to the life you want to be living.

Activities such as warm baths, music appreciation, self-care, nurturing food and beverage, self-help group meetings, prayer and meditation and inner-child dialogue are valuable for those who are over-grounded. Combined with extra attention to body energetics and sensations, they offer even more fruitful rewards. I strongly recommend that every person in recovery, whether ungrounded or the reverse, begin to practice any activities that increase body awareness, be it massage, yoga, stretching, body-oriented therapy or the above exercises. This is an important, often overlooked aspect of a full recovery.

By willingly exploring your energetic defenses, you are rewarded by gradually releasing your core energy. The expanding availability of this energy brings with it insight and wisdom. Develop an ear for this inner instruction and guidance. It will lead you to further mastery of your own body energies and feelings.

At our New York Institute, we have an advanced course called "Coming Home," which provides in-depth education and experience on our individual defenses. We share the experience of going to the core of ourselves underlying our habitual, involuntary body defenses. We heal them, disarming our defensive reflexes. This level of healing can only be integrated after a reasonable amount of our biographical healing is complete.

Station 3: Exploring the Sexual-Spiritual Split — A Milestone on the Journey to Self-Recognition

After facilitating countless workshops with hundreds of people in recovery, one thing is certain. The healing of the internalized schism between our sexual and spiritual energies is the most provocative topic, and the most intimidating task we can address. I have yet to meet one recovering person who does not highlight this as one of their foremost challenges.

A deeply ingrained and culturally-induced rift between sexual intimacy and spirituality haunts us. Yet, these two human forces are two sides of the same coin. At its most fundamental, spirituality is the opening of the heart, it is also defined as the embodiment of "transcendent beauty." When two people come together with open hearts, sex *is* a sacred act, joining them in body and spirit. A healing experience may occur which is the very embodiment of transcendent beauty, which must be regarded with reverence and respect.

All too often, this is clearly not the case. Opening the heart and keeping it open can be challenging, particularly for those whose sexuality is connected to psychic and spiritual wounds inflicted by early experience. What I call the "sexual-spiritual split" arises out of early religious and cultural training, which teaches that God, love, and family are good while sex is dirty, bad, and perverse. As a result, we find it difficult to resolve our commitment to a "higher" power with the human need to express, satisfy and celebrate our sexuality.

The sexual-spiritual split is a deep psychic schism within almost everyone in our culture which prohibits enduring, loving relationships to form, which at the same time can remain sexually alive and growing. The schism between sexuality and spirituality is caused by cultural, religious, and early programming that plants seeds deep in the unconscious that makes merging the two after bonding virtually impossible without specific healing. "Reclaiming Adolescent Awkwardness" is a phrase I use to give people permission to go to the awkward "places" necessary to heal the sexual-spiritual split and to form authentically intimate relationships. Most will not do this without being given permission and without psycho-cultural education.

The British author Aldous Huxley wrote, "The aim and purpose of life is the *unitive* knowledge of God." This speaks directly to the spiritual dilemma of our time; how to unite the diverging polarities of our dissociative culture. Ever since Descartes said, "I think therefore I am," we have been separating the body, mind, and spirit. I'm convinced that the key to this earthsplitting dilemma we face is to re-unite the body, mind, and spirit, and the primary obstacle most people face is the matter of uniting the spiritual with the sexual. I call this "healing the sexual-spiritual split." We need to reintegrate God and the cosmos with our sexuality.

A Weekend to Remember

The concept of the sexual-spiritual split first inspired the creation of Authentic Process Therapy during a weekend spirituality retreat that I presented in 1984 at Veritas Villa in New York's Catskill Mountains. On Friday evening, I polled the group of forty women and men to determine what areas of recovery they would like to focus on. A young man in the back of the room sheepishly yelled out, "Let's talk about sex!" Since this was scheduled to be a workshop on "spirituality in recovery" everyone found the suggestion amusing. A raucous conversation took place in the room, after which the group implored me to address sex.

Always up for a good challenge, I agreed to schedule a Saturday afternoon workshop to investigate sexuality in recovery. In 1984 this was more challenging than it is today. Since the weekend had been created to explore spirituality issues, I felt additionally challenged to integrate the two. There was another aspect of challenge that tested me in the fifteen hours I would have to prepare for the Saturday afternoon workshop. My co-facilitator was a Catholic nun named Sister Greta!

A significantly painful aspect of my own internalized sexual-spiritual split was planted by a nun when I was about seven. I had never totally healed from that trauma — talk about synchronicity! Although I knew Sister Greta to be a highly compassionate addictions counselor, I could feel a critical mass building inside. The universe was going to heal me whether I liked it or not.

Friday evening, before I went to sleep, I felt deep within that this situation offered a serendipitous occasion for healing. At that point I still didn't know what to do to create interactive participation around this theme of sexuality within the framework of a spiritual retreat. With all the symbolic transference that Sister Greta elicited, the lingering awareness that she would be observing and participating, embarrassed and unsettled me. It triggered all my unconscious fears surrounding my own split. It was hell!

In the few spare moments I had between facilitating other aspects of the retreat, I observed my experience with sex as it relates to my concept of spirituality in addictions recovery. I decided that I would share my personal experiences with the group as a stimulus for discussion.

As the afternoon approached, I could feel both a fear and a mysterious power building inside of me. At lunch I told Sister Greta how nervous I was discussing sex with *her* in the room. Of course, I see in retrospect that this was highlighting my own sexual-spiritual split even before I had named it. She fortuitously replied, "Oh, go ahead, go for it Michael! You aren't going to say anything I haven't already heard; and if you do, I look forward to hearing it."

As the session started, I stood in front of the room nervously holding a piece of chalk. Sister Greta was sitting on a piano bench in the back corner. I looked back at her and we both began to laugh, and at that moment it came to me. I would share with the group my most recent discovery — how I have been separating the concepts of intimacy, sensuality, and sex in my own mind, and how helpful that realization has been to my own sexuality breakthroughs. I darted to the blackboard and put those three words, intimacy, sensuality, and sex, in that order, from left to right at the top of the board, and started discussing the words.

Initially, the group was enlivened though chaotic. They tended to want to lump the words together. I could actually see participants' faces twisted in confusion as they attempted to define these words as independent concepts. When the confusion was well established, I suggested that group members call out words they associated with the word "intimacy." As they did so, I wrote the following words under the intimacy column on the board: "warmth," "communication," "honesty," "caring," "smile," "knowing," "trust," "openness," and so on.

Then we moved to the center column headed by the word "sensuality." As people got silly and awkward they began calling out these words: "touching," "candlelight," "smell," "lick," "biting," "tickling," "music," "whispering," "massage." The list went on and on.

Last, I called for words associated with sex, requesting that we not repeat words already used even though they may have sexual associations. People were obviously embarrassed, as I observed them slyly looking at each other. The presence of Sister Greta was ominous. One woman in front of the room whispered "penis," and everyone in the room giggled as I put it on the board. Then Sister Greta shouted out "orgasm," and the room went into a roar. I listed it on the board, too. Then the words just started coming: "vagina," "cum" (and everyone was curious as to where that spelling originated), "fuck," "suck," "fantasy," "cunnilingus," and a few others. Sister Greta laughed and laughed with a magical healing energy. Without needing to overtly acknowledge or define it, everyone knew that a very special healing was touching us all.

This laugher fueled another insight in me. I was reminded of my own recent thoughts on how difficult it had been to merge my sexuality with an on-going, loving relationship. My fear of self-disclosure relaxed and I saw how I might bring the group to a second (and even third) tier of discovery by sharing my own polarizations in these areas for the group to identify with.

For a few more minutes we lingered with our creation on the board. There were still some confused expressions in the room and some quasi-enlightened remarks. Sam, a 22-year-old former marijuana addict shared, "I have never thought of separating those ideas before. To me they are all the same thing. Looking at them separately sort of twists my brain. I don't know what to do with it, but it looks like an important discovery. What should I do with it?"

Allowing this question to provide a transition into the next level of the exercise, I asked Sam if he would join me in the front of the room to help demonstrate an answer to his question. He agreed. Sam and I stood facing the blackboard. I suggested that he was representing the entire group in this exercise.

I already knew that Sam was not married, he did not have a significant other, and he wasn't dating at the time. I asked him, "Sam, if you met someone that you were attracted to, what would you aim toward first, intimacy or sex?" While doing this I paced back and forth in front of the board pointing at the three headings, first in one direction, then the other. As I "walked the board," I demonstrated the "journey" from each side, first starting with sex (a very common starting point when one has an addictions history), through sensuality and finally to intimacy. Reversing myself, I started at intimacy, moved through sensuality, and then to sex. I then asked Sam and the group to tune into their bodies and feelings and imagine that they were entering a dating situation from both sides, and note their feelings and sensations.

Sam blurted out, "I can't do it. I can't go either way. I can start OK, I can do that from either side, although the intimacy would be new to me. But I don't think I can have both. When I was using pot, it was easy to just have sex. Now that I'm clean, it doesn't work that way. My sponsor says I should date and get to know someone first, but I get terrified and just shut down."

As I continued walking the board, I asked all the participants to raise their hands as soon as I got to a place where they felt they got stuck or paralyzed. In one walk across, every hand in the room, including Sister Greta's, went up. Everyone looked around in surprise — no one more surprised than me. Every one of the forty participants experienced the same paralysis that I had thought was my unique struggle. Everyone in the room acknowledged that they had all thought it was their unique struggle. We were all suffering from a sexual-spiritual split.

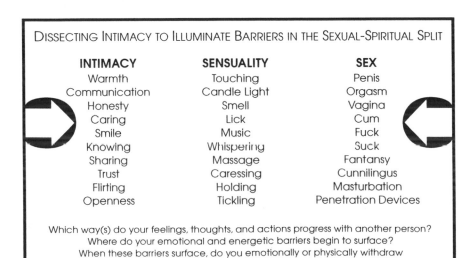

DISSECTING INTIMACY TO ILLUMINATE BARRIERS IN THE SEXUAL-SPIRITUAL SPLIT

INTIMACY	SENSUALITY	SEX
Warmth	Touching	Penis
Communication	Candle Light	Orgasm
Honesty	Smell	Vagina
Caring	Lick	Cum
Smile	Music	Fuck
Knowing	Whispering	Suck
Sharing	Massage	Fantansy
Trust	Caressing	Cunnilingus
Flirting	Holding	Masturbation
Openness	Tickling	Penetration Devices

Which way(s) do your feelings, thoughts, and actions progress with another person?
Where do your emotional and energetic barriers begin to surface?
When these barriers surface, do you emotionally or physically withdraw
or do you forcefully override them?
What historic memories and/or feelings are in the friction-point of the emerging barrier?

I shared some of the other damaging sexual messages that I received early on: that God was synonymous with love, warmth, family, goodness and wholesomeness, and that sex was shameful, disgusting, sinful (mortally so), ungodly and spoken of only in whispers, dirty jokes and sneers. I also told the group that I had uncovered this internalized unconscious split in myself only recently, and that this discovery was finally allowing me to merge these two dynamic, energetic birthrights.

We all have our own version of this internalization. With such a deeply embedded, dualistic concept, how can one possibly bond in love and bring shame-based sex into a relationship? The unconscious sends up powerful, though often deceptive, barriers that prevent a fulfilling merger. A good example of this comes from my own childhood. When I was about seven, I attended catechism class, which was a requirement for all Catholic children. The class was taught by a nun in full habit: an imposing authority figure to a little boy! The class had about thirty students; in fact, I can remember sitting in the middle of a row on the left. The nun was explaining the difference between venial and mortal sin (venial being the lesser one, while mortal seemed to mean that you would be doomed to eternal hell). With these definitions on the blackboard, she pointed at them and strongly proclaimed, "To touch your private parts, or someone else's, is a MORTAL sin! MORTAL, mind you, not venial."

I was in shock: I was already doomed. Not only had I touched my private parts, but I had explored the private parts of friends during our games of "doctor." It was devastating to me: not even eight years old, and I was going to hell. I spent many years thereafter trying to repent to God, making deals to not do it again, only to fail in humiliation and sinfulness. I regretfully share that I was 31 years old before I was able to uproot this demon and quiet the internalized havoc that it brought to my intimate relationships.

Patrick Carnes touched on the subject of the sexual-spiritual split in his book on sex addiction, *Don't Call It Love*. He writes, "Much damage has been done to sexuality in the name of religion. The result inhibits progress on both planes. To heal, start by acknowledging that sexuality is about meaning and that spirituality is about meaning. Search for areas of commonness between the two. Be gentle with yourself about old tortuous conflicts. They are not about you. They never were."

Initially, most adults in recovery do not realize that they have incurred this psychic split, nor do they remember its origins, but they certainly experience the results. You might find the scenario familiar:

once you begin to date, you may experience infatuation, even love and eros. Sex may be very pleasurable. Usually within three to six months, bonding begins as you share struggles and joys. At this point the unconscious polarity begins to haunt the relationship. Since you are not necessarily aware of your past damages or repressed traumas, you may begin to amplify your partner's imperfections in an unconscious attempt to sabotage the relationship. Or you might stay in the relationship and feel inadequate because sex is more work than fulfillment. You may even avoid sex altogether. Simply stated, once bonding occurs, either love or sex must be abandoned. Until we heal this sexual-spiritual split, they cannot seem to live in the same house.

People began to ask, "How can we do it?" In the uncanny, magical flow of that afternoon, I suggested that we move on to the final piece of the exercise and asked for another volunteer. A man in his mid-40s named Gary stood up. His wife Carol, who was sitting beside him, was aghast, laughing and turning red with embarrassment. Someone else roared out, "You can't do it, you're married."

Gary cut through the lighthearted bantering and replied, "Yes I can. I've been married 14 years and sober for 16, and this damn split has haunted every minute of every day of my marriage. I love Carol, but you would never know it by the way I act sexually and intimately. I'd really like to work on this." So we did.

During a break that preceded this part of the exercise, we had moved the chairs from the center and I procured some large 16" x 20" sheets of paper and some felt-tipped marker to make signs with. I asked Gary to stand in the center of the room.

I thanked Gary for his honesty and courage to take part in this psychodrama, and then asked him to take a deep breath and relax, look around the room, and notice all the friendly faces. He did so, beginning to smile and relax. I asked him to go deep into his memory and share with us an early message that he received about sex, and to just look within and say whatever comes up without censoring himself. Gary related, "You'll go blind if you play with yourself." I thanked him and wrote that message with a felt-tip marker on a placard.

Then I asked Gary to pick another participant to represent whoever gave him that message, and he selected an older women named Martha. I asked Martha to hold up the placard six feet in front of Gary and face him.

Then I asked Gary for another message that he had received while growing up. He responded, "Women are sluts." I put it on a placard and Gary picked another workshop participant to represent the person who had given him this message. This time he picked a big, strapping man in his late thirties named Mike. I invited Mike to hold the placard in front of Gary next to Martha, and begin to form a circle.

This continued with messages like "Sex is sinful," "Vaginas are ugly," "You are a pervert," "Women should be virgins," and so on until we had eight people circling Gary and holding placards toward him.

The last message he shared was, "You will do it if you love me." As I wrote the placard, I asked him what it meant. He answered, almost crying, "That's what my uncle would say to me when he molested me."

As Gary took some deep breaths to regain his composure he said, "I've never told anyone, not even Carol, about this before. I can't believe I said it." The visual image was quite profound: Gary in the center of the room being encircled by these early messages.

As Gary tried to compose himself further, I encouraged him to stay present and avoid zipping up his defenses. To enhance the experiential component of the vignette, I asked the "message bearers" to turn the placards toward themselves and loudly read the messages to Gary one by one. I instructed them to keep going around and reading them louder and faster until I asked them to stop. This continued for about two minutes, bringing everyone in the room (especially Gary) to a fevered pitch of discomfort. After stopping the action, I checked in with Gary and asked how he was doing. He replied, "I can't believe I carry all that with me all the time, especially to bed."

I then asked Carol if she would participate, to help us complete the exercise. She said yes, and I asked her to stand about six feet outside the circle facing Gary. I instructed the message bearers to go around reading the messages one more time. Then I asked Carol if all of this made her feel close or distant from Gary. I said, "Does it make you want to move closer or further away?" She replied, "I want to stay right here, I feel like there is a wall between us."

I then invited the group to share. Everyone was enlightened by the realization of how these deep inner messages make sexual intimacy impossible. They could see it and they could feel it; it was crystal clear. I suggested that we move on to a symbolic exercise that would release these unwelcome, uninvited demons. I directed Gary to slowly, one by one, tell the message bearers, "Take back your lousy message. I don't want it. It isn't mine and it never was."

I suggested that as he addressed each one, to tear up the placard and then either throw it on the floor or give it back to the bearer and dismiss them from their role. After Gary "gave back" the first two messages, I checked in with Carol. I asked her if she was feeling any different. She reported that she felt a little closer to Gary, that he seemed more open and available as he discharged the symbolic carriers of these messages. I suggested that she move closer as she intuitively felt his availability. When all the messages were confronted, Gary just stood there facing Carol and began to gently weep.

As all the walls and barriers melted, Carol gracefully moved towards him. As she did, Gary fell to his knees sobbing, "I'm sorry, I didn't know. I didn't mean to push you away like that. I have been bringing all of these ghosts into bed with us all these years." Carol joined him in a kneeling position. They embraced in a manner that included all of us in their intimate connection. The wall of shame was gone. The room glowed with a healing spirit. We all spontaneously became more open, affectionate, and tactile. I stood in warm embrace with Sister Greta. Other participants gently touched or leaned on each other as we all bathed in the intimate healing energy generated by Gary's courageous uncovery process. In those moments I experienced transcendence and simultaneously understood what the humanist therapist Carl Rogers meant when he said, "Whatever is most personal is most general."

As the afternoon session came to a close, participants were sharing their insights regarding their own repressed shaming messages, and wanted to know how they could continue this healing work on their own. I offered to share some techniques with them, and we designated time on Sunday morning for this purpose.

I was awed and positively overwhelmed by the grace and power in these various exercises which have since been incorporated into the Stage Two recovery workshops. I have come to realize the resolution of the sexual-spiritual split as a milestone in this work. I have not met a recovering person who was not shamefully and often unconsciously walled off from tender, loving intimacy (or hot juicy intimacy, for that matter!).

How to Unify and Heal the Sexual-Spiritual Split

Here are six relatively simple suggestions for healing the sexual-spiritual split. The are based on my own healing experience. I shared them that Sunday morning and have continued to refine and articulate them since:

1. Create your own exercises
2. Increase body awareness
3. Share your history

4. Dialogue in relationship
5. Rediscover adolescent awkwardness
6. Enjoy flirting

1. Create your own exercise. Consciously combine meditative, spiritual, or contemplative experiences with your own sexuality. In group settings, this suggestion brings laughter and confusion, further illustrating the split. People always ask, "How are we supposed to do that?" They often break out in further embarrassed laughter and disbelief when I suggest, "You could try experimenting with masturbating and praying at the same time!"

In addressing their defensive laughter, I point out, "Do you see, do you feel, how foreign my suggestion feels? That only emphasizes the reality of this internal polarity!" I encourage people to think about this in relation to merging their core sexuality with a spiritual, loving relationship.

Such experimentation was a very different and awkward experience for me at first, but in time I could feel a new and deeper diversity of both pleasure and release. Sexual experiences grew from being simply physical, with a genital concentration, to becoming a full body, kinesthetic event with cosmic fusion. That was quite a difference.

I also shared some other inventions that helped expose and fuse these opposing forces in me, and I suggested that people create their own. I have told workshop members how I would think about sex whenever I was in a church setting, or how I created rituals with candlelight, mirrors, and incense for sessions of self-loving and self-pleasuring. I shared how I slowly began to make a "special place" in my life for, and began to exalt in, my sexuality, alone or with a companion, as the ecstatic all-encompassing manifestation of my humanity.

2. Increase body awareness. Bring body awareness and energy to your sexual regions. Many recovering people have depleted energy levels and a diminished sense of aliveness in their pelvic area. This is particularly evident in intimate bonding situations. Because of this, sexual motivation usually has more to do with things like neediness, escape from other feelings, and proving one's self-worth, than pure pleasure. For many, pleasure can only be realized in highly charged scenarios that tend to become obsessions or are avoided because they are dangerous and/or self-destructive. Various energetic theories explain that in childhood, the individual's will to survive and endure difficult challenges brings an inordinate flow of energy to the head (or ego), thereby depleting the lower body. Another hypothesis is that all of the complex, repressed feelings about sexual expression solidify under pressure, creating a "wall of shame," that constricts the pelvic region. Whatever the reasons may be, the following exercises have proven helpful in energizing and awakening sexual aliveness in recovering people, and freeing them of this wall of shame.

In Latin and most Eastern and metaphysical philosophies, the word "breath" as we have seen, is synonymous with "spirit." Breathing is very important, and this exercise will help improve your ability to breathe. First, I suggest deep breathing exercises focused in the groin.

EXERCISE #4

Imagine that you can take your breath all the way down to your perineum, that lowermost part of the crotch between the vagina and the rectum or the scrotum and the rectum. This can be done while sitting on a bus, riding in a car, or for a few minutes before or after sleeping. While the results may not be immediate, with a little practice and patience, deeper breathing will lead to spiritual integration.

What I call the "rotation exercise" is an excellent exercise that can either be combined with the conscious pelvic breathing or done independently.

EXERCISE #5

Stand up straight, relax your knees and rotate your hips in a circular motion, stretching out in all directions as far as is comfortable. Imagine that you are standing in the center of an empty peanut butter jar and you want to use your hip and pelvis, in a circular motion, to clean the peanut butter off the sides of the jar. Keep rotating, first in one direction, then the other. Lower and raise yourself to completely clean the inside of that jar. Attention to conscious breathing will be helpful. Take a moment or two to giddily and randomly move your pelvis, tuning in to the energy and spontaneously moving it however it wants to move. Just go with the flow for a few moments. Subtly at first, you will begin feeling a renewed aliveness in this region that is sensual, sexual, and centering — all at the same time.

A last suggestion for energizing the genital zone is gentle, healing touch.

EXERCISE #6

Rub your hands together, heighten the friction and energy, and then slowly lay your hands on and explore your genital area. Tune in to where and when the energy in your hands connects with the energy in your lower abdomen, genitals, buttocks and so on. Let this energetic awareness guide your movement to where you feel that the body thirsts for touch. Linger there, acknowledging the depletion or absence of energy there. Some people find it more comfortable to do this activity with an "imbued love object" such as a stuffed animal, pillow or favorite blanket. These tender and playful exercises can help you take responsibility for, and own, your sexuality in all the splendor and challenge that it encompasses.

If you feel intensely charged in the pelvic region, you may want to do breathing and gentle self-touching that connects your "heart center" to the pelvic area.

EXAMPLE #7

Similar to the anti-collapse exercise (page 87), rub your hands together creating friction, heat, and energy. Then place them over your heart and consciously breathe deeply, allowing your heart to open, meeting it's energy with that of your hands. After you feel this opening and this connection of energy, gently move one hand to your pelvic area. Gradually, as your *inner healer* moves you, glide that hand anywhere that your genitals or buttocks wants to be touched. Stop the movement frequently to consciously breathe, allowing the open heart energy from one hand to connect in magical *healing imagery* with the hand now connected with the pelvic energy. If resistance surfaces to block the energy flow, simply make room for the resistance, allow it to be, and continue breathing into it. Make the resistance okay, embrace it, and you will become larger than your resistance, surrounding it with loving open hearted energy. Notice any images or feelings that come to you as the resistance relaxes. Whatever they may be, they are being presented to you for healing and attention. They are what needs to be healed next in the merging of your sexuality and your spirituality. If no particular images or feelings come to you, the earnest attention you give to these two energy centers simultaneously is extraordinarily healing in and of itself.

While at first you may be fearful of losing your prized intensity, gradually you will discover a new richness, sensuality and diversity permeating your sexuality.

While these exercises are outlined for individual use, they can also be a delightful, healing ritual with a partner.

3. Share your history. Begin a process of uncovering and sharing sexual secrets with "safe" people. It is important to do this work with those who are active, understanding and compassionate listeners. These "secrets" are rightfully too sensitive to be exposed to individuals who will not afford them suitable respect. Along with these secrets there is a need to bring awareness to religious and other spiritually infused influences on one's early sexual evolution.

For someone who wants to do dedicated work in this area, I suggest writing a narrative history, or outline, to put your sexual development in a historical perspective. This begins with the first remembered "exposure" to sex, sexual energy, or sexual material. Then, as best you can remember, indicate the development with subsequent incidents. This exercise will help put your current sexual expression in an understandable and historical context. By sharing this history with a safe person, you can further heal the sexual-spiritual split.

4. Dialogue in relationship. Risk cultivating meaningful dialogue around sexual issues in dating situations and with significant partners. Remember that the deepest interpersonal healing takes place in relationship. You don't need to like this fact, only accept it. Refusal to accept it is self-delusion rooted in fear. Finding or cultivating a safe partner(s) is, of course, pivotal. You can do a great deal of healing with therapists and within community. However, that healing will be limited by the appropriate professional and cultural boundaries of these relationships. To ultimately heal the sexual-spiritual split, explore relating to another human being while attempting to bring both polarized aspects of the split to this relationship without walls of shame arising. It is important to work through shameful aspects and feelings of inadequacy about sex with a partner. It is fine to move slowly. Your intention and willingness are paramount.

5. Rediscover adolescent awkwardness. Become willing to enter a period of discovery called "adolescent awkwardness." In dating or in a significant long-term relationship — a time comes when the healing of this split must be addressed for the relationship to grow. One must surrender preconceived concepts regarding sexuality and intimacy and join another person in authentic adolescent discovery. Recovering people missed a healthy adolescence and therefore cannot go further into intimacy without replacing this important building block. In station four to follow, you will be invited to take a trip back in time to adolescent awkwardness, to revisit your past and find more workable solutions this time around.

Harville Hendrix, who founded the Institute for Relationship Therapy, observed that we all are attracted to people based on an unconscious template. Our endorphins go up when this connection mysteriously reawakens early, primary, relationship dynamics involving needs that were met and those that were not, and we begin an unconscious reenactment of this aspect of childhood. This is not nature's dirty trick, but rather a reintroduction of these dynamics for conscious and unconscious healing. It requires relatively conscious and willing people. Stage Two supports us in this curative transition. There is a good deal of authentic relationship processing in Stage Two community.

6. Enjoy flirting! Redefine your concept of it, as I have learned to do. Realize that connecting eye contact between two people does not necessarily lead to physical contact. Eye contact can be a complete and spiritually energizing act in and of itself. These mysterious, momentary alliances acknowledge a shared "knowing" of intimate inner needs and/or traveled histories that may be telepathically transmitted and responded to. For many, shame and diffuse feelings surrounding sex and intimacy negate the delightful and humanizing effects flirting brings. Enjoy this wonderful human gift as you are able to, seeing sexuality as only one thread in the wider rope of this experience. Also notice your resistance to doing so.

This appreciation of resistance signals the most important awareness of this healing. All of the above exercises will initially bring your resistance to the fore. This is good: you want to bring your resistance up out of your unconscious, where it has ominous rule, and expose it in a process of resolution. By connecting with your resistance, you have the opportunity to discern and untangle the diverse feelings and incidents that have formed themselves into a wall of shame.

Whenever shame or blockage surfaces in a budding or long term intimate relationship, the struggle to share it is part of the process of healthy adolescent development. It is the joining of less mature and more mature aspects of self together in a sensitive, growing relationship. In this process, there is great value in the shame. Shame flirts with us. It lures us while at the same time it tries to hide. As suggested by the author Max Scheler, in his book, Sh*ame and Pride,* "It is from in and under the shame that our shimmering magic emerges."

Sexuality, Higher Consciousness, Relationship

I have learned how combining love with sexual expression can be an act of higher consciousness. In workshops, I help foster the belief (and in this work, genuine *belief creates experience* as we have seen) that when two human beings share love's energy combined with erotic energies, a transcendent experience occurs, one that is often profoundly healing. This is a very sacred sharing and the true goal of a *fulfilling* sexual experience. Reaching this goal is the result of a *give and take,* a negotiation of the open-hearted experience of interconnectedness. Accepting that this is awkward, we need to learn to communicate about our *needs, desires,* and *fantasies.* Under each of the three are powerful and subtle feelings and energies that want to be expressed. These expressions help us grow holistically; they teach us about aggression and passivity, about our feminine and masculine energies, and about pleasuring and being pleasured. They help us dissolve the shame in our contradictions and complexities and expose our need to experience them fully for healing, growth, and self understanding.

Contrary to what many naively believe in recovery, we need to learn that healthy loving expression includes the expression of our more *shadowy* desires as well as our tenderness. The delicate *opening up* of our repressed sexual histories, variations, deviations, and fantasies is extraordinarily enriching and healing. True and spiritual lovemaking is the interweaving choreography of our higher and shadow selves. A holistic experience involves bringing together aspects of higher and lower self — how beautiful and so very intimate to do so with open hearts.

When sex is not fulfilling in a monogamous relationship, the cornerstone of the union is weak and vulnerable. Most of us, consciously or unconsciously, commit to such a relationship, at least in part, so that we need not search for sexual fulfillment elsewhere. If fulfillment dwindles and becomes barely existent, the foundation of the relationship is betrayed. People will often feel imprisoned and act out in emotional or sexual ways. There is, or will soon be, trouble in paradise. Often, because couples lack the skill required for the sensitive dialoging, they go into denial, often for years. This is not necessary. New skills are available to them here.

I am happy to report that I have been living in a sexually fulfilling, loving relationship for some time now. All the work has been worth it!

Opening up the heart during sex, letting go of taboos, being shame-free, while also being responsible and self-respecting, is the key to both the kingdoms of pleasure and higher consciousness. It is no wonder that when some people are in the throes of orgasm they say, "Oh God!" In that moment of letting go and dropping defenses, the reality blurts out. To me, loving sex heightens consciousness, and for me God is consciousness, and pure consciousness is love.

Imagine yourself and your partner, with open hearts, choosing to pleasure each other. Imagine breathing and letting go into the pleasure, whatever it may be, and knowing that you are going to God. Your partner is joining and supporting you in this awareness and experience. Then you pleasure your partner in whatever ways are desired and appropriate for the two of you. If you really give yourself such a delightful experience, you will experience ecstatic sex, erotic energy, and you will have a rich spiritual experience that is also enlightening. Every time more veils are dropped between partners, more consciousness opens to them. It will reveal itself in the daily living of life and in creative expression. This is what sex and pleasuring looks like when you are healing the sexual-spiritual split.

I believe we can always further heal this schism, always drop more veils, and always enhance our capacity for pleasure and spirit. If all the veils were gone, we would be pure spirit and probably not human any longer. How interesting to ponder such ideas as we heal ourselves day by day, and with each healing, enhance our ability to give and receive pleasure.

In evaluating our progress in healing our sexual-spiritual split, we need to simply ask ourselves: What motives do I bring to sexuality? What do I want from the sexual aspect of my nature? We know that our healing is progressing when our answers to these questions emphasize spiritual fulfillment, integrating our aggression and passivity, power and surrender, femininity and masculinity, and the desire for shared experiences of pleasure and higher consciousness.

Station 4: Revisiting Adolescent Awkwardness

I have never met a recovering person who could explore the awkwardness of adolescence without some coaching. Our involuntary defenses inhibit such experiments with embarrassment.

This is an important rite of passage that enables us to engage in dynamic, emotional, energetically-connected relationships. This passage leads to deeper alliances with friends, peers and family, as well as an intimate sexual relationship. Recovering people need to be made aware that, for many reasons, each of us missed some important developmental building block in our adolescence. We need to realize that we may have never had an experience of bringing our most complex, authentic self into union with another's.

In fact, in our culture, we all missed the experience of healthy adolescent exploration. When I ask clients about their first sexual experience, or their adolescence, the innocent *give and take* of pleasure is usually missing, as it was in my own history. Many of us drank or drugged through it, our sexual self-image already damaged. Some just sexually withdrew. However, it is still not too late to "permission" ourselves to learn a new skill and a new language. The permission and encouragement is necessary because it is still an awkward dialogue. We may once again experience being an awkward adolescent. Reclaiming this missing part of our development makes sexual fulfillment possible. Learning what it is we want and need and being able to respectfully ask for it is the goal. We learn to pay attention to these same needs from our partners and open our hearts to meet them as best we can. Even the intent to do this is very fulfilling.

To discover your real need for physical and sexual pleasure, tune into the signals of your intuitive mind and body. Move away from both logic and habitual dictates, and immediately a new path can be cut. You may find yourself, for the first time, able to bring your heart, words, and needs to your sexual expression. You may come to appreciate a new wholeness in yourself and your relationships.

It dawned on me some years ago that with all of my therapy and self-discovery, I had eroded my defenses. I found myself completely disarmed in romantic or dating encounters. I felt open, vulnerable and a bit goofy. There was often a wavering thick layer of raw fear that bounced around my upper chest and throat. But there was also an element of youthful excitement to this openness. Accompanying this managed exhilaration was the fearful inability to articulate it. I needed a new language.

When I shared this dilemma with my therapist, she suggested that it sounded like adolescence. Returning home, I immediately went to my *American Heritage Dictionary* to refresh my understanding of the definition. It stated that adolescence is "the period or state of development from the onset of puberty to maturity." I wondered about my own pubescent development, and eventually realized that in terms of self-authenticity, mine had been absent. In a headstrong way, I had pulled myself through those years, never stopping to face or acknowledge the excitement, insecurities, and needs that resided within. This is where the new language began.

Never having learned a second language before, particularly one that incorporated personal sensitive feelings, I felt challenged. However, I intuitively knew that this was the only road to having my basic human needs met, and to this goal I felt committed. In practicing this sexual and emotional articulation, the demons of perfectionism, humiliation and embarrassment were the first barriers. (For most of us there seems to be an irrational feeling that embarrassment is the doorway to death. In Stage Two we reframe this self-defeating thinking.)

In honoring the voice and feelings from my inner child, I suddenly realized I could no longer allow my habitual perfectionist-self to govern. I knew that to authentically relate to another, I would have to acknowledge and share my fears, insecurities and feelings of inadequacy. This also might mean exposing my history of damaging sexual and religious exposures and abandonment all over again. By sharing these deepest feelings, I would certainly shatter whatever was left of my packaged, "in control," outside demeanor — what would be left of *me* then? Under the "perfect mask" that I still, to some degree, deludedly brought to relationships, I found a new layer of my shame. I was deeply ashamed that I fudged over learning to relate to other people. I had fears and inadequate feelings that I hid from exposure, and I felt fundamentally flawed and unworthy, and didn't want anyone else, even the therapist, to know this.

Humiliation began to gag me as I thought of exposing these deeply held personal secrets. The price seemed too high. How could I humiliate myself like that? On some deep level I still feared being scorned and abandoned. These were no small fears considering my developmental history. To open up emotionally and expose my sensitivities and neediness would risk triggering all the repressed trauma, loss, grief, rage and confusion from my childhood. These were the feelings that, having no safe outlet, had twisted and shaped my persona of controlled self-determination to begin with. I needed a key of some kind to free me from this double-bind. I knew that I needed to expose more of myself to form intimate relationships. Sometimes a simple therapy session can change your life. But, how would I overcome my fears and put this realization into action?

How to Reclaim and Enjoy Adolescent Awkwardness

Two realizations rescued me from this binding dilemma: calculated risk-taking, and distinguishing shame from embarrassment. These emerged from the transformational, experiential workshops that I explored in the 70s and early 80s. These workshops provided a safe environment that integrated Eastern philosophies with Western psychologies. I was amazed to realize that most of the participants shared similar fears regarding intimacy and exposure. With as many as three hundred participants in a large hotel ballroom, we were all sharing this fear that I held so closely. I was not as "uniquely" flawed as I once thought. Most of the other participants were not even addicts or former addicts. They were just people from all walks of life and they had fears and feelings of inadequacy, too. They too shielded their own self-sabotaging of their own intimate pursuits. If this were true, and it certainly appeared to be, then I might be able to expose myself. I wondered: Is this what healthy adolescent discovery was all about; is this what I missed?

It was still going to take courage to completely shift my psyche toward this willingness to expose. To do this would be nothing less than transformational. And that is exactly what happened. Again, I was in a large hotel ballroom filled with hundreds of people. Werner Erhart, the founder of Erhart Seminar Trainings, was presenting a playful piece on risk-taking and embarrassment.

He made a complete fool of himself in front of the room, and the reaction of the participants was awkward identification and smiles of endearment. He reflected to us how silly we are for being so reserved. This demonstration vividly illustrated to me that calculated embarrassment might be the doorway to empowerment and fulfillment. This was a curious and disarming revelation. We found ourselves loving this guy for taking risks with us. And he seemed so free, liberated and happy doing so! We all laughed, and in that laughter I had an awesome awakening. It was as if my inner child popped up and said, "I can do that. I want to!" And the adult part of me instantly responded, "Yes, we really can."

In that moment I *distinguished shame from embarrassment*, reframing embarrassment as a metaphor for coy exposure and liberation. I now knew that as long as I felt a person was trustworthy, my self-exposure would no longer be terrifying. It would always be exciting (excitement, after all, can include a negotiable measure of fear), liberating, and playful. It might even be endearing. Not only was I transformed, but I am pleased to report that this awareness has sustained me since that day. It has enriched and deepened all of my most cherished relationships.

This shift in consciousness and expression enabled me to begin the deeper healing of my sexual-spiritual split, and empowered me with two skills for energetically and emotionally opening up my relationships. I have used these skills of calculated risk-taking and self-exposure in my work to meaningfully share these ideas with others in recovery.

I discovered that people experience transformation in this area when they reach a point of critical mass with their own intimacy conflicts and double binds. I have been privileged to watch many people traverse these waters, buoyantly exploring the blissful feelings and revelations that are the underside of these awkward adolescent feelings. Individuals (often in workshops) who may not yet be at a level that can host this full-bodied revelation often hold the ideas as seeds for later cultivation.

Psycho-education, coaching, and cajoling are absolutely essential at this phase. It must be sought after and administered in sensitive ways that honor the defenses and challenges. This is well-done in community groups where the mirroring with peers graces the process.

I have noticed that among heterosexual couples, the adolescent awkwardness surfaces in ways that are influenced by society's idea of gender roles. Men (or those taking a male role in a relationship) often believe that their male identity is defined by controlling and masking their sensitivities. They believe that without such control, they will fall into a so-called non-male, feminine state of weakness that elicits ridicule, abandonment and psychic anguish. This is a deeply internalized barrier for most men, and it must be sensitively uprooted and reframed. The fragile ego defense must be counterbalanced with authentic self-assurance, self-respect and self-praise for courage exhibited in pursuing further self-discovery.

Women (or those taking a female role in a relationship) tend to display a different dynamic. Often they are more willing, and even desirous of entering into adolescently awkward discovery. However, they may unconsciously sabotage the discovery when wounds and sensitivities are triggered by the awkward and sometimes ignorantly insensitive expressions of their male partner. While these remarks are a bit overgeneralized, they offer some background to how the gender gap is important in understanding adolescent awkwardness.

In same-sex couples there is an interesting paradox. The dynamics are more complex because there are no longer traditional male and female roles to default to, though they tend to creep in. On the other hand, the healing or reclaiming of adolescence is often more fluid. The vast majority of sexually diverse people, until very recently, clearly didn't have a hint of healthy adolescence to refer to, and so the need for filling in the blank is abundantly clear. They adapt quickly to the process because, having had to sustain and define themselves outside the acceptable norms, they are not attached to a role or *how things should be*. They are accustomed to cutting new paths because, for their own survival, they have always had to.

When I work with clients in individual sessions, there is often an awkward feeling in the room when discussing their issues. It is often only after discussing and accepting this awkwardness that the client may reveal a previously undisclosed aspect of self. It is often at these moments of struggle that true authenticity emerges and my relationship with the client takes on deeper meaning and usefulness. Awkwardness when befriended is a true friend indeed.

This "reclaiming adolescent awkwardness" is a time to discover, with other human beings, the value and glory of risking awkward self-exposure. It is also a time to learn graceful timing: Learning to intuitively meter out pieces of yourself in an interactive and balanced repertoire with someone else; and learning to receive and respect pieces of the other person's inner self. When these two merge, it is, under the best of circumstances, gracefully awkward. That is why we must be willing to feel embarrassed and imperfect.

I encourage you to identify and begin a process of befriending your awkward situations and moments. Make up playful exercises to begin normalizing awkwardness. For example, if you go to self-help meetings, go to a meeting early and sit quietly in a chair while the room fills. Feel your awkwardness and your response. Most likely you will feel an overwhelming need to make meaningful contact with another person or you will want to flee in awkwardness. Instead, try sitting with these feelings and begin to quietly accept and explore them as part of the human condition. When we are needy for nurturing or attention, awkwardness prevails. There seems to be an internal give-and-take, or cat-and-mouse, with the cloaked sensitivities surrounding these needs. If we can make friends with — and not run from — this awkwardness, there will be a much greater possibility that our needs will be fulfilled. Make up your own exercises to neutralize awkwardness. By embracing this feeling we become empowered.

Station 5: Re-Experiencing Original Pain and Trauma

Why would anyone want to re-experience original pain and trauma? It does certainly sound difficult at the very least! Pain hurts, right? And yet it is unresolved emotions concerning old pains and traumas that block our core energy, and that energy is an incredible, unlimited source of power and wisdom that can make miracles happen and bring us palpably into the experience of holism and its total integration with the universe. Is it worth it? Certainly. How do you do it? That's not always so certain.

To demystify these ideas and make them less foreboding, let's start with some basic definitions:

Original: Preceding all others in time; showing a marked departure from previous experience; not derived from something else; fresh and unusual.

Pain: An unpleasant sensation, occurring in various degrees of severity and suffering or distress.

Trauma: A wound, especially one produced by sudden physical injury; an emotional shock that creates substantial and lasting damage to the psychological development of the person.

This station requires a transition into a state of willingness. When I suggest "re-experiencing original pain and trauma" in workshops, the energy in the room goes flat and faces become pale and expressionless. As we explore this concept further, participants begin to acknowledge in various ways that they either know or suspect that old pains and traumas are contaminating their current reality.

In the safety of the workshop, with focused community support, we find the courage to bring historic demons forward. At the end of these workshops almost everyone leaves more enlightened and renewed, with a more integrated sense of self. This for many is the beginning of what I call "creating a host environment." This creation, or shift in willingness, is the pivotal aspect of this healing phase.

Original trauma refers to the first time a particular type of trauma occurred. Many people perpetuate that original trauma over and over again. It can become part of their character structure. An original trauma can create reactions which create subsequent traumas which are often increasingly complex as to who is responsible — we become gradually mixed up in it. In healing the wounds, we work back to the original incident layer by layer.

There are times when our unconscious pains and traumas are triggered by circumstances that are beyond our control. A crisis or tragedy will trigger a suppressed feeling, forcing us to deal with it before we are emotionally prepared to explore this area. As Stephen Levine suggests, "Healing is to enter with awareness and compassion that which we have withdrawn away from in anger, fear and judgement." Author Dan Millman suggests that "Tragedies serve as an express elevator to spirit." Poet Kristen Zambucka puts it still another way:

Pain accompanies all birth.
There is pain when we are born...
and there is pain when we are re-born
as old facets of the personality die away...
or are brutally torn out of our life pattern...
to make way for the new.
In breaking down the old future, one's world may seem to fall
    apart.
Trouble will enter like a storm...
A tempest will rage...
Do not resist...
there is a balancing power at work...
your new self is about to enter the world.

At this station, we incorporate elements learned from repressed trauma therapy. This station offers a chance to reconstruct your life by getting in touch with the flow of the life force, and identifying where the flow is obstructed.

When a trauma is present, you may locate an interruption in the flow of memories and life history, an interruption in your emotional flow, and an interruption in the flow of energy within the body. When I ask people in therapy to go back to the point of trauma, they often feel the onset of a strong bodily restriction. By working on unblocking the flow within the body, the repressed memories and emotions are also unblocked.

In my own Stage Two recovery journey, this was at least a ten-year process. Fortunately, each new discovery along the way gave me back another piece of myself, expanding my choices and possibilities. For many of the people I work with today, Stage Two seems more like a five-year process. The way our shared consciousness is growing, and with the improvement of community technologies, the process will get shorter still.

It is in this aspect of our process that we begin to reclaim our dissociated parts and look under our defenses. The awareness of body energetics greatly facilitates this work. If we rely solely on our logical, cognitive mind, we will continue to do what we have always done, and the results will be as they have always been. If we look into and beyond our defensive posturing, we expand the possibilities for awakening truncated aspects of self. This awakening leads to a healing integration.

Before I suggest the additional ways that original pains and traumas are consciously awakened, I want to offer two more somewhat simplified pictures of early childhood development. Trauma specialist Judith Herman suggests that "A secure sense of connection with caring people is the foundation of personality development." She continues to explain:

> Traumatic events violate the autonomy of the person at the level of basic bodily integrity. The body is invaded, injured, defiled... Furthermore, at the moment of trauma, almost by definition, the individual's point of view counts for nothing... The traumatic event thus destroys the belief that one can be oneself in relation to others.

These feelings are also practically universal among people in Stage Two of their recovery. It seems that our addictions produce numbing effects that help recovering people dissociate from emerging traumatic feelings. This was certainly my experience, although I was in recovery some years before I became conscious of the process. In *Betrayal of Innocence*, psychologists Susan Forward and Craig Buck add to this important perspective:

> To a young child, adults, especially parents, are the embodiment of all wisdom and goodness. The child must believe that the adult is good, because the child is totally helpless and dependent on the parent. To believe, even for a moment, that a trusted adult is malevolent, would be terrifying and overwhelming. Therefore, if something bad happens, the child automatically believes it is because he or she is bad. Any other belief creates too much anxiety. Self-blame is a powerful defense for the child against what would be unbearable feelings of panic and terror.

Of course, for so many of us this original defense of self-blame is hidden by the shame of not being perfect, and the emotional spiral unwinds from there into betrayal and self-loathing. Because those first experiments with trust were so painful, we may have great unconscious difficulty bringing ourselves to trust again. We slowly learn to risk extending trust only to those people or groups that are reasonably consistent and respect authenticity.

Sexual, Endurance, Physical, and Emotional Trauma

There are four major types of trauma we may be repressing and possibly dissociating from, each with their own characteristics. These are: sexual trauma, endurance trauma, physical trauma, and emotional trauma. We will take them up one by one:

SEXUAL TRAUMA

Indications of sexual trauma are usually present in people in recovery, even if not overtly. Of course, the most obvious sexual trauma is incest, rape and other forms of physical and sexual abuse. Many people have also suffered covert or emotional incest. This means that they were exposed to sexuality and/or seductive sexual energy by a family member or other older person before they were mature enough to understand the activity. For the purpose of creating a community vocabulary, any incidents that injured or neglected one's innocence during the sexual development process I refer to as sexual trauma.

This activity can present itself in many ways. Perhaps the child becomes the surrogate partner for a spouse who is not getting his or her needs met — that is a seductive relationship. Sometimes the trauma is physical and sometimes it is strictly emotional or part of an energy dynamic — this too is part of sexual trauma. Sometimes a severe religious upbringing disturbs people's natural sexual development, bringing with it many of the attributes that are seen in cases of covert (or even overt) sexual abuse.

ENDURANCE TRAUMA

Most recovering people have had, at the very least, endurance trauma. This is the prolonged sense of feeling unsafe in one's world during childhood. It is that day-in and day-out, low-grade threat to our sense of safety and security. While it seems harmless and non-threatening, it is constant, and its continuity can create defenses and emotional/energetic distortions as severe as the most violent and overt direct abuses. An example of endurance trauma would be a child who grows up in a home with an unpredictable alcoholic, or otherwise impaired parent, one who sporadically loses control and threatens the safety of themselves and those around them. After one or two such incidents, the child *lives in waiting* — a constant day-in and day-out terror, anticipating the next episode. This terror over time *is* endurance trauma.

PHYSICAL TRAUMA

In attempting to classify and give language to our historic wounds, physical trauma identifies wounds, injuries, illness and assaults to our physical bodies, including perhaps the expressed threat to further punishment. This can also include childhood injuries and disabilities.

EMOTIONAL TRAUMA

While this identification could be a catch-all for many different conditions, it is useful for categorizing wounds that do not readily fit in the other areas. For example, when I was growing up, my two older brothers had little time for me. They were probably busy trying to hold their own lives together. Whenever I sought attention from them they jokingly — and sometimes not so jokingly — called me a brat. Although they were playful, I was wounded. I began to believe that I was a brat, and that my needs for attention were bad. I consciously created a cover-up and affected an independent, "I don't need anybody" demeanor. Fortunately, some years back, I emerged from these unconscious contortions and was able to begin consciously getting my needs met in adult relationships.

How to Heal Original Pain and Trauma

There are a number of ways repressed traumas become known to us in Stage Two Recovery: Permissioned Emergence, Creating a Host Environment, Spiritual Emergencies, Understanding the Logic of Feeling, and Flashbacks and Distortions, among others. All are gifts of healing which lead us toward a restored holistic relationship with the world.

PERMISSIONED EMERGENCE

The idea of "permissioned" emergence gives us a new perspective on what some traditional forms of psychotherapy would call analyzing one's history. In Authentic Process we don't look to analyze or dig up personal history. We allow (and consciously permit or "permission") historic material to surface into our consciousness in a natural way. Then we feel it emotionally and allow the experience to bring additional perspectives to our life. We do not necessarily analyze the material. It emerges, we observe it, and we accept it.

Although it sounds foreboding, the emergence of original pains and traumas can be an alluring and engaging time of self-discovery and self-appreciation. This process of self-illumination is frightening at times; the voluntary and involuntary resistance to discovery can be painful. The aftermath of a traumatic discovery may reveal chaotic episodes of complex feelings. Trust that out of confusion comes clarity; out of chaos order emerges. Without this belief, this work would be impossible. Some of the new literature on chaos theory helps ground us in trusting these possibilities. N. Katherine Hayles, a leading researcher in chaos theory, notes our cultural resistance to complexity and disorder:

That chaos has been negatively valued in the Western tradition may be partly due... to the predominance of binary logic in the West. If order is good, chaos is bad because it is conceptualized as the opposite of order. By contrast, in... Taoist thought, not-order is also a possibility, distinct from, and valued differently than, anti-order. In chaos theory chaos may lead to order, as it does with self-organizing systems, or in yin/yang fashion it may have deep structures of order encoded within it.

Creating a Host Environment

To heal addictive behavior you must gradually heal the underlying trauma which gave birth to it. In order to embrace the new revelations which arise from healing your past trauma, simply make a conscious choice to recover on multiple levels; take a bigger bite out of the "commitment apple." This conscious choice is the beginning of birthing a "host environment": surrounding ourselves with supportive people and therapies that nurture us and which respect both the challenges and goals of this Stage Two undertaking. This shift in willingness begins to shake us out of denial and self-delusion. The intention to realize the benefits of these efforts fuels the discovery. Dissociative or split-off aspects of ourselves become approachable, more recognizable, and more susceptible to reorganization and integration.

With this conscious, courageous posture of commitment and willingness, review your history through this newly created host environment that welcomes the emergence of complex and emotionally charged traumas and pains. To this self-inquiry, bring an awareness of "sense-of-self" spirituality, body energetics and sensations, and the internalized sexual-spiritual split. Even a moderate awareness of your unconscious or inner child will fuel this process of awakening unresolved shame-laden conflicts.

Understanding Spiritual Emergencies

As you begin to safely re-open and explore these wounds one by one, expect some feelings of fear or apprehension. There are times, which I call Spiritual Emergencies, when new trauma will inadvertently trigger either repressed memories of past traumas, or resistance to those memories such as dissociation and acting out. Many stages of healing could be involved, depending on where the person is in the process, and could create a cascading or simultaneous reaction. There are many variables. You may be flooded with a rush of intense, complex feelings. People report that they feel like "the rug has been pulled out from under them" as intense feelings crash through worn-down defenses. This usually happens when we are *not* consciously addressing Stage Two issues, often in combination with real-life events such as loss or grief. It is also commonly called a nervous breakdown, an emotional breakdown or a psychotic episode.

Transpersonal psychologist Christina Grof and her husband Stanislav Grof, the psychiatrist, were the first to recognize these instances as "spiritual emergencies." In Authentic Process Therapy, these emergencies are relatively rare. In my own five-year clinical study of one-hundred-twelve people in Stage Two therapy, only two experienced symptoms of this magnitude. Their experiences were relatively short-lived and they immediately received the necessary support to reorganize their systems and begin structuring new, more self-empowered defenses. They are more common when individuals attempt to sidestep emotionally complex trauma work after years in recovery. Unfortunately, many people long into their primary addiction recovery have such occurrences because there was no clear Stage Two model available to help them understand their feelings.

Consider the case of Jorge, who had been sober and in AA for 22 years. His daughter, who was 18 years old, accused him of having fondled her repeatedly when she was 7 to 10 years old. They were encouraged to see a family therapist. Though he denied it at first, in a session it came out that he really didn't mean it, he had acted on impulses and he didn't think she would remember. It later came out that he was continuously fondled as a child by his own mother. He had never shared that with anyone before in his years of recovery. Instead he reenacted it. He had not opened himself to Stage Two processes and the repressed traumas were forced out in a situation that was beyond his control. The result of this confrontation and the resulting process sent Jorge into a spiritual emergency or breakdown that led to months of psychiatric care. Finally, Jorge began to share and heal his own past.

Honoring the Logic of Feelings

The logic of feelings sometimes runs counter to everyday reasoning. Everyday Western reasoning suggests that we should avoid painful or unpleasant memories — since we fear that they will overwhelm us. However, I have discovered that feelings want to be *completed*. By avoiding these issues and the changes that they provoke, you set the stage for more out-of-control, intense emotions to overpower your defenses as they wildly try to complete their life cycles in spite of you. They want resolution and closure. Once you accept this as logical, you begin to unite your heart and mind so that they can work together towards the healing of your past trauma.

Part of completing feelings entails connecting to and with them. One of the best ways to connect to them is to have them heard and seen by another empathic human being, or fair witness. Each time such a connection is made, they lose some of their charge. Without such connections and completions, however, these intense repressed feelings stay lodged in the body-mind and continue to undermine your life. In the realm of feeling, this reaction is logical and predictable. It is the heart's own way of saying, "pay attention to me."

There are many ways to reach these original wounds and traumas: community process, attention to dreams, creative writing and expression, and most importantly, the daily living of life itself. As you observe the difficulties and defenses that you bring to everyday life situations, you may discover that energetically and emotionally your wounds are just beneath the surface. Previously, you may have viewed your limitations as character flaws. After exploring these original wounds and traumas, reframe your limitations as clumsy old bandages over your wounds. This reframing allows you to give up both the infantile self-blame and the adolescent shame of being imperfect. It allows you to remove the old bandages and thus shed a new healing light upon the old wounds.

Understanding Flashbacks and Other Distortions

Flashbacks are defined as recurring intrusive images that interrupt one's consciousness — fleeting thoughts that are hard to hold. Some people experience other things that are related to these: a sense of emotional numbness or unreality, or the sense that various body parts are growing, shrinking, burning or tickling. Still others experience hallucinations.

Obsessions and dreams are also important clues in our search for understanding. Watch for and become willing to tune into, the energy and feelings that are associated with them. With appropriate support, they will take you home to your core.

While these experiences are understandably frightening, do not let your fear keep you from exploring, in safe settings, the energetic and emotional foundation of these symptoms. By examining what lies under these flashbacks, defenses and distortions in consciousness, you can reconnect emotionally with historic physical, emotional and sexual wounds, abandonment and other forms of deprivation.

It is important to remember that in community these wounds can be reorganized and re-framed in a way that is empowering rather than debilitating. Some sexual and other abuse wounds can be horrifying in their diverse manifestations and our culture is only beginning to recognize their prevalence.

The process of psychic emergence can often be accelerated or slowed down, based on your individual needs — which may change from time to time. The responsive ebb and flow of life's daily challenges must be taken into consideration. Your defenses will typically re-emerge when you need to slow down. It is appropriate to acknowledge this, recognize it as a time of outer rest and inner reorganization, and wait for your defenses to relax. This need to slow down usually comes because your system feels overwhelmed and threatened. There may not be enough psychic energy or community support to adequately address all inner and outer demands. On the other hand, there are times when a recovering person has steady equilibrium, and is therefore more prepared to accelerate the discovery process. These are times to trust your intuition and consider incorporating some of the other dynamic modalities.

APT and other authentic process settings (you will discover some of these in the *Resources* directory in the back of this book) are excellent for re-invigorating the discovery process, and reconnecting with truncated memories and feelings. Community healing provides a supportive environment and corrective experiences that heal the feelings under the defenses, thereby consciously triggering resistance and illuminating self-sabotaging mechanisms. Only after this can we relate and grow in more deeply intimate ways.

Station 6: Grieving Unresolved Losses

Grief is a normal and natural response to any significant loss. It presents a conflicting mass of human emotions that follow any major change in familiar patterns of behavior. According to therapists John W. James and Frank Cherry, co-founders of The Grief Recovery Institute:

> We grieve for the loss of all relationships that could be held as significant and therefore emotional: moving from one house to another in early childhood can be such an event. Leaving the routine of the home to start school can cause grief for many children. Divorce can cause enormous conflict and confusion. Even marriage can cause feelings of loss for a familiar life style. Dealing with addictions to alcohol, drugs, food and so on can

lead to monumental grief. Often, these common life experiences are not seen as grieving events.

Recovering people will recognize this last sentence as a profound understatement. Every one I have come to know suffers from an unconscious, individualized "laundry list" of unresolved losses. These repressed losses are easily explained, since most of us lacked a safe and supportive enough environment during childhood in which to express and explore complex feelings.

Grief is intentionally separated from original wounds and traumas for the following reasons: Grief has its own unique characteristics and manifestations and is universal to the human experience. Ironically and magically, the healing process involved can be distinctively beneficial to all other healing as well as the grief which precipitated it.

The prevalence of unresolved grief in recovering people is additionally compounded by societal denial of the complexities of loss. As John Bradshaw suggests, "Grief involves the whole range of human emotions. The original pain is an accumulation of unresolved conflicts whose energy has snowballed over time. The wounded child is frozen because there was no way he could do his grief work. All his emotions are bound by toxic shame....We came to believe that we could not depend on our primary care giver. In fact, we came to believe that we had no right to depend on anyone. Isolation and the fear of depending on anyone are two of the main consequences of toxic shame."

Often, when we appropriately express our grief, our friends and family don't know what to say to us. They are afraid of our feelings. They will try to change the subject or intellectualize the process. They think that keeping busy helps. Practically no one wants to talk about death or feelings of loss. We are encouraged to pull ourselves together and get on with our lives.

Because we tend to want the approval of others, we rise above our grief, abandoning our aliveness behind in the shadows. We attempt to suppress our feelings only to have them haunt us later. We engage in acting-out behavior to relieve the psychic pain, frustration, and pressure. For many of us who had found at least temporary psychic relief in addictions, we were struggling to find some peace from the constant undercurrent of our unattended losses.

Though most of us come into recovery, and even into our Stage Two work, completely unaware of our repressed, unresolved grief, it will resurface if we are willing. We must resolve our grief so that the re-enactments and compulsively driven lifestyles can be transformed. With validation and support, each person needs to experience the feelings that were not originally allowed. We need to do this in safe community contexts. Some of the complex feelings involved in grief work are sadness, anger, remorse, hurt, depression and loneliness. The duration depends on the severity of the loss, and the degree to which it may trigger other unconscious losses.

In my own grief work, I was amazed at the intensity and depth surrounding these emotionally forgotten patches of my history. The first trauma surfaced when I was 32 years old and newly abstinent from drugs and alcohol. What erupted under me was the complex feelings of loss and grief surrounding the death of my teenage bride eleven years earlier.

We had married young, I was age eighteen. It was one of those wonderful and crazy teenage things, a time of great learning and great confusion. Sheila and I were aware of all of our immature traits, but our love and commitment were unquestionable. In the three years that we had together, Sheila suffered a leg amputation from a rare bone cancer, which later metastasized to her lung. She died after a year of tortuous physical, psychic and emotional pain.

She died without us ever having acknowledged that she had a terminal disease or discussing her impending death. Times were different then: we did not know how to negotiate such complexities. This emotional incompleteness caused me much pain. I had somehow shrouded the entire trauma.

In therapy, eleven years later, the entire experience unraveled. With deep feeling I rediscovered and shared many of the pains and confusions from the compounded traumas, as well as many of the sweet and tender moments that counterbalanced them. I remembered the day at the hospital when the doctor informed me that her leg would have to be amputated. It was the night of the East Coast electrical blackout. It took six hours to drive home with her mother, neither of us saying a word. The setting was strangely appropriate: My whole world was going dark but I didn't know how or where, to express my feelings. As I finally came out of my own "blackout" I recalled the struggles my wife endured when she was fitted for a prosthesis and had to learn to walk again, I remembered the coughing spells that signaled her pneumonia.

When all of this came back to me, my foremost emotion was shame. I was ashamed of my emotional incompleteness. I felt that I could have comforted us both more if only I had known how to communicate effectively. I felt I failed her. I was ashamed of the helplessness that I felt throughout the entire crisis. My complex thoughts and feelings of relief when she finally died compounded this shame.

In therapy, after experiencing my emotions, I was able to reconnect with the love and tenderness in our union. This came over me like a wave of peace. It felt as though the best and most loving parts of my deceased partner instantly surrounded and engulfed me. In the purity and amplification of these feelings, my soul was restored. I immediately felt more open and more alive. Love lived in my heart again. When I shared all of these feelings, I gained the ability to once again have a significant, loving relationship.

A second incident of unresolved grief that surfaced was related to my childhood pet and best friend, Shep. He was a collie who looked very much like Lassie of TV and movie fame. I was in a workshop when it hit me.

I recalled how Shep was getting old and losing the use of his hind legs. I remembered the day that the vet picked him up to "put him to sleep." Although I was only thirteen years old, I was the family member selected to supervise Shep's departure. I remembered the man muzzling Shep and carrying him to the truck. I closed the door and died inside.

When the rest of the family came home, they acknowledged Shep's absence, made some reassuring comments and jokes to one another, and continued their business. No one noticed that I was in a complete state of shock. No one in my family was prepared to soothe me or help me sort through my complex feelings.

Twenty-two years later, when I allowed my inner child to come out, I was able to grieve and reconnect with Shep. I have shared this story in workshops as an example of unresolved grief. It's been a beautiful way to honor Shep's memory. Because of this uncovering process, he still lives and so do important parts of my emotional self.

I have had many such discoveries in the gradual awakening of my emotionally incomplete losses. It seems that as time progresses, I connect with the oldest and deepest of them. I welcome this depth of character because I have slowly learned, and come to trust, that in these unresolved regions lie my true spirit, beauty, vulnerability and wisdom.

How to Work With and Heal Grief

Grief dwells in an inner reservoir. When you focus on one particular loss and reconnect with those feelings, you gain a clearer perspective on many other losses. The ones that you choose to reconnect with depend on your current needs and the issues at hand. There is always a sweetness and comfort in these reconnections once you process through the shame-bound complex feelings, and a part of you comes alive once again. It makes sense that grieving enlivens. If there was not significant and meaningful bonding in these relationships to begin with, we would not have experienced the loss as traumatic.

Furthermore, in the state of openness and vulnerability that is created through grieving, new learning and corrective experience come more easily. These can be times of significant change and transformation. Outer life experiences tend to be put in a perspective that reflects what is truly important in your life, and what is without significant meaning. When you re-enter and process unresolved losses, you simultaneously begin to separate "the wheat from the chaff."

Robert Gass, who conducts workshops on loss and "opening the heart" suggests that: "One may always feel sadness...yet rather than being crippling, this sadness may one day become like a rich color in the palette of the soul."

As John Bradshaw suggests, there is very good news in this merging with nature's healing process. Grief is a healing feeling. If we allow ourselves, it will come naturally.

Healing grief is a very individual process. Each of us must be reassured that the sun will shine again, for while we are in grief, only clouds prevail. We must be comforted by an outside source, written or spoken or sung words that healing *will* organically occur. We need to *be with* our unpleasant feelings and even allow ourselves to get lost in them as need be. We must also rise above our grief as need be. We must pull ourselves out of it to periodically socialize, even if we don't feel like it. We must dance with suffering, allowing it to lead sometimes in our private moments and in the nurturing presence of our community. However, it is also important to distinguish the grief healing that occurs in grieving unresolved losses from feelings connected with a current, significant loss. Though the healing principles are the same, a present loss, even one that is grieved in a healthy way will take longer to heal than unresolved losses from the past. This is because a current loss is anchored in present reality that must be lived day to day, while unresolved losses from the past are not anchored in a current reality that must be dealt with. You must only "make room" for the feelings to move through you and be respected. The revisited memories are ghosts from the past that bring us profound and important connections with lost parts of our selves. With this reclaiming of our soul, we develop an expanded sense of aliveness. This process continues to quicken as we become more grounded in our wholeness.

Grieving the Lost Years

There is a particular emotional experience in Grieving Unresolved Losses that is worthy of special mention. This is the experience of Grieving the Lost Years. It is important to understand this specific manifestation of grief and sadness so that it is not misunderstood.

I am speaking about the unique grieving episodes that accompany *new good things* happening to us. For example, we experience the visceral feeling of hope for the first time. The initial feelings are ones of happiness, possibility, joy. For many, immediately following these feelings, comes deep sadness of a grieving nature. Another example is truly experiencing being loved and loving for the first time. Again, a time for good feelings to emerge, often followed by complex grief and sadness.

This grief and sadness is the appropriate expression of our newly discovered awareness, on a feeling level, of our years of deprivation of hope or love. The moment we first truly experience expansive new feelings, the emptiness of the lost years becomes acutely apparent and felt. We would not be able to feel the grief without reconnecting with the feelings of aliveness and empowerment. However, they instantaneously lay before us the lost years of inner deprivation and spiritual death.

Grieving the lost years is an important part of the process in coming into our completeness. It is *very important* to distinguish these grieving moments from all others so that they are not misinterpreted in ways that thwart our healing. This particular manifestation of sadness moves through the system very quickly if it is understood. It is like a necessary wave that has been waiting to wash through. The other important reason for this understanding is so that we do not misinterpret the feelings, thereby using them to confuse or diminish our rich new experiences. For example, one falls in love for the first time and soon finds oneself weeping. If you do not understand the connection of this weeping to love's lost years, you may think you are not really in love. You will feel confused. You might say "If I am so happy, why am I crying?" Old negative thinking patterns may come in and suggest that falling in love is hopeless. Or, one might take the sadness to mean one doesn't deserve love. The negative scenarios that the unrecovered mind can make up to attach to feelings it does not understand are truly amazing. That is why we need to learn the logic of feelings in Stage Two healing.

Waves of sadness for the lost years will often follow our first adult experience of a particular joy. We want to honor the appropriate passing of this necessary wave of feeling, and notice how quickly it moves through and integrates with our organic system. It all makes total emotional sense. The lost years need to be respected, grieved, and honored in order to move on to the fullness of one's self.

To learn more about healing grief, read on to the next chapter, specifically the first emergent station.

Connie's Story

Connie is an African-American women in her late forties. She was a participant at an experiential workshop I facilitated, called "Healing Through Stage Two Recovery." The weekend event was produced for the alumni of a rehabilitation center that Connie had attended three years earlier for help with a heroin addiction. She had been clean and sober since. In the opening session on Friday evening, Connie shared that one of the goals she brought to the weekend was to work on her self-imposed isolation. She didn't know why, but almost every weekend she became deeply depressed and remained a prisoner of her own small apartment. She told us, "After working all week, I just want to go home and pull the covers over my head. I don't know how to deal with people in a comfortable way. It's just too hard and confusing. I am here to deal with that. I just want to make a life I can feel better about."

On Saturday morning the group was asked to meditate and recall an image from childhood. When I asked for a volunteer to share an experience, Connie was the first to raise her hand high, and I called on her immediately.

> **Connie:** I have an image of myself sitting on the stoop of a house we used to live in. I'm just sitting there with a frowning face.

> **M.P.:** Can you tell me about how old you were and where this house was located?

> **Connie:** I was about seven. The house was in Riverhead, New York. That's where I grew up.

> **M.P:** Can you tell me what you were wearing, Connie, and what was the weather like on that day? Tell me more about the image.

> **Connie:** I was wearing jeans, kind of dirty jeans, and a red top with a print design on it. The weather was grey and cloudy — it was late morning.

M.P.: O.K., Connie, this is very good. Now take a comfortable breath or two and continue to stay with me. Now listen, you have shared this first image of your inner child with us. She is about seven, sitting with a frowning face on a porch at your childhood home in Riverhead, New York. She is wearing jeans and a red print top and the morning is cloudy. Now, Connie, I want you to close your eyes for a moment, relax and take a few deep breaths. Good. Now I am going to ask you to turn inward and to enter a private dialogue, similar to the one you and I are having, with your inner child. Ask her gently and directly: What are you doing on the porch, and why are you frowning? Then just be still for a few moments and listen for any inner responses.

At this point an energy came over the room. Everyone was aware that something significant was happening inside Connie. Her body shifted in her seat and her shoulders began to softly sway, almost as if she was fainting. I suggested that she take a deep breath or two and when ready, if possible, share whatever came to her from within. I also suggested that the entire room do some conscious deep breathing in acknowledgment of the shared awareness and feeling in the room and in support of Connie's discoveries.

Connie: At first I began to feel sick. It was as though all the blood was drawn out of me. I felt weak and dizzy. Then I remembered, [at this point Connie began to cry profusely, her body shook. However, she continued sharing with intermittent punctuation of gentle gasping] I remembered the fire. It was right next door. Cynthia and her little brother Tommy burned to death. She was my best friend. That day on the stoop, that was the day of their funeral. I wasn't allowed to go. Everyone tried to protect me and I just felt so broken inside. Every day I froze inside as I walked passed the charred rubble of her house. Oh God, I missed her so and there wasn't anyone to talk to about it. We moved shortly thereafter, and gradually I put those broken feelings behind me, or at least I thought I did.

M.P.: Connie, before I say anything else I want you to know that I am deeply touched by your sharing. My heart goes out to you in your profound loss. Thank you for your courage, and the willingness to trust us with such a tender part of your being. [Pause] Now, Connie, do you feel composed enough to take this exercise a step further?

Connie: Yes! Somehow, I feel like I can do anything now. Let's get on with it.

M.P.: Good. O.K., now, Connie, I am going to ask you once again to close your eyes, breathe consciously and allow your whole body to relax. I invite the rest of the room to share in this exercise incorporating their own visual images from their own childhoods. Now, I want you to begin to re-engage with "little Connie."

In your own words, however they come to you, I want you to let her know that you have heard her pain. Tell her that you understand. Share with her how healing re-uniting with her has felt and suggest that perhaps it can be the beginning of a growing dialogue. Tell her how strong you are — how you have recovered from your addiction and how you know how to find appropriate support... Tell her that you don't want to leave her again and that, perhaps together, a whole new life might be possible.

At this point in the exercise Connie looks absolutely radiant, sitting in her seat, eyes closed, relaxed, with a faint, knowing, unapologetic smile on her beautiful face. A healing calm has come over the room.

M.P.: Now, I want everyone to tell their own inner child that you need to re-engage with the group for awhile. Make a deal with her (or him for male participants) that either one of you, in quiet moments, can re-enter dialogue, and the other will join in. This will help the growth benefits and healing of this union to continue.

Connie's story, while quite dramatic, is representative of both the nature of the inner connection and the profoundness of the restoration that takes place in the Fundamental Stations of Stage Two, the recovery of the whole self. Next, we move into the Emergent Stations. There we will see how these connections will expand all dimensions of personal power, aliveness and wholeness.

7

Transformation
The Six
Emergent Stations

The Six Emergent Stations presented in this chapter represents a series of breakthroughs in awareness which will unfold within you once you have recognized, faced, and begun to deal with the Six Fundamental Stations of your healing crisis. In this phase of the process, you begin to transform your life and way of being to bring it more into harmony with your vision of the holistic state. More and more, your actions begin to reflect your search for your rightful place in the universe.

These stations are called "emergent" because they help you come out of hiding; they help you express who you are and what you've learned in your journey. Your spiritual evolution unfolds more and more visibly, using the energy and awareness that have emerged (and will continue to emerge) from the first six stations. They teach how to best manage emergent complexities as they evolve, moving you toward a state of holism and a shame-free presentation of self.

People mask their early wounds with necessary defenses; then the innate dynamics of denial wrap the emotional wounds with shame. Gradually, voluntarily exposing these wounds facilitates healing. Repressed trauma causes a dissociation of aspects of consciousness; in everyday terms, the psychic numbing phenomena so common among recovering people.

In addressing the constrictive tendencies (becoming devoid of emotion and meaning) that accompany truncated memory, Dr. Judith Herman, author of *Trauma and Recovery*, observes:

In avoiding any situations reminiscent of the past trauma, or any initiative that might involve future planning and risk, traumatized people deprive themselves of those opportunities for successful coping that might mitigate the effect of the traumatic experience. Thus, constrictive symptoms, though they may represent an attempt to defend against overwhelming emotional stress, exact a high price for whatever protection they afford. They narrow and deplete the quality of life and ultimately perpetuate the effects of the traumatic event.... The testimony of patients is eloquent on the point that recognition of the trauma is central to the recovery process.

Reclaiming your individual history, by restoring a sense of continuity with the past, is vital to empowerment. Stage Two is a time of awakening the unconscious. We all need to be coached inward sometimes, to follow the twisting path of recalled feeling and sensation, step by step, back to the conflicted roots of our present-day situation. This journey cannot be made intellectually or analytically, rather it is like an emergence. Clues and memories emerge like fossils unearthed by an archaeologist. It comes through the support of safe community combined with the willingness to expose pieces of the truth and put them together.

With each such experiential discovery, self-understanding and self-compassion begin to replace self-diminishment. Your habitual behavior is reframed in the light of historical precedence, and as the truth of your original innocence emerges, you gradually dissolve the blanketing membrane of shame. I sometimes refer to this in community workshops as "popping shame caps." It is in this engaging pursuit of authenticity that the uncovering of repressed trauma often takes place. These shame caps are unconscious lids or barriers to our fuller self-expression. They are the results of misguided, though possibly well-intended, attempts by our family and society to control our behavior in developmental years. Authentic Process Therapy helps us to pop open these barriers and connect with our own past, our healing, and most importantly, our personal power and intuitive voice. Through this work we begin to discover our purpose for being. The ultimate goal is the shame-free presentation of self.

Station 7: Letting Go and the Authentic Presentation of Self

There are moments in the Stage Two recovery process when you will experience a breakthrough in awareness. In this revelatory instant, there is an emotional and sensory insight that helps you understand and accept your developmental history and resultant personality traits. It is suddenly much easier to shed the mask of composure and let others see who you really are.

The expressions that I have observed coming from people at such times of discovery range from "I can't believe it" to "Oh no!" to "I am awed by this awareness." The facial expressions accompanying such pronouncements are surprise, openness, calm and deep understanding. Sometimes there is a mischievous little authentic smile that seems to say "Oops, I've been caught." At these times we often find it easy to express ourselves with genuine authenticity.

Sometimes, however, these breakthroughs also bring an experience of complex grief, which can be harder to express.

John Bradshaw, in *The Family* writes that it is the "unexpressed feelings that keep you compulsively 'acting-out,' your emotions can only be your emotions by expressing them. Denying our emotions is a way that causes us to lose control over them. Once repressed and denied you no longer have your emotions, they have you."

Denying is lying. You no longer have the memories, but the repressed emotions form a frozen energy core that unconsciously runs your life. Compulsive/addictive behavior is by definition outside one's control. Emotional energy has to go somewhere. You either repress emotions (act them in); project them onto others (you label others as needy when you feel shame over your own neediness) or "act them out" (you deny being angry and then throw things around or commit subtle acts of disrespect or harm towards others).

Becoming aware of these things begins to give you an understanding so that your feelings can be respected and integrated. The expression "acting out" as used above is an excellent term that can describe a person's behavior. However, I have found it to be a somewhat destructive, shame — compounding term when we direct it against ourselves during the recovery process. In many Twelve-Step groups, "acting out" has become the new "bad" behavior because it suggests losing control. Remember the popular Twelve-Step axiom: "Take what you want and leave the rest." This is excellent advice and I wish to apply it here against the oversimplification and right/wrong thinking that sometimes occurs when a person is in the process of trying to accept the emotional complexities of authentic, advanced recovery. It takes a long time to get all of our impulses manageable. Compassion, not criticism, is the key.

Returning to some problematic behaviors during Stage Two recovery is absolutely unavoidable. Until you earnestly work through these stations, defensive patterns of behavior are one method for finding equilibrium when you feel threatened or are going through changes. Sometimes these patterns are the only safety mechanism you have. I encourage myself and others to be mindful and respectful of these patterns, always making sure we bring them to safer and less destructive levels. Stage Two recovery is about self-compassion, never about perfectionism, so when doing this work, try to reframe the concept of "acting out." I am not suggesting you excuse destructive or abusive behavior, but rather find a less shameful way of navigating out of these defensive, shame-laden barriers.

We need to allow ourselves to mourn for that which has been robbed from our lives. I encourage compassion for unconscious acts of covert and dishonest self-presentation. Once we realize what they are, the important thing is to move toward a more authentic representation of self, to bring a more honest perspective to our important relationships. This honesty and openness can supply the magical healing ingredient in a relationship: intimacy.

In her book about intimacy and independence, *You Just Don't Understand: Women and Men in Conversation*, Deborah Tannen, Ph.D. writes, "Intimacy is key in a world of connection where individuals negotiate complex networks of friendship, minimize differences, try to reach consensus, and avoid the appearance of superiority, which would highlight differences. In a world of status, independence is key, because a primary means of establishing status is to tell others what to do, and taking orders is a marker of low status.... All humans need both intimacy and independence."

Through Stage Two work you will gain the confidence to know that through honest and equal sharing, others will come to see and appreciate areas where you excel and will listen to your wisdom. This usually happens to the extent that you see and appreciate the strengths and wisdom of others. Part of this process, however, is seeing where others may be blocking a supportive non-competitive environment and having the confidence to negotiate the situation by means of specific observation and the authentic expression of feeling.

Vying for status within a relationship or a group is deadly as far as the development of intimacy is concerned, and yet total equality is very rare. The achievement of true intimacy — having the strength to be vulnerable and having the confidence to feel equality and oneness with others in spite of obvious differences — this will give you a more satisfying sense of self than winning all the "one-up" battles you ever face.

True intimacy allows for the authentic presentation of your true self, "warts and all." We expect to be accepted because we accept ourselves. We love to the extent that we can love ourselves. We trust to the extent that we trust ourselves and our ability to express our concerns and limitations. Intimacy is only possible to the extent that we allow it, and the tragedy is that most of us don't allow it except in times of tragedy, times of grief.

Grieving allows people to embrace their authenticity, bring deeper compassion to their inner child and adult self, and explore loving, authentic relationships with others. While this mourning can shake a person very deeply, these experiences also intimate our "wholeness" in ways we never believed possible. Being able to express the wholeness of our experience — the joys and griefs — without defensiveness, trusting in the process of life which brought us to this present moment, leads to the authentic presentation of self. This is the doorway to the holistic state.

Station 8: Learning More Effective Behavior Through Corrective Experience

Simply put, corrective experience occurs when the recovering adult finally learns, for the first time, how to get basic human needs met. In *Homecoming*, John Bradshaw opens the chapter on corrective exercises with an appropriate quote from his colleague, Kip Flock:

> The best news is that since the child was wounded through neglect and learning deficits, we can learn to get the child's needs met as an adult. We can develop skills in all areas of human interaction. It's not a question of unlearning; it's a question of learning things for the first time.

Before giving my own observations and experiences on corrective experience, I will again borrow from Bradshaw, who has contributed so much in this area, to set the tone:

> Corrective work is the most hopeful aspect of inner child work. Our wounds are partly the result of learning deficits, and we can

correct those deficits with new learning. We do some of this new learning incidentally as we respond to the social demands of growing up. But for most of us with a wounded inner kid, there are still large areas where the lack of these developmental skills causes great pain and discomfort. Many adult children do not know that their abortive behavior is due to learning deficits. They relentlessly shame and blame themselves for their failures and character defects. Doing corrective exercises helps your wounded inner child to understand that your defects are actually deficits. The behavioral contaminations of your wounded inner child are actually ways he learned to survive.

This chapter from John Bradshaw's book offers an extensive series of exercises to address varied stages of development. The chapter also suggests other authors who have written extensively, offering rich exercises and understanding on corrective experience. Experiential workshops are an excellent way to access corrective experience.

I define this station as the time when we compassionately recognize and accept our learning deficits. Building on our own individual history, it is a time to consciously apply ourselves to learning how to get both our wounded inner child and our adult needs met. Affirmations and new learning are particularly helpful in this station.

Recovering people mistakenly attempt to rush into this work. They may try to jump over the deep process work in the earlier stations or, more often, are not even aware of their necessity. The processes explained in stations seven through twelve are not very effective without some progress in the first six stations. Using affirmations, is a good way to correct the way you respond to complex situations such as dating, intimacy and dealing with authority figures. But people who depend on affirmations without first completing the earlier stations run the risk of becoming discouraged, cynical, and increasingly shamed because they will very likely come to feel that their efforts in this area went unrewarded. They may blame themselves and again decide that they are uniquely flawed because they never learned the correct sequence and the importance of the developmental stations in Stage Two recovery. Corrective exercises tend to be short-lived and only cognitive in nature until we have completed a portion of our grief work.

Consider, for example, the pessimistic person who reads daily affirmations about positive thinking only to find that negative feelings continue to overpower positive thoughts. Eventually he gives up, deciding that affirmations do not work, or that, as he previously thought, he is just hopeless. In order to have these experiences that are possible with affirmations penetrate the core of his being, an inner opening must occur. Uncovering original pain and trauma, processing unresolved losses, and grieving through the growing pains of early developmental stages provide just such an opening.

Once you move through the prerequisite stations, the corrective experience becomes natural, easy, and highly nurturing. It is no longer just a cognitive struggle to learn new behavior by rote. In moving through and resolving your grief, you relax your ego defenses and become an open vessel for inner nourishment and learning, and your behavior changes accordingly. The grieving enlightens you about what is really important and what is not. Begin to naturally focus on, and feel deserving of, having fundamental needs met.

In workshops on "Healing Through Stage Two Recovery" or "Healing the Wounds of Sexual Abuse," we conduct very concentrated and specific original pain and grief exercises before offering the corrective experience training. In the emotional choreography of the workshops, corrective experience brings the calming salve. It brings closure to catharsis and heals the raw grief through finding practical solutions to life's eternal struggles. These Authentic Process workshops mirror our processes through these stations in everyday life. Opening up, expressing and nurturing our authentic self always follows original pain and grief work in safe, community settings.

These processes of corrective experience in workshops are nothing less than profound. I often get letters from people months — and even years — later offering appreciation for a workshop and expressing thanks for the resulting self-empowerment. The magic that takes place on the group and individual levels enables people to have their deep needs met through corrective experience.

When you are receptive to correcting the conditions in your life by correcting your actions, be prepared to take additional risks. Corrective experience is fueled by the thirst for knowledge, and accelerated by healthy risk-taking, meditation and contemplation. This is a time to make new relationships and nurture old ones with people who are committed to their own growth. New relationships mirror and validate your emerging, authentic presentation in a unique and important way. Historic interdynamics are absent, allowing you to maintain a clear view of the present moment.

At this station, you begin to make course corrections in your life's direction. It is often at this juncture that you begin to sense what you might find interesting and enjoyable. Out of your earlier grief experiences and simultaneous realizations of what is and what is not important, you will begin to shape a future-oriented, self-created life.

In my own visits through this station, I always come out with a clear perception of the injustices, ignorances, and abuses in our world. I see more clearly what is not important and what is destructive. I realized in my grief that I was always a "good boy" because as a child it seemed that my survival depended on it. I always worked hard not to offend anyone. When I realized just how much effort this took and how dishonest it made me feel, I decided to expose more of my "bad-boy" qualities, thereby creating a balance. The awareness that I was putting so much effort unconsciously into a behavior that was unrealistic and unsatisfying angered me. The inner anger in turn energized me. It propelled me on my own path toward what I have deemed to be important. This is my inner need for continued growth, self-expression and spiritual manifestation. The anger generated by our grieving of developmental stages can actually thrust us further into our natural loving nature. It brings a purpose to life that gives meaning and self-respect. It makes us feel comfortable and content in our own skin.

I have been asked in workshops, "How do I know if I am acting in a way that is corrective or in a way that may be counter-productive?" I suggest that if we look at our behavior, and if it is respectful to ourselves and to others, then we are operating from a corrective position. If our expression or behavior is disrespectful to ourselves or another, we need to seek out a corrective experience. Respect for "self" and "other" is the best indicator.

In *Man's Search for Meaning*, psychiatrist and concentration camp survivor Viktor Frankl articulates his perception of how women and men require this sense of purpose to feel whole and complete. The essence of being human, he believes, lies in searching for a meaning and purpose in life that is larger than ourselves. Corrective experience unlocks the doors to this search.

Station 9: Separating Adult Needs from Childhood Needs (Milestone on the Journey to Self-Transformation)

I often use the expression "separating adult needs from childhood needs" to highlight the need for discovering the early unmet needs that we all, often unconsciously, bring into our adult relationships. They usually confuse and sabotage these unions. Separating them out is a liberating experience that makes satisfying adult relationships possible.

How do we separate them? This frequently asked question presents a challenge because the actual experience is very personal and occurs in a very private part of ourselves. The best answer I can give comes from my own experience and from concepts I have learned from lectures by Eva Pierrakos.

We must realize that what is a natural need for a child may not be an appropriate need for an adult. I have heard many recovering people jokingly say, "I'm looking for someone to take care of me." This is often not such a joke. The unconscious can cloak a powerful, needy force that "wants to be taken care of."

I've counseled couples in which one proclaims how independent he or she is, yet all the while exuding an energy and body language that says, "please take care of me, don't leave me, I can't survive without you!" Obviously, this person is giving very mixed signals to their partner. Simultaneously, the partner lives with a gut feeling that they can never live up to the projected nonverbal needs, no matter how independent the talk might be. Until the unconscious childhood demands in both partners become conscious, the dynamics within the relationship will be very difficult. Usually the partner of a "needy" person will have childhood dynamics that nonverbally say, "Don't you dare fence me in. I won't be encroached upon. I won't give up my freedom for anyone. I don't want to feel manipulated or duty-bound." You can imagine what a dynamic and twisted "dance" this creates. These are not adult needs, they are charged remnants of unmet childhood ones. Neediness is not good or bad itself, but we need to take responsibility for it so that it does not unconsciously sabotage our best efforts.

Perhaps you had an unfulfilled childhood need, the thought of which brings pain even now. No matter how much you might deny that pain, it remains. It does not disappear. The denial of this pain perpetrates the need and projects it into future adult relationships where it recreates the original pain of deprivation. We become deluded when, on some level, we believe that the pain can only be eliminated when we are given the specific nurturing that was lacking. This, of course will never happen.

It is important to take compassionate responsibility for these inner needs, while realizing that one cannot wait for good feelings to come from outside. By taking responsibility you become less dependent on being praised and loved, or rebelling against that dependency, because you are able to give it to yourself. Learn to accept and relax the demanding needs of your resentful inner child. This brings you to your core in another way by increasing your ability to have strong currents of good, warm feelings. This helps nourish your desire to share these feelings rather than withhold them. One gives up secret, childish, greedy and spiteful ways of administering feelings. Gradually the childhood emptiness is filled, but through self-love and the fulfillment of adult needs.

When I study the authentic expressions of people I have counseled, the adult needs become apparent. These are needs for personal growth, self-expression and the realization of our spiritual potential. The attainment of these needs brings fulfilling relationships, love and pleasure.

As you separate out your childhood needs, the clarified adult needs begin to signal what your unique and personal path in life might be. You begin to find your purpose. This is felt on intuitive levels and tends to integrate your life experiences and your passions and desires.

As the material surfaces, with help from the community or a practitioner, you begin sorting out the real, adult needs from those needs that were unmet in childhood. For recovering people, this emerges like a tangled ball of yarn. Imagine one primary-colored thread representing appropriate adult needs, and the remaining, neon-colored threads representing unmet childhood needs: this is the unconscious self. At first the ball seems hopelessly tangled. However, the ball has the potential to unravel quickly, depending on your abilities to accept guidance and feedback; by risking new experiences you become more open to self-examination and self-honesty, leading you to a greater awareness of hidden motivations.

In my case, once I learned to separate and respect deprivations from childhood, I was able to free my adult self to bring more passion to my life and work. The courage and clarity to write this is a direct manifestation of my own work in this station. It also gave me an opportunity to appropriately share my childhood experiences in a forum that is responsible, healing and perhaps beneficial to others. Whatever contributions I make to my world are direct results of my meeting my own needs on both levels and not confusing them. This integration has blessed me with great clarity and energy in areas that are important to me.

Adult needs *never* require others to comply with you or give you what you want — that is a childhood demand. The adult need for love and companionship can only be fulfilled when we are ready to love and share. This is very different from the childhood need to be loved. If you think you are ready for love, but through some fate of the universe it has not come your way, you are still operating with a cloaked childhood need: you are looking for a perfect parent. When you separate this and accept your neediness, and when you stop projecting your neediness into adulthood, love comes to you and your adult needs are fulfilled. I observe this happening over and over again.

To begin to separate your needs, be willing to assess and be honest with your own inner cravings. Tune in and listen to your own needy inner child, with compassion and without judgement.

 The willingness to enter this awareness will begin an energetic process where inner constrictions relax and love flows. That is the great mystery of it all. Embrace this mystery in the same way you embrace the mystery of your very existence. When we come out of our own delusion, we can trust the organic, self-organizing universe to meet our needs.

In my own significant relationships I sometimes observe deep needy feelings from childhood begin to surface because I am feeling insecure or overwhelmed with life. When I observe the needy pull from within and compassionately acknowledge it, something instantly loosens up inside and I realize I have a choice: I can either act out the feelings on my loved ones, which is always bound to confuse them and leave me unfulfilled, or I can love that part of myself, and experience the *shift* within where the need relaxes. Instead of demanding love, I can give it. Mysteriously, with a little patience and without requesting it, love does come my way in a manner I never would have imagined. In doing so, it meets my adult needs, maturing me in the process. The results validate both my adult sense of self-responsibility and my respect for resident unmet childhood needs. Do they ever completely go away? I'm not sure, but they can definitely become manageable in a very playful way.

I am always amazed to watch people at this station of their development. Their world begins to meet them with exactly what they need. They begin their own unique, constructive needs-fulfillment process. It is as if they draw to themselves pleasurable gratification, in whatever form, that is more expansive than what they had previously been able to embody. It seems that foreward-moving gratification and enlightenment come from relaxing the unconscious childhood demand for retroactive fulfillment. As this process continues, they are surprised that they can obtain fulfillment, contentment, pleasure and happiness despite having unmet childhood needs. Once the unconscious demand for the fulfillment of childhood needs is uncovered and relaxed, new possibilities reveal themselves.

A good time to uncover these childhood needs is whenever you are stuck in a relationship dilemma, or hit a wall. When you find the part of yourself that says: "It must be this way, not that way. Life must give me this; I must have it," give it a hug: that's your unfulfilled inner child.

To help you clarify your feelings, ask yourself: Do I remember this charged feeling from my childhood? Actually permission yourself to *ride the energy of the feeling* (not the words in your head) backwards in history to see what images, feelings, and body sensations surface. When you find an earlier, previously repressed incident or truth associated with the feeling, ask yourself an even more important question: How much of my present demanding is based on past factors or is charged with earlier emotions, and how much of it is present-day appropriate? In most cases the ratio will come back in the 80/20 range, with 80 percent originating from unmet childhood needs. That's where the release or shift occurs.

When we hear the demanding voice of an inner child and recognize it for its fallacy, something loosens up instantly. We can liberate our creative energies by questioning the validity of these childhood needs — ones which we may have taken for granted as being adult, until now.

This station begins to open the door to one's life purpose. I am reminded of an old spiritual axiom that says, "The diamonds are in your own back yard." It is with the clearness of vision that comes through untangling our adult and childhood needs that we are able to see the *diamonds.* We claim them one by one, mounting them brilliantly on the more holistic, integrated future of our personal evolution and manifestation.

Station 10: Integrating the Shadow Self

Carl Jung referred to the "shadow self" as a dumping ground for all those characteristics of personality that we disown. He believed that to honor and accept one's own shadow is a profound spiritual discipline. Author and therapist Robert A. Johnson called this acceptance "the most important experience of a lifetime" because it makes us whole again. Some theorists refer to the shadow self as the lower, destructive self, but the pejorative connotations of "lower" create a strong negative value judgement that can prevent us from understanding what it really is.

In my own definition of the shadow self, I suggest that the attributes assigned it are different for each person. For some people the attributes are aggressive, violent and destructive desires. For others, these at-

tributes are sexual secrets and desires, possibly ones such as incest, pe-
dophilia, fetishism or sadomasochistic adventure. Some reserve this
cabin of consciousness for their masked cynicism, jealousies and mean
streaks. For still others, their psychic organization may assign tenderness and loving exploration to the shadow self. Whatever one's shadow
self attributes may be, there appears to be a powerful sexual force — or
the denial thereof — central to the understanding and discovery of this
realm. It is a mythic, primal force. Only when we are willing to pierce
the membrane of shame that encases the shadow-self will our liberation
process further unfold.

Seen in the light, without judgments, the shadow becomes alive,
passionate and juicy, creative, and precisely intuitive. Once freed and
accepted, it can guide our lives truly and richly. As the unconscious
holds our rejected parts, it also holds our wholeness.

I see the relationship between the shadow self and complete recovery
as follows: The mask of composure that we present to the world was
created by our ego defenses in childhood to keep us safe and help us get
through life. The shadow is the flip-side of our mask of composure, an
underbelly containing all the repressed opposites. Sometimes these
shadow elements seem extreme or very charged because of repression's
inherent defiance and the force that it builds. Though this is an oversimplification — a quick glance over our shoulder at our shadow — it begins to illustrate the importance of its integration.

The shadow-self encases our soul, or spirit. The shadow self is our
undeveloped part which still contains negative emotions, thoughts and
impulses such as fear, hate or cruelty. As we bring it to conscious awareness, as it becomes united with our adult self and our core essence or
divinity, we become whole.

When we came into the world as infants, we were whole. As we
encountered our world, we received messages that certain expressions
and needs were good or bad. As we learn to divide our self-expression
into good or bad, we begin to create our shadow self. We decided which
of our characteristics were good and God-given and acceptable to our
society and which ones needed to be hidden away. In cultures that are
anchored in binary, right-and-wrong thinking, this is the way good is
separated from evil.

Unfortunately the characteristics that are considered bad will never
go away. They create their own domain in the dark corners of our personality and they eventually take on their own life. Because the shadow-
self has enormous energy potential, it can become a monster in the repressed regions of our psyche when it is out of control.

Since we were forced — as our culture dictated — to create a shadow-self during childhood, we can devote our recovering adulthood to restoring the wholeness of our personality. Studying mythology from other cultures and their dark but celebrated underworld creatures can be a real education when undertaken in this light. Bears, dragons, minotaurs and ogres all possess this subconscious power. The effort to integrate our shadow self is well worth the struggle. In our sober maturity we can responsibly handle the integration that we were ill-equipped to accomplish in childhood. In doing so we enhance our mythic essence, or core energy, laying the ground for our own spiritual experiences.

Bringing the Shadow Side to the Surface

Carl Jung used the term "shadow side" to refer to our fragmented unconscious feelings that are too painful or confusing to confront on a conscious level. As more and more of your unconscious material rises to the surface, your "shadow side" must eventually become conscious.

For the Stage Two process to continue, at some point you may need to "permission" the emergence of deep inner truths in a conscious effort. As each station is traversed, often time and time again, an integration of our complex feelings, experiences, and expressions makes you whole.

Often these shameful feelings are erroneous social concepts — prejudicial thinking or ugly stereotypes — that were internalized before you understood their full meaning.

For instance, as children, we may have been told, indirectly or directly, that all Christians go to heaven, and all non-Christians go to hell. As adults, we recognize this thinking as biased, prejudicial and erroneous, and we refuse to believe it. However we might deny it on the surface, remnants of this erroneous concept may still lurk in our deeper, unhealed unconscious, and cause subtle feelings of shame. We may not be responsible for the erroneous teaching of these shameful concepts, yet we must take responsibility for their effects and work toward a new self-understanding and self-forgiveness.

While doing my own therapy, I sometimes resented having to work so hard and commit financial resources toward repairing something caused by the cultural ignorance of others. It was during inner conflicts like these that I slowly realized that I had to, and wanted to, take responsibility for societal injustice and ignorance even when I was not the offending party. It was in my own best interest to do so.

My personal struggle to call up and embrace my shadow self has been slow, painful and enormously gratifying, but what I once experienced as my own fragmented shadow self has, with acceptance, given me a valuable energizing wholeness. With every emergence of another piece of this unconscious content, I confront my denial and self-delusion.

I pride myself on being honest, but every time I discover a new self-delusion or deception within my shadow self, I have to take responsibility for it. For me, this has been the opening to a deeper, richer honesty and integrity, remembering that in the shadow self we hide things even from ourselves.

For example, I have come to respect women and cherish their companionship, where I once unconsciously minimized their worthiness and wore blinders to their contributions. My own hidden violent and enraged feelings toward my mother, who had abandoned our family, were unconsciously projected onto almost all women, though I denied this. In my own perfectionist flight I unconsciously diminished women — and my culture supported me in doing so. As I began to honestly and spiritually connect with women, I spontaneously became more trusting and respectful of the intuitive reality of my own nature. This has been a gift.

Similar to my process of reconnecting with the feminine, there have been other painful and glorious awakenings from self-delusion that have further integrated me. Even as I write these words I can detect a remnant of my "I'll show you how smart I am" shadow self. The angry, insecure show-off part of me resides there. Perhaps it is rooted in being the youngest of three boys in a home that didn't have time for me.

Within the shadow self lie the roots of cultural pain. I have learned this from African-Americans, Asians, gay men, bisexuals, sexually abused persons, fetishists, heterosexual men, mystics, Latinos, the Irish, my own Italian heritage, Native American traditions, lesbians and most recently transgender people — who along with the entire feminist movement have been great teachers. They have confronted me and helped me to face my own deep and complex misconceptions and cultural delusions. I appreciate the courage that each displayed in confronting me in my ignorance and I am forever grateful for the learning opportunities. It takes courage and self-respect to educate and inform others who may be ignorant or misguided about sensitive cultural issues.

Each person that enlightened me, knowingly or unknowingly, shared an authentic piece of their personal oppression pain with me, opening my heart and awakening me to our shared humanity. By sharing these pains and rages, we became more a part of a human family together. By owning and working through our confusions and wounds we bring clearer, more human perspectives to our spheres of influence.

While these cultural examples are illustrative, there have been many other incidents having to do with selfishness, jealousy, sexual feelings, violent thoughts and terrors when my shadow self exposed itself to me. Each experience was emotionally unsettling at first. However, with integration and corrective experience each shadow insight has further freed and empowered me.

With every one of these enlightenments, I have been forced deeper into myself through layers of historical and cultural self-delusions, each time finally arriving at my real self. Each time I reorganized my concepts and beliefs, I always knew when this was happening because I *felt* it. All of a sudden my heart would open and I would see and feel the truth. From that moment on I would feel connected to the part of myself or culture that my shadow-self had once diminished. The moment these other aspects and cultures became a part of me, my richness and diversity expanded. The awakening emotional impact of diverse experiences and multi-cultural encounters broke through even before I embraced them as important intellectual constructs.

As you apply yourself to Stage Two recovery, complex sexuality issues and cultural prejudices tend to emerge from the shadow self. Often you discover deep repressed prejudice about your own heritage that may have been covered over. In Stage Two Authentic Process groups, diversity and sexuality become milestones for community building.

Unless we make a sincere effort to acquaint ourselves with our shadow-self, we may come out of the process somewhat stunted. For example, a person who considers herself a feminist but who rages against men has neglected the part of the process that calls for investigation into the self to discover what personal repressed, or incomplete, wound might be projected onto all men.

All men are not oppressors and most who are act out of their own cultural delusions and ignorance. They do not need to be raged against, but firmly and clearly educated. They also need to be compassionately forgiven, for they too have lost valuable parts of themselves to their shadows.

We must take responsibility for our rage and investigate the history of each particular issue to discover why it is so charged for us. In my case, I had projected hurt and rage regarding my mother onto to all women. Once I took responsibility for where the power of this rage was coming from and consciously integrated these feelings, I was better able to see all women for who they really are without my projection. Although misdirected, I believe my rage was useful and indeed enlightened me. But fuller self-discovery was even more useful in a yet more powerful way, as I identified the source of my rage — my mother's abandonment.

As you move into the deepest part of this work, the opportunity exists to reeducate and reorient this previously destructive part called the shadow self. This is particularly true regarding the sexual secrets, desires and shame that fuel and compound some of these conflicts. Most of this can be examined safely in Authentic Process groups. The facilitation and educational components of these groups create the safety and support the process of emergence. We need to continue creating such healing assemblies.

One way or another, in the course of healing we will come to embrace the shadow. Like a cat that has a good night of hunting, it will set before us a number of things we would rather not see. We must make ourselves larger, sometimes very large, to contain and accept these unconscious aspects of self — primitive, contradictory, devouring, destructive, and weak — along with those that better reflect how we *like* to think we are. We must make ourselves *so* very large that all our parts can exist altogether so that they may make us whole. We want to always remember that we can be and in fact are *larger than our conditions.*

The shadow cannot be won over nor can it be gotten rid of. Do not be surprised if it comes back in a form you thought you had already met and made peace with. If it were possible for the shadow to be brought fully into the light, then something else would probably have to drop into its place to oppose our outward energies. It seems we all need the contrast, the tension of opposition; consciousness feeds on it. Learn to dance with the shadow, to allow its energies honest expression, without feeling hopeless about yourself, because you include those energies. Coexisting contradictions are not a final state or achievement; they are a dynamic process. Like a high-wire act, we achieve a balance through ongoing creative tension. A sense of humor can be a tremendous advantage!

Station 11: Updating and Re-Tuning the Unconscious

> I will listen and love today. I will give people the greatest gift I
> can — my attention. I will also make sure that I am listened to
> and loved. I will ask for what I need.
>
> Affirmation by Perry Tilleraas, from *The Color of Light*

When you take a meditative moment in the morning to recite an affirmation, like the one on the previous page, you are likely to have one of two inner psychic responses: You will either be moved or unmoved. The response you experience directly relates to your work in the ten preceding stations. If you have been unaware of the necessity of recovery and rediscovery work, or if you've avoided it, an affirmation is likely to remain mere words that sound good but stop short of heartfelt connection. In this case, the affirmation is merely a cognitive exercise and is quickly forgotten. This is why so many people abandon affirmations or begin to feel hopeless when they use them.

Some people, however, find affirmations to be one of the most powerful means of changing their lives. To empower our affirmations, it is helpful to understand how they help us connect more meaningfully with ourselves and with the recovery process. They are not a short cut. If you apply them in Stage Two, they will resonate with other inner dialogues at the core of your being. The words will be digested with the energy with which they were written. This energy or synergy will inspire a more natural enactment of the affirmation. In computer terminology, you could say that the first way is similar to temporarily inserting a diskette, while the latter is re-configuring the hard drive.

Any life crisis in Stage Two recovery offers an additional opportunity to update and re-tune the unconscious. As you pass through these stations, unify and reorganize your consciousness. When you take responsibility for your cosmic role in crisis, you nurture and sustain wisdom. I have found this to be particularly true in matters of profound loss and illness.

I have watched many recovering people literally reclaim their life after a significant crisis of this nature. From a more enlightened Stage Two perspective we realize that crises make internal, psychic, structural change possible. It shakes up stagnant energy and fearful defenses, calling us to a higher lever of awareness. Without these significant jolts in recovery we would not be able to reach a balance at our next level. With every crisis we are challenged to update and re-tune ourselves with meaningful new awareness.

When you face crisis, look within and ask: What old and painful psychic structure does this crisis want to break down? How can I make an attitudinal shift out of this crisis that will bring more bliss into my life? The answers that come will be the ones you have been waiting for. Growth, at these levels, must honor crisis as a spiritual necessity; transformation is fueled by it.

Many events — my healing from cancer and the loss and death of loved ones — have shaken me to the core, and frequently have shattered my old reality. During periods of upheaval and grief I was able to accept self-responsibility for ingrained limitations. Wretched grief has several times enabled me to fruitfully reorganize my psyche.

Awareness and growth through Stage Two processes can transform your abilities and intentions when facing crisis. Before such awareness, crises may have been feared and not fully embraced. I do mean embraced, because when you consciously grow through these difficult times, and look back on them, you realize how they taught important lessons. In the larger picture, crisis, however painful, can be your friend. Remember that just because something shakes up the status quo and brings upheaval it is not bad. *The belief that things should stay the same is misguided.* The awareness of impermanence is an important part of the holistic state that APT strives toward. We always want to find the possibility of rewarding growth in whatever our world presents to us.

I do not mean to infer that embracing crises is an easy thing to do. In times of crisis, all of my deepest defenses express themselves, causing significant pain . However, as you become aware of the role of crises in your personal transformation, you become capable of a more complex experience. On one level you may feel pain and also the resistance to the pain. On another level you will recognize the personal significance of the inner reorganization. This is both painful and holistic in a very healing way. By accepting this inner duality, you will find a larger truth of how you change and grow over time. These are times when you seek help and need comfort, support and grounding. It is a time for prayer and meditation which will often bring peace and grace.

In updating and re-tuning the unconscious — whether through therapeutic probing, meditation and affirmation, or even crisis — there are three primary categories of permission as clarified in Bradshaw's writings, that give wings to this process. They are:

1. The permission to play, break out of old rules imposed in childhood and be authentic in our expression;
2. The permission to give ourselves nurturing discipline in the respectful management of our inner forces; and
3. The permission for the safe expression of complexities, and even chaos, in feelings from within.

The opening affirmation touches on all three.

Permission to Play

In the first instance, giving permission to play means just that. Perhaps you received early inhibiting messages about play. Give yourself permission to break out of these psychic prisons and hear your inner playful voice. Surrender to life's energy while at the same time setting realistic self-respecting disciplines, remembering to respect the needs and boundaries of others.

More and more, allow your playful authentic self to emerge. This includes sexual play. Sexual play is important, as is finding one's own safe sexual barriers and boundaries. John Bradshaw calls this "championing" your wounded inner child. Listen for the emerging inner voice, weak and tentative at first, give your adult attention and energy to it, and you will indeed be championing your most valued asset.

Permission to Manage Your Inner Forces

Part of championing your inner child is to become your own nurturing parent who incorporates a nurturing discipline that is respectful of self and others. This form of discipline allows you to move through life more gracefully in the natural pursuit of fulfilling your deepest needs. It allows you to be who you are without being disrespectful of who others are.

Although discipline is frequently confused with abuse, nurturing discipline is an expression of self-love. It is a commitment to following the truth of yourself. It entails the understanding that not every one of our impulses is worthy of action, and some actions are worth repeating on a regular basis, whether we always want to or not. Nurturing discipline helps us learn to distinguish between inner guidance and willfulness. This manner of discipline nurtures self-respect and self-esteem and can grant us wisdom and patience with ourselves.

Permission to Express Complex and Chaotic Feelings

In the sixteen years between the publication of *The Road Less Traveled* and *Further Along The Road Less Traveled*, M. Scott Peck changed the thrust in his opening words. The first book began with "Life is difficult." In the second book, he began with another, greater truth, another translation: "Life is complex." He went on to suggest that "The journey of life is not paved in blacktop; it is not brightly lit, and it has no road signs. It is a rocky path through the wilderness."

Stage Two work is bound to be complex — and chaotic — try to accept and welcome this chaos. Emotions are complex, and do not follow a linear route. When you engage and welcome your own inner child self and actively explore its complex expressions, you begin to release its energy. Once you surrender judgement and explore your emotions with a sense of wonder, interest, and investigation, you will become whole. Your energies and interests freely continue their movements, forever teaching you what you need to learn next. This is indeed a new paradigm with which to approach your recovering self and your world in a meaningful, compassionate way. In embodying this, remember to give yourself the time and rest that your organic system requires. Affirmation from others will also be required for equilibrium, hence the need for community.

Complexity Tolerance

To facilitate this third aspect of your unconscious reintegration, it is important to develop a tolerance and acceptance of the complexity and diversity of life both within you and in the world around you. A basic understanding of the emerging scientific paradigm known as complexity theories will be very helpful.

Science has explored the microcosmos and macrocosmos... The great unexplored frontier is complexity. I am convinced that the nations and people who master the new science of complexity will become the economic, cultural, and political superpowers of the next century.

Heinz Pagels, *The Dreams of Reason*

Complexity theories can help our society move from a binary, mechanistic thinking to a world-view that accepts diversity and multiculturalism. As we embrace and appreciate complexities, a new world emerges.

While the millions of recovering people and others of varied spiritual disciplines bring respect and understanding to their own complex inner selves and we and our leading scholars and entrepreneurs begin to bring this understanding to our social order and societal needs, there can be a great opening of shared consciousness and power. This power or force is generated in the deeper regions of the personal and collective unconscious.

In Stage Two recovery, as we rid our unconscious of all (or most) of the repressed debris from this lifetime, we access a more complete energy source that is more focused. With this awareness, we discover our life purpose, if we have not already done so. Once we have taken responsibility for our histories and updated our selves, we begin to get new, personal glimpses of life's mystery, how it is living itself out, and the part we uniquely play.

In the constellation of desires that people bring to Stage Two, the attainment of this deeper unconscious awareness begins to fulfill the last three desires of the constellation: the shame-free presentation of self, the discovery our individual "life purpose" and to know "who we are" in a real and spiritual sense.

It seems that the deeper unencumbered experience of this non-ordinary consciousness puts us in touch more with the collective consciousness that we are all part of. The interconnectedness becomes more real. When we allow ourselves to pull back from the everyday world through meditation, workshops, and other healing modes, we can visualize the larger forces of life at play and see how we fit into them. It does not make life less of a mystery, it places us in the center of the mystery and grounds our existence.

Station 12: Experiencing Self-Love and Self-Assertion

As we peel away our denials, confront our addictions, and surrender our attachments, we become more honest about our lives. Embracing the truth of suffering as well as joy, we wake up. As we realize and accept the spectrum of the human condition, the door of compassion opens. Recognizing the pain of the world, the disease, warfare, death, and misery, our hearts stir. We are all in the life boat together.

This quote is from the late Tibetan Buddhist Lama Chogyam Trungpa. It is included in Christina Grof's excellent book on addictions called *The Thirst for Wholeness.* She adds:

I am afraid love is not really the experience of beauty and romantic joy alone. Love is associated with ugliness and pain and aggression, as well as with the beauty of the world.... Love or compassion, the open path, is associated with 'what is.' By accepting what is, we tap the love inherent within us and a deep sense of belonging and relationship with ourselves, others, and our surroundings.

If you apply yourself in community to the preceding stations, and to your recovery in general, the experience of self-love and self-assertion will naturally emerge. For most, it begins early on when they renew their compassionate relationship with an inner child or their unconscious, though they may not be cognizant of it at the time. The work thereafter gradually fortifies this connection, producing a flow of energy, personal power, and love. The self-expression of "who I am" is fueled by and necessitated by this powerful proliferation of energy and its outer connections. The authentic nature of the expression itself, when shared with others, creates an energetic circle of love that is nothing less than life transforming for everyone touched by the sharing.

These expressive moments may seem frail at first. With each one, your capacity and self-confidence grows, your love energy increases, and in a short time you are making a noticeable difference in your life. Simultaneously, you begin to affect the world around you. You seem to have changed somehow, and others are affected, impacted, and encouraged.

No action or quality is more essential to complete recovery than self-love. Self-love is not necessarily ego, nor is it a shopping spree on a credit card or a box of Godiva chocolates. Self-love entails a commitment to being fully present, commitment to the full embrace of oneself. It means refraining from lopping off thoughts, emotions, body sensations, or any other experiences at all just because they are painful, unpleasant, or hard to take (pleasure for many is extremely hard to take). Self-love is a prerequisite to love of others and love of life.

If you think of love as an energy, you will begin to break away from old paradigms and rules that lead us into destructive and codependent relationships that re-enact the unmet needs of childhood. In the adventure story *The Celestine Prophecy*, James Redfield describes the transforming recovering population approaching the 21st century. Love is described in a way that perfectly fits in with the Stage Two community experience:

> The role of love has been misunderstood for a long time. Love is not something we should do to be good or to make the world a better place out of some abstract moral responsibility, or because we should give up our hedonism. Connecting with energy feels like excitement, then euphoria, and then love. Finding enough energy to maintain that state of love certainly helps the world, but it most directly helps us. It is the most hedonistic thing we can do.... The more we can love and appreciate others [in all of their diversities and complexities], the more energy flows into us. That's why loving and energizing others is the best possible thing we can do for ourselves.

Transforming these words into personal experience, a recovering person emerges out of Stage Two into the more blissful experience of complete recovery. It is a "shame-free presentation of self." We reframe our experience of sadness and rage and begin to appreciate each as an access point to our authenticity. As we cherish our rage and sadness, we become centered in the core of our being. The conscious and unconscious shame is gone. Creative change and regeneration will naturally and organically take place as we trust our intuition and accept energetic emergence (mysterious, powerful and guiding inner signals) and synchronicity. The change presents itself as strong or all-pervasive feelings that move us toward an activity or an expression. We no longer lack or fear our genuine personal power and expression.

Stage Two Recovery encourages self-expression. Until our world becomes a safer place for complex expression (which is gradually taking place), authentic expression will almost always require a degree of personal struggle. We support and understand this effort in community. We cherish this struggle and embrace it as a badge of courage and contemporary wisdom. With each expression, there is a gradual expansion in our ability to contain, process and express our core energy of love. Conscious expansion of this energy can take place in prayer, meditation and the appreciation of manifestations of nature, and objects and people in which one perceives complex beauty. This creates a mirroring, circular, expansive regeneration of creative, loving energy.

In *An Introduction to a Course in Miracles,* Helen Schucman expressed a voice from within herself. She describes it with powerful energetic authority.

Nor did I understand the calm but impressive authority with which the Voice dictated. It was largely because of the strangely compelling nature of this authority that I refer to the Voice with a capital "V." I do not understand the real authorship of the writing, but the particular combination of certainty, wisdom, gentleness, clarity and patience that characterized the Voice make that form of reference perfectly appropriate.

The following four quotations from *A Course in Miracles* give another voice to the importance and value of redefining our concept of love as an energetic current:

Everything you teach you are learning. Teach only love, and learn
   that love is yours and you are love.

Having rests on giving, and not on getting.

To have, give all to all.

All your past except its beauty is gone, and nothing is left but a
blessing.

As you emerge into the ongoing experience of holism, your view of
life expands from a construct of basic insecurity and self-absorption to
an outpouring of energy and exploration. Energy that once fueled negative or "impossibility-thinking" now charges an adventurous, energetic
engagement in meaningful discovery and awareness of the possibilities.
Instead of approaching your goals as impossible dreams that you could
never dare to attain, you can set realistic intentions and work to fulfill
them. The personal power and innate creativity that come forth leads to
bliss. Bliss — which I define as private moments of ecstatic universal
connection or oneness with all things — creates a yearning for peace,
love, truth and beauty. This hunger, as John Bradshaw calls it, or thirst,
as it is referred to by Christina Grof, inspires further empowerment.

As John Bradshaw writes:

Bliss engenders empowerment. We move from our childhood
belief that we will always be victims to a childlike spontaneity
and optimism. We embrace our imagination and creativity. We
refuse to be victims any longer. We become the artistic creators of
our own lives. We take risks. We go after the things we really
want.

Acknowledging that there are indeed limitations in our human nature, he continues, addressing the awesome outpouring of creative energy by offering models.

Our great musicians were limited by the laws of musical scale,
but within those limits the variety of their compositions are
almost unbelievable.... Our great painters were limited by their
canvas, but walking through a museum of fine art can be an
awesome and overwhelming experience. Within our human
limits, there are still miracles to come. You are one of the miracles!

Forgiveness and self-forgiveness are the fullest expressions of self-
love. However, beware of false forgiveness, if it is done because it is the
right thing to do, or because you do not want to feel the hurt. True forgiveness can take place only after due process and expression of the hurt
feelings. In forgiveness, you recognize the unity of self and other and
that there is no wrong-doer and no wrong done. Recent findings in
physics show us that the events of the past can be influenced by the
present. In forgiveness we can rewrite the past.

These stations, as they present themselves, transform and activate. Return to them in times of need or confusion. They offer a framework and vocabulary for feelings and experience. Tune into the station that intuitively resonates with your feelings. Notice your emergent awareness when you do this. Trust your intuition, your inner healer, to bring to the surface whatever needs to be integrated from the unconscious regions. Share your awareness in safe community and allow clarity and self-understanding to evolve.

Those who have done a considerable portion of the Stage Two healing have the blessing of living in holism much of the time. This includes the attributes referred to as "The Fruits of the Tree" in the graphic model of staged recovery on page 15 and in the next chapter: Boundless Creativity; Awe and Bliss; Feelings of Accomplishment; The Shame-free Presentation of Self; Experience of Empowerment; Intuitive Inner Knowing; Body, Mind and Spirit Connection; Serendipity, Grace and Synchronicity; Awareness of Impermanence; Service to Others; Ongoing Maintenance of Stages, and others.

We recovering people have the opportunity, responsibility and adventurous pleasure of being in a position to transform our lives and our world for the better. We include a wide range of people-people who are recovering from addictions, people recovering from co-dependency and people who want to grow out of emotional and psychological systems that are no longer working. We are the most massive and expansive, positive, human energy force that this planet has ever encountered. I perceive us as a "tribe of healers," coming from many backgrounds, who together in healing consciousness will significantly impact positive movement in the new century. As many of us have at some level perceived ourselves as victims, the old concept of "the meek shall inherit" will speak to us in a humble and realistic way.

A Return to Love

In my own initial stages of recovery, I told my therapist that I had had a normal childhood. While I acknowledged that my parents divorced when I was four years old, I clung to the idea that my family was normal. During the first few years of therapy I refused to acknowledge the pain. Then one day the traumas of my childhood hit me. I went in to that therapy session feeling "squirrelly" inside; my depression and anxiety had exacerbated. In that session, almost out of the blue, I blurted out, "I can't believe I didn't have a mother." Concurrently, a deep sadness swept over me. As this feeling filled me, I began to observe the many memories it contained. I remembered that at five, six, seven, eight years old, and so on, my biggest fear was always that a new friend, classmate or teacher would ask me, "Where is your mother?" The shame would be overwhelming: shame that my mother didn't love me enough to stay with me, shame that to give an honest answer to the question would let people know about the adultery, which was shameful in itself. (In 1950, almost all divorces signaled adultery, so I felt that everyone would know.) People would always look at me funny when I said, "I don't have a mother, no one has to take care of me." The pitiful look I received from the mothers of my playmates was particularly unsettling.

The memory of my mother's affairs and my reactions to them began to sadden and enrage me. All of my painfully confused loyalties for many years after the divorce suddenly came to awareness. In that same session, I told my therapist about the terror I had felt toward my father during those years. He was very hurt, confused and embittered by the divorce and my mother's activities. His emotions tended to be out of control. I never knew when he would have an outburst of fury or withdraw in anger. I just knew I had to please him, I had to be good. He was all that I had. My two older brothers considered me a burden. I really couldn't count on them for much. We were all on our own.

I was always trying to get attention, and I became angry when I failed to get it. I became a showoff. If it sounds as though I have completely uprooted my shadow self through my own earnest self-empowered brilliance, it's really the show-off in me. Actually, most of my insights came from a synchronous series of painful confrontations, a few big ones and many smaller ones. Each one made me take a new and hard look at myself and propelled me deeper into regions of my shadow-self, where all the rages, insecurities, delusions, prejudices, and sexual secrets lay.

All of these recollections and their associated feelings instantaneously presented me with a new reality. This new self-perception was feeling-based. It had an aura of authenticity. No longer were these hidden dissociated memories, they were now a very alive part of me. I felt more centered, more anchored.

After sharing some of these feelings, another bolt of awareness came to me. I said, "Oh my God! I can see how this has affected *all* of my relationships." Many close relationships flashed before me, and for that moment all that I could see was aspects of my own nature. I felt dishonest that I was covering up my real self. Instead of acknowledging my pain, I covered it up and made excuses. For so many years I had told people that I could take care of myself. I had pretended that it didn't matter that I had no mother. Now I felt sad that I had to hide my true emotions. I could see how my emotional and energetic defenses blocked any real intimacy and how they covertly kept anyone who might become intimate at a distance. I wondered how all these people had been able to deal with the mixed messages I must have been giving them. I mourned for my lost childhood. I mourned for all that I missed in my adult relationships that I had unconsciously sabotaged with my cover-up. As confusing as it may sound, I even grieved for the loss of the self-delusions I was about to surrender.

Therapist and author Alice Miller, in *The Drama of the Gifted Child*, articulates my experience beautifully:

> The achievement of freedom... is hardly possible without the felt mourning. This ability to mourn, i.e., to give up the illusion of a happy childhood, can restore vitality and creativity... If a person is able to experience that he was never loved as a child for what he was, but for his achievements, success and good qualities... and that he sacrificed his childhood for this love, this will shake him very deeply.

In his book, *The Family*, John Bradshaw offers this view of grieving:

> This work is painful and that's why we hold onto our denials and delusions. Why go back to the past? Why go through all the pain again? The fact is that we really never went through the pain. We developed a fantasy bond and used our primary ego defenses to avoid the anger, hurt and pain of our abandonment. Then we avoided our avoidance with our rigid roles and defenses. We missed expressing the feelings at the crucial time.
>
> We missed it because our caretakers would not allow us to be angry or sad. They justified this with poisonous pedagogy. We also missed it because it was so painful.

The story I just recounted tells of the first time I recall grieving the lost years. I actually grieved for what I had lost for years because I developed in a particular way. There have been many similar incidents since, some more profound than others. It seems that whenever we first observe one of our unconscious defenses in an emotionally connected way, we also immediately sense all that the defenses have cost us in terms of love, intimacy, and authenticity.

I have been able to create a relatively safe and secure world for my-self and loved ones. In the midst of the societal chaos that often sur-rounds me, I feel stable and centered. This has been a gift to me, re-ceived in the process of accepting and honoring my own history: a gift of my own Stage Two recovery.

In the next chapter, we will have an opportunity to explore and enjoy more of the gifts or "fruits" that we discover in the process of complete recovery.

8

The Fruits of the Tree

Holism, the Reward of Recovery

Someone once said, "A persuasive speaker is one who can tell you to go to hell in such a way that makes you look forward to the adventure." Well, recovery is not hell, but the fruits of the tree are a most persuasive reward, and if one gets an early taste, one indeed looks forward to the adventure.

I have often been asked, "At what point in the journey does a person ascend into the experience of holism?" (In other words, "Are we there yet?")

I answer, "For me, it began somewhere half-way through the Stage Two work." This seems consistent with the experiences of others I have facilitated, although they often do not immediately realize it because they are so focused on their work. For many, there are glimpses some-times of the holistic experience, prolonged throughout both stages of the process. These glimpses inspire us to continue.

To respond to this question more completely, I have included toward the front of this book the "Tree Diagram," which shows the journey to-ward complete recovery as an *upwards* journey. In this journey of growth, the eleven stations of Stage One and the twelve comprising Stage Two are part of the trunk of the tree; you might consider these as the struggles the young tree makes towards the sunlight as it grows in the "jungle." I know many can relate to this quite easily.

In the next stage of growth, after reaching its full height, the tree bears fruit. The type of fruit will be different for each type of tree, but it will be delicious. The fruit shown in the Tree Diagram is described in the following pages.

At times it all seems overwhelming, all these levels and stages of growth, many of which still lie ahead. Sometimes we think we'd like to have it all over and done with. But believe me, you wouldn't want it any other way. There will always be another step, always another mountain to climb, and when the healing work is done, the one thing that changes is that you completely look forward to the journey.

This is not a theoretical model, but an experience which actually changes things: it transforms your life. As the fruits of the tree start falling ripe into your hands, a certain amount of the old fear gets stirred up. Most of us have all our old defenses against freedom and pleasure still in place. They are rooted deep within us. Ask yourself, "Why wasn't I ready for pleasure and freedom at that time, when these defense mechanisms were put in place?" Then ask yourself, "Am I different now? Am I ready for freedom and pleasure now?" Perhaps the answer will finally be, "Yes. You bet!"

If you do feel ready; if you are no longer afraid of freedom and pleasure, you are ready to join the feast of life. You are ready for the fruits of the tree, the "states of being" that you can realize from earnestly applying yourself to Stage Two healing.

How to Recognize the Fruits of the Tree

Even if you have never experienced joy and abundance in your whole life, it doesn't necessarily follow that you never will. An oak never grows a single acorn until it matures. A "Christmas Rose" doesn't grow any flowers until Christmastime. The Forget-Me-Not, the Foxglove, and the Burdock do not blossom until their second year. Likewise, the tree of the recovering human spirit doesn't necessarily begin to grow fruit until somewhere in the middle of Stage Two. Some of us are just "late bloomers."

If you are like many people emerging from an addictions-based existence into the fruition stage of your own life, you don't know what to look for. There may be signs all around you that something is happening, but you don't have any name for it, and you let it slip by unexplained. For this reason, I will try to name some of the most important benefits you can expect from your own complete recovery. It is important that you are able to name them for yourself when they are happening. This *naming* is what builds the new foundation for a life of holism. We continue to expand from this foundation once we begin to establish it. Without acknowledging and naming our *fruition experiences,* we will lack the solid grounding for the possibility of more pleasurable and fulfilling ones to come. Remember that naming our experiences makes them real, and reality is something we can build on. The names I have bestowed upon my *fruition experiences* are based partly on my own experience, the experiences of recovering people I've worked with, and other sources. As with the twelve stations, the order is not significant.

Experience of Empowerment

As you make your way through Stage Two recovery, one of the most important things that can happen is to recognize what it feels like to be empowered, to acknowledge that feeling and to grow in it. Prior to engaging in Stage Two work, many people don't have a clue as to what empowerment is. They know the word but don't know the experience. Empowerment is the energetic experience of bringing yourself out into the world and seeing yourself making a difference in the world around you — *and* being able to acknowledge that.

It is important to formally give yourself permission to be empowered now, because when growing up you may have received "permission denied" messages; you were disempowered.

Along with the experience of empowerment is the experience of exhilaration and connectedness. There is something in the human spirit that loves to connect with and make a difference in its environment. It just feels good.

The experience of empowerment makes you feel part of the larger whole. You may limit this in your mind at first to how you connect with those around you, but from a holistic perspective, you begin to see how the rippling effects of your actions affect the world at large.

When you're experiencing empowerment, you are also connecting with that core of energy deep inside you which is your very essence. It is a spiritual powerhouse like the heart of the sun, which powers the entire solar system. Empowerment is not about manipulation or ego. When your motivation comes from that place of blazing light and life deep in your core, you don't manipulate, you motivate.

When we're "in the core energy," as we say, and allow ourselves to be conscious in that place, we *do* feel connected with the whole. We can't help it — our actions start to have far-reaching effects. Of course it is possible to feel empowered in a strictly social and psychological sense, but if we're thinking in terms of holism, then empowerment takes on new dimensions.

This is where psycho-education comes in. Most people have never been educated about complete recovery, or holism. Therefore they don't have the context in which to make the transition from empowerment to holism. Like the core energy, the potential for complete recovery has always been within you. All it takes is the permissioning of empowerment to awaken it. True empowerment is not something one reaches for, it is something that naturally and organically happens from doing the healing work.

Service to Others ("Giving Back to the Universe")

When you find your core energy, you must do something with it. It wants to flow through you, usually in the form of "service to others." Everyone I know who has done this work (at least to a certain degree) is now doing something that makes a difference in the world, whether they are doing it through art, volunteer work, or healing. Instinctually they know that by giving away the energy that they have, giving away the love, they will receive more.

Once you do the deep healing in Stage Two and face your pain, you become very aware of the suffering that surrounds us all, and your view of others is transformed. When your spirit opens up in this way, a natural empathy and sense of responsibility organically leads you to appropriately interact with this suffering. There is a saying in the Twelve Step programs, "In order to keep it, you have to give it away."

True love and service is not something you have to aspire to do, out of a sense of guilt or obligation. Undertaken as an obligation it won't feel good, and won't stoke the fires of your core energy. You naturally evolve towards giving away these beautiful gifts of service because you need to do something with the energy, and it feels good. You enjoy connecting with the larger world, the larger spirit, connecting your core energy with that of others, and being of service to others accomplishes just that. It also awakens others to the possibilities of how much fun "random acts of kindness" can be.

Why is it that a human being can't be truly happy unless they have a purpose larger than themselves? Whatever the reason, it is not until we come out of the minuscule thinking of "taking care of number one," which only wants to know one thing: "how am I going to get my needs met?" that we truly find peace and contentment. When we possess enough energy and self-confidence to be able to put it on the line for a larger purpose, at that point we are really alive.

Of course, many people are afraid that if they give the energy away they are going to lose it, or are going to get hurt. While there are certainly situations where personal energy can be abused, experience shows us that the happiest people are those who find a purpose larger than themselves and give themselves over to it, within reason. It then gives them a logical framework in which to draw more core energy out of themselves, to experience the deepest kind of giving and receiving possible. The more you give the more you get: this is the universal law of abundance. It also illustrates the law of necessity: you create or connect with the need and then you find the power to fill that need. It draws out the best in you — more of you than you even knew was there. In the end, you learn of capacities you didn't even know you had.

For those of us who are afraid to give too much of ourselves, a fuller comprehension of the universal law of abundance is helpful, refreshing, and liberating. Eric Butterworth and Charles Fillmore, authors and ministerial leaders of the Unity movement, have helped in my understanding of these principles. In speaking of universal abundance, Butterworth says:

> We live in a universe that is opulent, limitless, and accommodating. It will manifest for us exactly what we have the consciousness to encompass. There is legitimate, royal abundance for every living soul. We live and move and have our being in it. Of course at this point, it may be nonmaterial, spiritual substance. It is an energy-potential that requires mental and material precipitation. And the supply to meet our demands is right *where we are* and *what we need*. When you know the secret the supernatural becomes natural and the miracle becomes commonplace.

Fillmore says:

> The important thing is, since substance *is* — opulent and limitless and everywhere present-the great miracle-working power is faith. Faith is the ability to perceive substance, to draw it forth, to form it and shape it into what we need.... We need to stir up the faith to believe that we are in spiritual unity with the whole; that our mind is a channel through which great ideas flow; that we can find this substance-first in the form of ideas, guidance, and the creative skill of our hands, and second, as the outward manifestation of the means of exchange, the money to do what needs to be done.

This restates the third "power" for dissolving barriers, that shared belief creates experience.

In bringing these thoughts on abundance to a close, Butterworth says it best:

> As more and more people lay hold of the concept of the Divinity [within]... and begin to see themselves in a new context of wholeness, they will not only begin to claim their inheritance of abundance, but they will also become an uplifting influence for opulence in the world.

Sharing our healing with others is what completes our search for wholeness.

Intuitive Inner Knowing

Inside your ear is an organ that tells you when you are off-balance and corrects your movement, usually without your being aware of it. Likewise, there is a mechanism within your spirit which tells you when you are getting out of balance spiritually. I call this "The Inner Compass." Many in recovery have lost that sense, and one of the marvelous fruits of the tree is finding it again. Once you find the Inner Compass, you begin to trust it to tell you when to move, when not to move; when something is correct, when not correct. It can save your life.

When you want to commit yourself to something, you no longer need anything from the outside to tell you, "this will be for your long-term benefit." You know from the inside, and trust that, even against opposition. Before Stage Two, you looked for the right way to do things, but from an external source; a rule or authority, never learning to trust your inner voice, your inner wisdom. Once it has led you safely through danger enough times, you begin to trust it. You also may begin to see the Compass as an inner healer.

Part of the Compass may be the instinct to know that you need to go to a retreat and do some healing. You may be feeling blocked and know that you need to be healed inside, even if you don't know what it is. The inner healer will know what needs to be healed next. Invite your intuitive Compass or inner healer to revisit the twelve stations of Stage Two at such times, and see where the needle points. Notice what direction your point of awareness is magnetically pulled towards.

Years ago, when I was first diagnosed with lymphoma, I used the available complimentary or alternative medicine at the time. I went to a nutritionist and had an enormous regimen of vitamins and minerals prescribed, which I took for a time. After some years had passed, I intuitively cut certain things out, changing and altering the doses, because something inside told me what I needed and what I didn't. It was that Compass. I never needed anything to validate that, or to go to a nutritionist to have it altered. One learns the ebb and flow of their own healing, and what one's needs are at different times. Then one finds what one is looking for.

Self-empowerment depends upon strengthening the sixth sense that refers us inward for answers and guidance. Each person's inner guidance has its own language: it may come as pictures, as words, or as energies felt in the body. We can learn our own inner language. As with any skill it takes earnest effort over time.

In doing Stage Two healing we often first make contact with our intuitive inner knowing during our first" inner child" awakenings. For many, these are the first vague sounds, feelings and sensations of the voice. But as quoted earlier by Zambucka, Fox, Bradshaw, Pierrakos and myself, once awakened and earnestly listened to, this voice grows within you — and some day respectfully takes into its hands your whole life. As we learn to trust it more and more we come to a special place of existence. In regard to what is right for us, we rise above all authorities. This is not an egotistical arrogance, but a natural inner knowing that draws on your whole historic and present being and the wholeness of creation. Who could argue with that? While to the timid this often feels like high-risk poker, because there is no higher authority giving permission, I refer to it energetically as *riding the edge of self-responsibility*. This means that you listen to your inner voice, the one you've learned to trust, and decisively act upon it. Nonetheless, it won't work for long unless you take full personal responsibility for your actions and your life. It is a very exhilarating way to live, effervescent with the feeling of aliveness.

Awe and Bliss

Bliss is a deep personal feeling of ecstasy, an ecstasy, a heavenly rapture, a spiritual joy. When we are consciously in bliss we realize, in a fundamental way, that we are in this world, but not of it. We are part of something greater. We toy with moment-to-moment, back and forth awareness of the material plane and the spiritual. We become light-hearted and free of confusion. Bliss is something we can only experience for ourselves. Bliss of course can be a group experience, but I think of it predominantly as a private, personal ecstasy. This at least is the foundation for a blissful life.

In a workshop recently we were talking about bliss, and decided to explore it. Several people, when asked to get in touch with bliss — their private moments of ecstasy — contemplated and came up with the memory of driving in a car alone, past a bridge over a body of water. For some reason, this exact experience gave each of them a moment of bliss.

This is interesting for several reasons; first of all because there is no outside influence telling them to look for this experience, and; secondly, because, well... there is this *particular* bridge that does that for *me*, when *I* drive by and view it from *my* car. These moments can be so simple, but unfortunately, our culture has never been encouraged to acknowledge and build on these moments. We've never been given permission to create and value a foundation of bliss, the way we've created a foundation of various forms of unhappiness.

Most Stage Two healing takes place in a non-ordinary environment, because as soon as we look to our ordinary environment, our cultural context, for guidelines on living, we lose our bliss. The ordinary guidelines for what creates happiness — monetary success, looking great, weighing exactly 130 pounds — are not what life is really about. Bliss may exist within the capitalist system, but conventional success is not a necessary requirement. Taking time to look at and admire your personal "bridge" may require stepping out of context of what other people think is valuable. You may even have to struggle at first to give yourself permission to feel that feeling, but it's real.

In that same workshop, most of the participants realized that they spend approximately five per cent of their lives in bliss, a fact which they had never noticed before. That isn't bad, and it is certainly something to build on, but it seems that most people have more personal ecstasy than they normally acknowledge. You might say they are in denial about their bliss. This same group also realized that by bringing their awareness of the 5 percent of bliss to the other 95 percent, all was transformed.

Follow those private feelings, and moments that bring you more bliss. If viewing a bridge brings you bliss, then why not hang out by a bridge? Why should you discount your experience just because a bridge isn't on the list of things you've been told are supposed to be edifying, along with Picasso and Haydn? If dancing brings you bliss in some private place within, you'd be a fool not to follow that. What else on earth would you follow? What else would make sense?

If you follow your bliss, be prepared for surprises, because you don't know where it will take you. You can't always logically construct the best possible future; you don't have all the pieces of the puzzle. But if you follow your bliss, step by step, you will receive the best indicators of where you should be, call it a "Geiger counter of the soul," telling you when you're getting "hot" or "cold." Developing this homing instinct requires stepping outside the cultural context, and trusting an inner world more than an outer world.

Consider the possibility that the most important thing in your life on a day to day basis is how you feel. If you adopt that priority, rather that those priorities enforced externally by our culture, you may find yourself moving towards things that make you feel better, especially in relationships. For some, this is a radical shift.

So often, taking the high road in a conflict makes us feel better than the egotistical, "I've got to be right" mode. Whenever you are in any conflict, ask yourself the question, "What is going to make me feel better?" After asking, you'll find you are always moved in a direction that makes you feel better, a more blissful direction.

Often, our bliss comes from a direction we don't think is logical, but as we have already stated earlier, there is a logic of emotions that is different from every day reason. As the French say, "The heart has reasons reason cannot understand." When dealing with the inner world, trust the logic of that inner world. Following your feelings every day and having that work for you is an extraordinarily logical goal, if you stay with it, for it will bring fruition and satisfactory completion to all your endeavors. Why? Because the logic of emotions is to seek completion.

We are evolutionary creatures. But how do we know what the next inch of evolution is going to be? We're not supposed to know. We just know that more of us will burst forth in some way as long as we are growing.

Bliss inspires creativity. Creativity inspires bliss, and they interconnect. You never know how the creation of your life will turn out, but you can be sure that if it is truly creative, bliss will be part of the equation.

I live in awe because bliss is a constant current running through my aliveness. What I mean is that first and foremost I feel comfortable in my own skin. I feel whole. From moment to moment, most of the time, I feel the essence of my being spring forth from a source deep within me and also beyond me, that connects me to all other beings and things, that feeds me just what I need, that makes my steps sure, and that keeps me safe, no matter what happens. I like being me, and that liking is now so thorough, the beingness so free of shame, I'm quite sure no person, place, thing, or event could spoil either.

This ease in my own being more often than not permits me to relax in this world with other beings in such a way that life *does* become a dance, a joyous and sometimes awkward dance that delights and fascinates me, testing my muscles, endurance, rhythm, attunement to mood and music, and skill at matching steps with my partners. Even when I do lose the beat and stumble, when life for a time is just hard — and I do not want to mislead you, sometimes it is — I still carry the imprint of when it was blissful. I still carry the awesome, unshakable knowing that blissfulness is the truth.

Feelings of Accomplishment

Prior to Stage Two, most people don't acknowledge, feel, and get grounded in their accomplishments. After Stage Two, one's accomplishments become a much more foundational part of their energy.

If you can walk around every day making choices based on how you feel, while wrestling with your environment as we all do, and still come out feeling you did your best, that's a great accomplishment. It should give you a wonderful feeling. Allow yourself the pleasure. Just doing Stage Two work can bring a tremendous feeling of accomplishment, knowing that most of the world has not even had the opportunity. You can feel good for yourself, but also feel good that you have something to offer those who haven't had the privilege. Even if your actions don't make the front page (and most of the really important ones don't), they may be shifting the universal energy in ways unknown to you.

Many people do not allow themselves to feel accomplished until someone else can validate it. How often have we secretly felt, "It's not real unless someone else can validate it"? Once we separate our adult from childhood needs we can still ask for acknowledgements from the outside, but much more of it we give to ourselves.

Who is to judge whether you feel good or not? Who can possibly judge that other than you? How else do you know if you have achieved what you set out to achieve unless you feel that you have? If you can go to bed at night knowing that you felt as good as you could all day by making choices that made you feel that way, you'll go to bed feeling accomplished.

We often hear of those who seem to accomplish so much, accumulating gold records and blockbuster movie credits, only to self-destruct at the first sign of rejection. The explanation is simple. They are people who haven't had the opportunity to do their Stage Two work. Their feelings of accomplishment were shallow, based on external criteria.

They had not gone to the depths of themselves to find out what they really wanted, or what would truly brings them bliss.

We assess other people's accomplishments, especially those we see in the media, and we compare and condemn ourselves, but we don't have any idea how they really feel, or what they were really shooting for, or what their motivation was, so we have no basis for comparison, nor do we need to. We can only compare ourselves with our histories. No other comparison is fair or meaningful. We only need to know what's going on within us.

Within the conventional social context, accomplishment often means "doing better than someone else." It means there can only be one winner — which makes everyone else a loser. But winning and losing is irrelevant. All of the fruits of the tree are accomplishments in a sense, but they are all personal, and are not measurable by or against anyone else.

The Shame-free Presentation of Self

This is the experience of meeting the world on *its* terms and your own. To more fully understand this state of being, try this quick exercise: Sit in a relaxed position, take three deep breaths and shake loose your everyday logical mind. Now, image yourself standing full-bodied, totally in the present moment, without a hint of shame or embarrassment about who you are, who you have been, or what your needs are. Take another deep breath. See yourself with the ability to clearly express those needs respectfully and without hesitation. Know yourself in this image as one who feels entitled to be seen, heard, and taken seriously. Lastly, take another deep breath, and imagine your feet firmly planted on the ground supporting your ability to hear and *effectively* engage with a complex and conflicting world.

In such imagery you will begin to find your own shame-free presentation of self and claim *ownership* of the ground that you walk on, for in the spiritual dimension, the universe belongs to all of us in a real and sensory way. We *know* this and *stand in this place* when we enter the complete phase of our recovery.

As you grow into complete recovery, you gradually find a balance between the wholeness within and the wholeness without. You find that you can literally bring yourself to the world, engage with it, and then accept how things really are, without losing your own sense of what's right for you. It's a delicate balance, but there's no contradiction. Again, it's not a question of right or wrong, it is two realities coming together. The world is going to go on being whatever it wants to be, but you don't have to let it defeat you.

Whether the world is represented by a person or a culture, you don't have to give up yourself in order to interact — you negotiate yourself into it. Relationship is the interaction between two different entities. You don't have to invalidate yourself or the world to develop that relationship. The shame-free presentation of self means putting your history underneath you without shame, wherever it happens to have been. You allow yourself to evolve from that place knowing it is a perfect place to be evolving from.

When you engage with the world from this place, know also that in the process you are changing the world around you. Neither you nor the world will ever be exactly the same again. This is healthy, natural and organic evolution. As you move through your stage two healing, just keep saying "yes" to who you are — bringing that out into the world — and you will be joining in the magical dance of creation.

Awareness of Impermanence

The acknowledgment that everything is impermanent is absolutely vital. This is most applicable in terms of intimate relationships. One of the challenges of Stage Two is connecting on an intimate level with another human being, and I don't believe we can do that totally until we accept the impermanence of our lives and theirs, until we can open up enough to know that we won't be able to hold onto the other person. We can only affirm that while they're here, we're going to enjoy them as much as possible. This principle holds not only for relationships, but for whatever we are doing in the moment. We can't embrace the present moment if we're going to hold onto the last one or the next. Our worst fears are always in the past and the future, seldom in the here and now. If we look at our life experience, the truth of impermanence is already proven to us in our history. Nothing has ever stayed the same. No relationship has stayed the same, no job has stayed the same, so the illusion that we are going to be able to hold onto things is truly a delusion, one that does not serve us well.

Life itself is impermanent, and the sooner we accept that, the sooner we can live life more fully. We live in a culture where we don't want to think about death, while at the same time we know that, like all plants, animals, and events, we come here, go through our growth cycle, and we die. The sooner we get happy with this fact, the more fulfilling our lives will be, for when we lose the fear of death, we lose the fear of life. We live so much more fully when we know we are not going to have this particular life forever, and therefore every minute is precious.

Awareness of impermanence and non-attachment go hand in hand. If we are aware of impermanence, we will not attach ourselves to things as if our life depended on it. It's hardly possible to be truly detached without a deep awareness of impermanence; they go hand in hand. Some try to force on themselves the sense of detachment and become numb to the moment. But true detachment comes from a lack of fear, a deep understanding of impermanence, and that lack of fear leads to total involvement, total in-the-moment presence, and total enjoyment. Enjoyment and non-attachment are not contradictory, they are both components of the holistic state.

Serendipity, Grace, and Synchronicity

Serendipity is when you wish for (or dream of) something and another thing even greater occurs. I love it when that happens! For example, before I even went back to school, I dreamed of working with people — that by the time I was forty I would free myself from what I perceived as the world's slavery, and have a healing practice that I loved. I'm doing that today. I could never have fathomed then that I would find the enjoyment in life I'm experiencing now. There are also everyday experiences of serendipity, usually on a smaller scale, which we need to stop and appreciate once in a while.

Grace is like grease. To me it is a lubrication for the soul. It is an unexpected gift from the universe that comes and helps smooth the way through difficult transitions. The more you trust grace, the more you have it. When you have faith in the self-organizing universe, you come to believe you don't have to do it all yourself, that there is an energy available to you that can boost you through a difficult time, painful as the challenge may be.

Two years ago I had a heart attack, just as the first edition of this book went to press. I was swept up in almost a year of discomfort, pain, confusion, and the trauma of open heart surgery. Yet, at the same time, I was mysteriously graced. I went through the experiences in several dimensions of awareness. Except for relatively short periods of intense confusion and fear, I maintained my connection to wholeness, I watched for the lessons to be learned in the process (and there were many), and continually prepared to re-enter the world with an even fuller sense of myself. I am forever grateful for the grace that I experienced those times when my essence was aligned with that of my higher power, the universe, or the Great Spirit, and grateful that it seems to have succeeded in becoming a regular part of my life.

So often we are harder on ourselves than life is. Grace is more forgiving toward us than we are toward ourselves. If we can accept ourselves as evolutionary creatures, evolving beings, manifesting, stage by stage, like a flower, then grace comes by trusting that we too are part of that process. It is not meant to be torture — only resistance is torture.

Carl Jung first coined the word synchronicity in 1952, though synchronistic events have been occurring since the dawn of human existence. To Jung, and to the many who have benefited from his discovery, synchronicity is a "meaningful coincidence." According to Robert H. Hopcke, the director of the Center for Symbolic Studies and author of *There Are No Mistakes: Synchronicity and the Stories of Our Lives,* "a synchronistic event is a coincidence that holds a subjective meaning for the person involved... that is to say, valuable and/or significant in its effect." Hopcke describes the four features that generally make an event synchronistic:

> First, such events are *acausally* connected, rather than connected through a chain of cause and effect that an individual can discern as intentional or deliberate on her or his own part. Second, such events always occur with an accompaniment of *deep emotional experience,* usually at the time of the event itself, but not always. Third, the content of the synchronistic experience, what the event actually is, is always *symbolic* in nature, and almost always, I have found, related specifically to the fourth aspect of the synchronistic event, namely, that such coincidences occur at points of *important transitions* in our life. A synchronistic event very often becomes a turning point in the stories of our lives.... Meaningful coincidences, which always occur at points of change and transformation, are thus symbolic of our profound connection with others and reassure us that indeed we are never really alone in the midst of such transitions.

Synchronicity is a wink from the universe that tells you you're on the right track. It is the feeling that you are in synch, and that things are happening around you which all conspire to help you fulfill your destiny. It is a very private feeling, one that can't always be proven or evaluated by others. I don't necessarily say you should go looking for synchronicity, but to take notice when it comes.

There is a mystic aspect to all of this, because it is not in our everyday understanding. There is a certain trust of the unknown which goes with it all. Synchronicity, serendipity and grace are around you every day; they are the ways to describe our personal experience with the self-organizing universal principle.

When we trust and believe that we are part of a self-organizing universe, and that all we have to do is manifest where we stand and continue to grow where we are planted, how simple life will be.

The Experience of Holism and Transpersonal Healing

Once you heal through your biographical healing, which is Stage Two, you begin the organic healing of the universe, and of consciousness. That's where transpersonal events occur. They transcend the body. For example, I did a week-long breathwork healing workshop a few years ago with Stan Grof, for personal healing, and had a transpersonal experience that changed my life and gave it focus. In that workshop, I went back to other lifetimes, or to a collective consciousness back in time. I was castrated, and I experienced the castration personally. It was a numbing experience, and not a pleasant one, which stayed with me for months afterwards. It was very instructive to me as to why my present life is so anchored in healing the sexual-spiritual split. The castration had to do with sexual ritual that was culturally accepted in that life time and that was not by an oppressor of the time. I was punished for what I was doing. It was so real. I went back to it three times during the breathwork and lived out different parts of it. To me, these kind of visions and out-of-this-life experience are part of the transpersonal healing, healing beyond our own bodies.

The experience of holism, or complete recovery, includes not only accepting all of the physical, emotional, spiritual, and sexual aspects of ourselves in awareness, but also accepting our responsibility for the healing of the larger self, the other, the universe. For in reality all is one and inseparable.

Albert Einstein, in describing what he called "our task," foresaw the need for the holism that our complete recovery embraces:

A human being is part of the whole, called by us 'Universe,' a part limited in time and space. He experiences himself, his thoughts and feelings as something separated from the rest, a kind of optical delusion of his consciousness. The delusion is a kind of prison for us, restricting us to our personal desires and to affection to a few persons nearest to us. Our task must be to free ourselves from this prison by widening our circle of compassion to embrace all living creatures and the whole of nature in its beauty.

While these ideas may seem new to many of us, a Buddhist sutra recorded over two millennia ago tells us:

> In the heaven of Indra there is said to be a network of pearls so arranged that if you look at one you see all the others reflected in it. In the same way, each object in the world is not merely itself but involves every other object, and in fact *is* every other object.

In other words, of the myriad of pearls in Indra's heaven, we each are one. In this holographic nature of things when one individual changes, that change is reflected in everyone and everything else. Wow! *That's* holism!

Ongoing Maintenance of Stages

Once you have gone through stage two, you are sometimes going to come across experiences in life that trigger a traumatic memory that is not already resolved. Complete recovery includes the ongoing completion of our feelings and experiences. This means you will have to go back down into Stage Two stations, to work through that situation to its resolution, and come back up again. The reason why this is considered a Fruit of the Tree of awareness is that you can now go through this process quickly from a place of wholeness, rather than confusion. From this perspective, you can also work with any addictive tendencies on an ongoing basis.

The ongoing maintenance of stages also serves in preserving one's humility, the antidote to ego. We will always be in the process of becoming, and healing and change are the dynamic tensions that give birth to becoming. We need never be perfect, except in being the perfect manifestation of who we are in the present moment. We need never be fixed, except continuing to adjust ourselves out of culturally prescribed norms that may not fit who we presently are. Why would a human being ever want to be *fixed* in the first place? I find great comfort in knowing that, like every other human creature, I need to continue to earnestly process complex feelings in order to be the best I can be. Being the best we can be allows us to live with a feeling of emergence, of being part of an evolutionary process.

This ongoing maintenance is not the chore it might seem, but the guarantee of being able to maintain a very pleasurable level of aliveness — with the additional guarantee that we can continue to expand it with every day and year that we live.

Boundless Creativity

Upon experiencing complete recovery, your life becomes one of continuous creating in a gradually expanding way. Creation can be many different things at different times. I don't know how to define my own professional creativity sometimes, so I think of myself as a social artist. By the nature of our being, and being evolutionary creatures at heart, we are always on the edge of newness, and most of us, until we work through Stage Two, are not awake to that. There is an eternal stream of evolution happening all around us. That's why I love Jean Houston's quote about people she feels are really alive, "They have a sense that they are dancing on the *fulcrum of evolution*." How could you not be creative all the time? Once you accept impermanence, things are always changing. If the universe is evolving, and we are part of the universe in a holistic way, how can we not evolve?

In our evolution and our creative state, we are, inevitably and inextricably, connected to all the other creation happening around us and interacting with us all the time. It is a creative universe, so we are in a real sense, co-creating with the universe. At a certain point, we reach complete recovery, and life is art. If we keep moving forward on this path, these moments will indeed happen. Co-creation is one, two, or more people creating with a power greater than themselves. Certainly as the universe is greater than ourselves, our creativity can be as boundless as the universe.

Personal Spiritual Intimacy

When you work through your own barriers to intimacy, spirituality, and the authentic presentation of self, that labor of love will bear fruit. Part of this reward is called personal spiritual intimacy, the connection with spirit that is highly personal, that doesn't have to be explained or have to be part of anything else. It doesn't have to be part of a religious experience, although it might be. The basic spiritual essence is personal and intimate. It is being intimate with yourself. We are talking about a basic inner process.

When you reach this stage of your own development, you have a personal, intimate, loving relationship with yourself. This means that you're honest with yourself, you're close to yourself, you love yourself, you have an equality with yourself, you're supportive and understanding with all parts of yourself, and know where your blocks and foibles are, and make room for them, engage with them, and love them too. What I'm trying to describe is just a wonderful feeling of self-acceptance that permeates your being and allows you to be totally you.

This *being totally you* is highly spiritual in itself. When you can love yourself enough to do this, you discover a deep well within — a very personal one — which contains your unique wisdom, sense of self, sense of wonder, and purpose for being. The richest blessing of having a personal spiritual intimacy is that you can draw from this well eternally, it is part of the wellspring of creation, and love is the connection.

Body/Mind/Spirit Connection

To discuss the body/mind/spirit connection in clear terms, I need to make the distinction between the four levels of connectedness.

The first level of connectedness is where we are "unconsciously unconnected," which is the way many of us begin our Stage Two recovery. Basically, we don't even have a clue as to what the words body/mind/spirit mean in relationship to connection. We don't remember ever having had the visceral experience. We have no framework for the experience.

The second level is "intermittent connection," in which we have felt the connection (and are no longer clueless) but only experience it intermittently without a sense of mastery or conscious management of the connection.

The third is what I call "growing connection," the condition of almost always being at least somewhat connected and continuing to grow with that connection. In this state we have and are always gaining a sense of mastery of our connectedness. We are very conscious when we feel disconnected, and will look to Stage Two stations or other healing to move through whatever is disconnecting us. Perhaps we would sign up for a workshop or retreat that provides a nonordinary healing environment so our inner wisdom can bring to the surface whatever needs to be healed next.

The fourth is being "totally connected" — a nonordinary state of consciousness. When this happens we are totally at one with ourselves, our bodies, and the universe, feeling our feelings, thinking our thoughts that are related to our feelings — all in the essence of love. Our hearts are open. We see how everything fits together. We intuitively understand Einstein's theory of relativity. (I will give some personal examples of these experiences in the next paragraphs.)

While no linear progression actually exists because each person's experience is sacredly unique, I can nonetheless generalize a possible healing scenario based on my experience and observation. As one enters Stage Two one is often "unconsciously unconnected." Early on in the work one will have "intermittent connection" which may come from consciously doing the work. It also may arise from finding a new perspective on the process of life itself. If someone remains earnest in their journey toward complete recovery they will probably have periodic episodes of "total connection" and gradually begin living in what I call "growing connection." This is where I live. Though I have had many experiences of "total connection" I don't believe my body or the rest of the world is quite ready for me to live there.

The importance of making these distinctions and developing the awareness of levels of connectedness is so that we can name our experiences — and we *must* name our experiences. Only by naming them can we validate them. Only by validating them do they become real. Only by becoming real can we grow from them. By validating connecting experiences we build an inner invisible (but very real) platform. Over time it becomes unshakable and this grounds us in "growing connection." Without the naming and the validating it would be impossible to live in this state of inner connectedness.

The experiences of "total connection" are valuable because they shake up the status quo of energy systems and structures in the body. This does two important things. It shows us where we're going and where we're not, at least not yet.

This experience brings forth feelings and insights that would not have been available in a less connected state. Often it will bring forth traumatic patches of history that are now ripe for healing. If they were not ripe, the organic system would not bring them forth. Sometimes experiences of great pleasure and joy emerge.

The second important value of these experiences is that they teach us where to grow. Once the body has these experiences it will naturally and organically grow toward the connected condition. Once the natural state is reawakened, we grow toward the light just like flowers grow toward the sun. We have barely survived in the shade of false authority and shame for far too long. But we have survived. The sun feels good and we eagerly grow toward it.

One of my early experiences of total connection, which I also experience as a sacred opening, was in 1978 when I participated in a weekend workshop called the Advocate Experience in San Francisco. In many ways this was a pivotal evolutionary experience. The Experience was created by David Goodstein (who also founded the *Advocate Magazine*, the first national gay and lesbian publication) to deshame the experience of being gay or lesbian, thereby empowering participants with a richer sense of self. It was nine years after the beginning of the gay liberation movement, marked by the Stonewall riots of 1969. It was three years before the community was to face the challenge of AIDS, which I believe the Advocate Experience prepared us to do. Participants went on to found or co-found most of the gay and AIDS service organizations which lived up to this enormous challenge with a dignity, wisdom, and creativity never seen before in such a catastrophic human epidemic.

My experience in that weekend was profound. Less than half way through, the effect of having all these people (about 100, all told) in this beautiful hotel ballroom together, all of whom grew up feeling different in the same ways that I did, hit me. They all *knew* my deep inner isolation. They *knew* how much the sound of the words sissy, fag, dike made my skin crawl, whether it was addressed to me or not.

There were no positive models for being sexually different when I grew up. It was a very lonely and isolating idea. We lived in terror of anyone finding out the direction in which our affections and fantasies traveled. Somehow in realizing that all these people made it through such childhoods made me admire their courage and stamina.

Then all of a sudden it mysteriously mirrored back to me. Finally, I admired my *own* courage and stamina. I had enormous compassion for myself and everyone in the room. I felt my heart open and then I felt my vertebrae open up like they were four inches in diameter. This incredible energy went through my spine and through my body. It was love. In those moments my spirit connected with my body and my mind. I felt like I was dropping several tons of shame, not only for myself but for others too. All the painful, isolated moments of growing up different flashed before me and they too were healed. I was never the same again.

I went on, with several other participants, to bring the Advocate Experience to New York where several thousand people experienced similar healing over the next few years. I also went on to co-found several service organizations for sexually diverse people. That healing has never left me, nor has the empowerment that resulted. I believe that it was that experience that moved me into the "growing connection" of my body, mind, and spirit.

Another experience of total connection for me was on a massage table receiving Polarity Massage. The practitioner was guiding me in breathing and reporting to her any sensations I felt in my body as she moved the energy in my body through gentle manipulation and touch. About fifteen minutes into the process, as she was balancing and relaxing the energy in my left leg, a strong current of energy came through me. I reported it to her and she asked me if there were any images associated to the sensation. Then the images came.

I was sitting once again in the first house that I bought at the age of thirty-six. It was the day of the closing. I was single at the time and this purchase was a courageous adventure for me. She asked if there were any senses or feeling with the images, and yes there immediately were. I could smell the cedar wood which this lovely little house had in abundance. I could see me on that day, alone, just returning from the lawyer's office, sitting on the floor in the empty house smelling the cedar. Being in touch with the loneliness and joy of that moment, I began to cry gently. That house had meant so much to me, there were so many happy moments associated with it. In those moments on that table my mind, body, and spirit were totally connected. Everything was perfectly clear.

New images and feelings came to me as she continued to work on my body. It was while living in that house that I was treated for cancer. I then saw myself in the hospital getting my first chemotherapy treatment, my whole body twisted in anxiety. I hated the thought of these toxic chemicals entering my bloodstream. All the traumas of the treatments, surgeries, infections, and medical intrusions to my body swept through me with quickly shifting images, and I cried. At the time of the treatments, I was strong. I had to be. It was only now, five years later, that I could grieve for what I went through. While the entire experience was cathartic and sad, it was simultaneously renewing and enlivening. I was so thankful for having these memories come out of my body to be healed, and I felt the healing immediately

Many other images related to other incidents at that house came to me and my mind was able to put them in a totally new context which gave new depth and substance to those years of my life. I left that massage therapy session with all my faculties in tact and available to me. All of my life made sense. I could see how each thing built on the other to make me the person I am, the person I need and want to be. My universe was in order and I was grateful for this perspective. It was this same session that began my years of exploration of body-centered healing techniques. I was "sold," you might say.

In my early years, I'd had a number of total connection experiences under the influence of hallucinagenics such as LSD, but never totally integrated them until I began to have sober experiences of transcendence many years later. These were experiences where my body, mind, and spirit were united and I was also present to witness it all on still another level of consciousness. I will always be grateful for the wisdom, awarenesses, and healing that came from my many incidents of total connection. They have guided my mind, spirit, and body in a unified intention to live in as connected a state as is possible at any given moment. The whole of myself enjoys moving with this intention.

Whatever your experiences with body/mind/spirit connection, even if you feel unconsciously unconnected, know that further experiences wait for you. They want to inform and enlighten you. I believe they are gifts from the creative universe, or from our creator. You only need to have the willingness to allow it to happen and the courage to put yourself in non-ordinary environments and states of consciousness. This can happen in workshops, body therapies, breathwork, vision quests, sweat lodges, and so on. Let your own intuition and the synchronicity of situations made available to you be your guide. You will develop a trust and knowing as you become more conscious that the body/mind/spirit can respond in an instantaneous dance whenever you provide a setting for the occurrence.

Respect for Self and Others

The concept of respect for self and others is one of the most important guiding principles in this work. You can't achieve complete recovery without it. When we are respecting ourselves and others we always *know* we are on healthy, whole, solid ground. We are in tune with our higher self and all that it signifies. When we are not, it is a signal that we need to tend to ourselves, to see what correction needs to be put in. Without respect we cannot be or feel whole.

Respect is the state of being regarded with honor and esteem — a willingness to show consideration or appreciation. This is what we are required to bring to ourselves and others if we want to fully enjoy the fruits of the tree. This is not such a difficult requirement in that it feels good to do it. We only need to work out of some old culturally induced ego defenses that want to make someone (or ourselves) right or wrong, better or worse, or more than or less than.

I recently read *No Word for Time: The Way of the Algonquin People* by Evan T. Pritchard. In this insightful book Pritchard shares his reclaiming of his native ancestry and the wisdom he accumulated on the journey. Though thousands of years old there is much we can learn from indigenous cultures. In this book is outlined the seven principles of respect that are close to the heart of Native American wisdom and the Algonquin art of speaking. With reverence to their tradition of origin, I share them because they express so clearly my own concept of respect for self and other:

1. Respect for feelings, and for suffering. Always show compassion. Do not add to the suffering.
2. Respect for individual space. Practice non-interference and non-control. Don't use people. Respect each being's life, limb, land, privacy and property, including your own.
3. Respect for limitations as well as strengths. Honor both in yourself and others, and no one will be abused.
4. Respect for boundaries and individual differences. Take responsibility for your own choices and disentangle yourself from the choices of others.
5. Respect for truth. Show directness and integrity in speech and action.
6. Respect for the earth and all paths, peoples, cultures, and customs growing here. All have a place in the hoop.
7. Respect for yourself, for all aspects, high and low. We all have bodies, hearts, minds, and spirits for a good reason. Spirituality is the relationship between each of them. Conduct your life fully, but with dignity.

With these principles put forth, I trust that the necessary understanding of the respect for self and others required to be a whole and fulfilled person is perfectly clear and realizable.

The Seeds Fall Close to the Tree: Creating Conscious Consciousness

Each of the Fruits of the Tree in themselves bear fruit; they grow our consciousness. Whatever fruits we are experiencing, such as personal spiritual intimacy, or bliss, are simultaneously continuing to expand and enrich our consciousness. This consciousness is the critical awareness of our own identity and how that relates to others and to the whole that embraces everything. So whatever fruit(s) blossoms into our awareness will in the same moment continue to raise our awareness and sense of aliveness.

We can emerge out of Stage Two healing, learning how to make our conscious mind and unconscious work together for us. For example, one of the ways that I do this is by respecting my unconscious creative processes. I always prime my unconscious so that it can respond to particular challenges in a prepared way. In the writing of this book, I always defined the challenge of the next day's writing early in the preceding evening in as clear a way as possible. The following morning as I sat at the computer ready to address the challenge, my unconscious would always spring forth with the important points I wanted to make. Sometimes it would feed them to me during the evening or night and I would make notes. It never failed me.

Since most of the material and synthesis of this book comes from my unconscious, (and the larger collective consciousness) one might say it was "channeled." The ideas came through me. But I do not use that word because the way I am using my unconscious is so basic and practical, and channeling sounds so mysterious. Also my unconscious often responds in a delayed fashion; I do not possess the skills that I have witnessed with people who have the gift of instantaneous channeling — although, I often have that delight while working with a client or facilitating a workshop. The perfect words for a situation come through me and I have no idea where they come from. It is very exhilarating. It is those times that I feel the Creator's breath. I have come to learn and respect many ways that my consciousness works. Where I do so, I elicit it to help me feel good about my life.

If you do not understand what I am saying, and that is very possible, make it okay. You are not deficient, you may only be lacking a certain experiential frame of reference. If the fruits of the tree feel attractive to you, make it your intention to experience them for yourself. Create the image and believe that the possibility for these experiences are within you. Stay with the Stage Two healing process and you will know exactly the truth of what I write. It will be your own very unique experience, but you will know exactly what sensations and feelings I am expressing.

The next century will be about consciousness and how to best appreciate and use it. Complete recovery is about continuing to heal and awaken consciousness, always intending to reduce our own suffering, that of others, and the planet. We are being prepared for the challenges of the 21st Century.

Support
&
Empowerment

When we get out of the glass bottles of our ego,
and when we escape like squirrels turning in the cages of our personality
and get into the forrests again,
we shall shiver with cold and fright
but things will happen to us
so that we don't know ourselves.

Cool, unlying life will rush in,
and passion will make our bodies taut with power,
we shall stamp our feet with new power
and old things will fall down,
we shall laugh, and institutions will curl up like burnt paper.

D.H. LAWRENCE
Earth Prayers From Around the World

Earlier in the book I discussed the four "powers" of advanced recovery: The power of community-based healing, the power of shared intentionality, the power of shared belief, and the power of Authentic Process. In using the tools for the inner journey outlined in this chapter, I encourage you to be mindful of these four powers and how they relate to and enhance these awareness-building activities.

Before using any tool, stop, and become conscious. Breathe deeply at least three times and allow your psyche to relax and open to these powers of authenticity that are within you. Embrace whatever tool your inner compass, or intuition, leads you to, with the energy imbued in these powers. For example, when writing a healing poem, experiment with making it into a instrument for sharing your beliefs, your intentions, your heart, and authentic feelings with your chosen spiritual family. When you bring your expanded conscious awareness to your inner adventures you will be rewarded again and again.

All people need love. We all need support and empowerment. At the same time, we cannot expect others to be our caretakers, or to be there for us at the moment we need help. There are well-established self-loving and self-healing techniques that work wonders for the soul in our personal journey toward complete recovery. If that is not enough, and pain and depression become overwhelming, medication is an option as a way to buy time to heal our wounds. It is also empowering to know that each person involved in the recovery process is part of a global awakening, that you are not alone.

9

Tools for the Inward Journey

There are a growing number of "tools for the healing journey" that are available outside of the Authentic Process Therapy Community, activities that enhance the process of recovery. I will share applications for each, to illustrate their value in advancing growth in Stage Two recovery. These nine ways to enhance and accelerate the self-healing process are:

1. Artistic and Creative Expression
2. Journal Writing
3. Creative Writing
4. Emotional Release Work
5. Esteem Work
6. Meditation and/or Visualization
7. Sense of Self Spirituality
8. Body Energetics/Body Work/Body Movement
9. Martial Arts and Self-Defense

1. Artistic and Creative Expression

For several years, I have been collecting samples of creative expression given to me by clients and workshop participants, and have learned a lot about recovery in the process. I hope to publish a "coffee table" book at some point, an anthology of writing and art in recovery to share these varied creative expressions. I know this will serve as an inspiration to others to take advantage of this powerful healing tool for their own empowerment.

In my own recovery and in the facilitation of others', I have found that any form of creative expression, when integrated with authentic Stage Two process, makes a difference. For individuals who have difficulty allowing feelings and energy to freely move through their body and consciousness, creative expression can transcend these limitations. For example, when we are emotionally charged, we can channel our energy into "stream of consciousness" expressions and record our feelings in writing, painting, dancing, or other artistic media. In doing so, we have a personal experience of integration and self-realization. These experiences are vital in our movement toward a sense of wholeness or holism. Sharing these creative expressions helps build a sense of community.

2. Journal Writing

While I encourage most people I work with to do some form of journal writing, many have resistance. Others find great solace in regular personal writing. There are times when journal or letter writing is the only way out of a sticky psychodynamic. For example, a parent or family member might trigger repressed and complex feelings, feelings that can lead to withdrawal. However, withdrawal is not an acceptable option because it often brings accompanying self-punishment for not being able to better address the conflict. Often even a therapy session does not provide sufficient time for sorting out the complexities of all the current and repressed feelings. But a letter written (but not always sent!) to the person or an essay about him or her (to be shared initially only as healing process), when earnestly done, will often unravel the conflicted feelings. Sharing these various writings in therapy or community often illuminates still other layers of complex feelings. The sharing and sorting out of these deeper feelings brings the picture or situation into a clearer, more realistic perspective. From this vantage point you may or may not choose to take specific actions toward conflict resolution and personal empowerment, but at least now you will have a choice.

If you've ever tried journal writing you may have found a certain level of resistance within yourself. For most of us, liberation comes from finding creative ways to get through, around, or over the resistance.

When I set out to sort out my feelings using inner-process writing, I often make a deal with myself. I first acknowledge that when it comes time to write, I will have resistance and that part of me will find distractions and excuses. The more conscious part of me, the one that wants to work toward resolution, often pales in the face of this powerful resistance.

I discovered a simple trick to help me get beyond the resistance. I acknowledge that this conflict will most probably emerge as the time for writing approaches, and I vow not to participate in the internal debate. I give myself permission to transcend the debate and to write, at the scheduled time — *no matter what I feel internally* — to write because I know that it will take me where I need to go. If I don't take myself there, no one else is going to. I tell myself, "I am just going to write, period." I share this with you in the hope that it may be helpful in its simplicity.

3. Creative Writing

Poetry, poetry, poetry — what an incredible gift! These words come from a person who, some years ago, was too rigid to even consider writing poetry. It came to me one day, more out of necessity than from conscious creativity.

My old tried-and-true way of processing deep conflicting feelings through journal and letter writing had become somewhat laborious and boring. I had just done it too many times. It still worked, but I wanted a fresh vehicle, possibly one that felt more concise and efficient. I decided that, for my own use, I could write short sentences as well as the next person, and perhaps these economical sentences could be imbued with personal transcendent meaning.

I began writing short sentences in an effort to understand and come to terms with feelings of rage that had recently surfaced regarding my father. This man — whose rage, confusion, and frustration dominated my developmental years — also provided me with food, shelter and an honorable, basic value system after losing my mother.

This inner conflict had surfaced in stages. I dove into poetry because I feared I would otherwise be writing for eternity. A series of six poems in four months time brought peace to my weary heart and soul. It also led me to a process that gifted me with an entirely new and richly personal relationship with my Dad.

However one chooses to do creative writing — whether poetry, short story, essay or songwriting — bringing the intention of healing and integration to this work will enhance its therapeutic value.

4. Emotional Release Work

Emotional release is the backbone of the healing process, particularly those healing from childhood emotional and sexual trauma. These could be blocked feelings of vulnerability, fear, grief, or even love, but quite often the feeling that is most repressed is rage.

I often find myself wishing there were more safe and structured environments to express repressed rage. Rage, fury, and anger tend to be messy. When these feelings surface after years of repression they can be downright frightening. For this reason they are often avoided or shunned in our society, and the crippling and destructive effects of the repression continues. Our society and many of our therapies do not make a serious effort to support this emotional release. We agree to live in denial and avoid the messiness, and yet these out-of-control feelings may fester within. Some rage hovers near the surface and is triggered by seemingly insignificant events, while some never comes to the surface except in therapy. Authentic Process validates and encourages the safe expression of repressed and triggered rage.

Like many others in recovery, I have had to learn to befriend my rage, to learn to rechannel this energy and use it for self-protection and self-actualization. We do this A, because we have to, and B, because it works. When the rage begins to surface in the process of recovery, our survival and continuing development as spiritual creatures demands that we place these feelings in a new context. To continue to avoid them is to consent to living in depression and isolation.

While some of this work can be coached by a willing practitioner, time restraints involved in squeezing authentic rage into the "therapeutic hour," and space and noise restraints within a professional office, can often be inhibiting. However, you *can* do it on your own.

In my own early emotional release work, my therapist suggested I get a punching bag. I did so, and it was a liberating and enlightening experience. As I gave myself permission to express fury while hitting the bag, I was amazed at the images that flooded my consciousness. Though mildly jarring, it was at the same time enlivening and energizing. As I continued to encourage myself not to judge the images, I found myself raging more freely. Slowly stories emerged from the images. To continue augmenting and supporting this process, I learned and incorporated many techniques. I beat the bed with a tennis racquet or a rolled up towel. I had screaming marathons into my pillow. I walked as fast as I could and grunted. I ran like hell. I did all this and more, to free myself and integrate my feelings.

The rewards of doing this messy work are beyond words. I feel as though anything I write will just be that, words, while my emotional release work goes so much deeper.

Because of my passionate appreciation for the benefits of emotional release work, I enjoy passing on the secrets of primal expression to others. I find I always benefit. When skillfully facilitated, everyone present experiences the healing. The best and deepest emotional release work of this nature can come about in planned, structured workshop settings where the facilitators and other participants have agreed to share this dynamic and empowering work. Within such a structure, the power of group dynamics and the skillful coaching of the facilitators allows participants to access and process deeper rage than would be otherwise possible. In anticipation of the workshop, participants consciously and unconsciously prepare themselves for this process. Opportunities for such workshops may be found through the Resources directory in the back of this book.

5. Esteem Work

In our world where diversity prevails, so do prejudices. Therefore, as I have discovered, most recovering people have cultural pain issues that need to be put in a new perspective. For example, I have worked with African-Americans, Asian-Americans, gays, lesbians, Irish-Americans, and Jews who wholeheartedly believe they have accepted who they are. However, in the heart of Stage Two process, a more confusing level of feelings often surface, feelings of cultural shame and self-rejection. While these feelings may be apparent to the practitioner, the client may at first deny them. There is often a great barrier of unconscious resistance to reconnecting with these early feelings. After all, they are feelings which led us to build our self-esteem on the foundation of the person next to us, rather than upon our own. Psycho-cultural education is helpful at this point.

I have found that we can work through these feelings relatively quickly if we avail ourselves of the group process. Support groups are a great way to rebuild a new and appropriate sense of self-esteem. They provide support and education from peers who are also rebuilding their own esteem from the ground up. What I am saying is that no matter how good a practitioner I might be, an African-American in recovery may need to engage in some peer support work exclusively with other African-Americans. The same is true for women, gays, and Latino-Americans. Adoptees have special self-esteem needs all their own.

Peer support groups and ethnic events are an important part of a multi-cultural society. There is a powerful mirroring effect that takes place in these exclusive settings, one that facilitates healing and leads to a fuller recovery. While I may be able to guide a person in this process and understand and identify with them, the deep identification work is best done in healing community with cultural peers.

6. Meditation and/or Visualization

Meditation and Visualization are the twin arts that help us tune in to our innermost feelings. It could be said that Meditation and Visualization are what tie each of the other "tools" together; they enhance each process we undertake. With practice, they provide both inner awareness and the experience of transcendence.

In the words of meditation teacher and author Stephen Levine:

To deepen awareness is to awaken. To awaken is to maintain "a continuity of the heart." To meet whatever comes, not only the confusing condition of the mind, but the spacious unconditional presence that lies beyond. Meditation is not a denial of anything, neither this tangled oft-conflicting conditioning nor the ever-healed that exist just over the horizon. It is an entering directly into consciousness with mercy and clarity. It is a deep seeing of what turns pain to suffering. And how we cling to that suffering rather than let go into the vast unknown. So, we explore the mind, not to master it so much as to not be mastered by it. We are not making war on the mind, we are making peace with it.

In my experience, this passage speaks not only to meditation, but to the essence of Stage Two process. My own first experience of this came in the depths of confusion during my first year of Stage One work. I relied on the Serenity Prayer and used it often to calm my restless heart and soul. It became a mantra in troubled times:

God (or Great Spirit), grant me the serenity to accept the things I cannot change, the courage to change the things I can, and the wisdom to know the difference.

After I repeated it over and over again, it gradually penetrated my deeper consciousness and I began to have an altered experience of reality that was more heart-centered. As I began repeating the prayer to myself, it was like flipping a switch inside. A calm would come over me and a transcendent experience of clarity and understanding would prevail, as if my heart were floating on a perfectly still pond. Since those first momentary "still water" experiences, I have respectfully and slowly cultivated my own personal meditative life. It is the well I drink from. All of my Stage Two struggles and instances of "working through" have been graced by this energy.

Like the other practices, meditation takes diligence and effort. While it may not be for everyone at all times, meditation and visualization provide great curative powers for those who apply themselves. I recommend that people approach meditation and prayer in whatever way comes easiest to them and to always think of it as practice, never perfection. The practice itself tends to bring us more into our body and into the here and now, which is where the heart takes root and opens up like a flower. Self-critical judging of this experience diminishes its natural centering effect, yet, most of us tend to do this until we realize the subtle benefits of suspending judgment and just being.

Each of the creative art modalities I have mentioned are a form of meditation. The incorporation of one or all of these arts will provide us with power and inspiration. In this way, insights from the unconscious the higher self and the inner child will emerge and rise to a new level of brilliance.

7. "Sense of Self" Spirituality

Definitions of spirit and spirituality differ from person to person — some look to God, while others consider Love to be the highest power. Some search for the Great Spirit or Universal Spirit, while others seek Nature. However we define this higher power, to reach it we must come out from under a defense-driven isolation. We must admit that we cannot successfully confront our personal barriers without the help of others. Once we admit this, our defenses will relax and we will have an opportunity for a spiritual awakening. This is often the threshold to Stage One and Stage Two recovery. If we are earnest in this desire for help, and if empathic support is available, this spiritual, energetic and experiential metamorphosis can start taking place.

I use the words "energetic" (relating to actual feelings of energy currents and restrictions in the body) and "experiential" (relating to a felt experience rather than an intellectual idea) because this transformation can occur without any reference to God or spirituality. It often takes place in groups like "Rational Recovery" and "AA for Agnostics." It happens through the compassion and understanding of others who can allow a person to be as they are (even when this includes *not* believing in God or spirituality). When we are understood and accepted in this way, we feel an opening, however slight, of an inner energy that connects with a similar energy or feeling in others who are sharing in community recovery. Some people, in response to unconscious fears, will deny or minimize this experience. In these instances, I suggest reframing this feeling, in alignment with the Stage Two goals. Experiment with trusting what it brings and you will be rewarded.

While some of us usually have some measure of a personal, spiritual experience in Stage One, by the time we reach Stage Two, we are ready for a deeper experience of what I refer to as "Sense of Self" spirituality. In this phase of Authentic Process Therapy, psychodynamic, humanistic, transpersonal and existential psychologies converge to trigger a person's deepest realization of self. This is a time for awakening the unconscious — with the help and support of community — to dissolve or transcend existing barriers to fuller self-expression. Often there is great resistance to this deeper self-discovery. Once again, the effort will entail reaching out for help and letting go of the ego; but this is necessary for one to move into and through this work. And, again, the empathic nature of the support that is received from the group significantly affects the process.

At this point in the process, many might ask: "Why? Why should I spend time and energy probing my depths? I just want to get on with my life."

This reaction is understandable, because the process is painful. The resistance makes it so. But once you begin, you will open up to new energy and information. And though pain is processed, in community it is also embraced with understanding and the humor of human identification. In a sense, the healing can be fun. As AA's founder, Bill Wilson, once wrote: "Sobriety is only a bare beginning; it is only the first gift of the first awakening. If more gifts are to be received, our awakening must go on."

In my own recovery, I struggled to define God (and spirituality) for myself. After distilling my many years of searching and striving to understand, I was left with two ideas that I continue to juggle: compassion and understanding. The first is a feeling of kindness, love, and empathy towards myself and others; the second involves the unraveling of my own unconscious material and bringing it to light, a process which conjures up for me an experience of a transcendent energy, spirit, or force.

Many ancient philosophical and religious writings espouse that "God is love," but it took my own rigorous study of my personal history to breathe life into these words. When reviewing my life for God-like experiences or moments, I discovered that most of them entailed someone extending themselves in love to me, or conversely, extending my love to another, in an open-hearted connection of love, or spirit, one-to-another. The other God-like experiences were times when I allowed nature to love me, for this too is a God-like experience. As I accept the "nature" of my own organic growth and evolution, I do this more and more.

Likewise, the term "self-discovery" is used in casual conversation these days, but talking about it is far removed from the actual unraveling and restructuring experience it brings.

I have learned to bring both compassion and understanding to my own repressed conflicts, defenses, and deeper secrets, and have experienced a deeper space within from which to view the world, and from which to share this loving, spiritual, and energetic connection.

M. Scott Peck impressed me with a similar description of sense-of-self spirituality. In *The Road Less Traveled,* he wrote something that I felt others had stopped short of saying. He suggested that, "If you desire wisdom greater than your own, you can find it inside you. The interface between God and man is at least in part the interface between our unconscious and our conscious. To put it plainly, our unconscious is God."

This has been true for me. The more I have "permissioned" or allowed my unconscious to become conscious, the more I feel connected to forces and experiences that are highly spiritual in nature. As Carl Jung suggested, when speaking in these metaphysical terms, perhaps we ought to switch from speaking of the "unconscious" and instead speak of our "higher consciousness."

Although I have used the word "God" sporadically in my own discoveries, it is important to remember that often this word can be abandoned for ones that are more practical and meaningful to the individual. Many people, whose childhoods were marked by inconsistencies, abuse or neglect, may feel betrayed by God. Discovering this deeper sense of self is sometimes best accomplished with words that have an experiential feeling to them. Ones that I have successfully used are "spirit," "Great Spirit," "universal spirit," "energy," "connection with self and others," "letting go of willfulness and ego," and "being open hearted." There are so many cliches with the word God in them! When you dig deeper for words both reverent and referent to the Supreme Being, it also makes you think about what you're saying.

The above realizations are the spiritual grounding for the sense of self that is helpful for Stage Two Authentic Process. When we consciously commit ourselves to this journey, we want to be realistic. We must be ready to surrender some illusions and expectations, especially those that are based in self-delusion and denial. We will need to surrender some of our fears about what we should or should not be experiencing and what our lives should and should not look like. In making the commitment to fully respect and appreciate our own complex nature, we will find ourselves on a most exciting and meaningful inner journey. In exploring our own depth we find our significance. Once we begin, we will have all the help we need. If we are willing, the help will come to us intuitively, mysteriously, and organically.

These words begin to lead us toward a fascinating healing mode discussed in Chapter Eight: the concept of serendipity. This is the gift of finding valuable or agreeable things not sought for. Carl Jung referred to this phenomenon as synchronicity. M. Scott Peck calls it "being touched by grace." Eva Pierrakos takes it a step further by including the ego-reduction, saying, "When your spiritual center begins to manifest, your ego consciousness integrates with it and you begin to be lived through, as it were, by the spirit."

However you describe this concept, it is one that people in recovery report regularly, once they reach out for empathic help. They will often say "miracles happen" or "there are no such things as coincidences." They experience circumstances, opportunities, and people coming to them in their moments of need and readiness.

Simply stated, the minimum sense-of-self-spirituality that we must bring to APT is the willingness to be open to and to reach out for help. In this humility, our determined, willful and sometimes hidden egos will begin to relax and integrate with our energetic core. As recovery continues, this willingness, humility or surrender will become elusive at times. When deeper issues and conflicts are exposed, we must then balance the determined, frightened aspects of the ego's defenses with the deeper desire for connection. Meanwhile, we continue to open up for help and clarification.

Twenty years after the founding of Alcoholics Anonymous, Carl Jung suggested that since alcoholics had a greater thirst for the spirits than others, perhaps alcoholism was a spiritual condition. Drawing on this perspective, it follows that so many recovering people unceasingly explore the gamut of spiritual traditions, both new and old. After all, Bill Wilson established AA after reading William James's book, *The Varieties of Religious Experience*. From James, Wilson discovered that in order for a spiritual awakening to take place, people must face calamity or crisis. They must admit that they feel defeated in addressing the crisis alone, and thus appeal to a power greater than themselves for help.

There are those whose character structure and defenses make even the most minimal sense of self spirituality difficult to access. The tangible experience of love, spirit or connectedness eludes them; instead they rely almost exclusively on logic to survive. Out of necessity, they may have psychically dissociated from the bodily energetic flows necessary for spiritual selfhood.

There are two ways to support people who are challenged in this way. One is to introduce the exploration of body energetics and awareness. If this is insufficient, I might also suggest a thorough psychopharmacological assessment, possibly followed by the introduction of one of the nonaddictive, antidepressant or anti-anxiety medications. (This will be discussed further in Chapter Ten: The Use of Medication in Recovery). Body work helps by validating and normalizing feelings, sensations, and energetics that may have previously been compartmentalized and minimized, while the medication can help by reducing biologically-reinforced stress on the system, thereby enabling a freer flow of emotions.

8. Body Energetics, Bodywork and Body Movement

My initial awareness of body energetics happened quite unexpectedly — as a by-product of singing lessons. (I am not a singer, but my recovery process has led me to do things I've always yearned to do). My voice coach incorporated Polarity Massage to help open and free the voice, and her process revealed that the restrictions in my voice resulted from blockages in my body. The freeing of these blockages opened my voice and piqued my interest in body-centered approaches. This interest and exploration in body energetics helped me to integrate my many years of varied psychotherapeutic journeying into a more energized, holistic perspective.

Simultaneously in my private therapy practice, I became more aware of my clients' body posturing and physical gestures. I would observe clients sitting across from me recounting stories and traumas from their history with barely a tinge of emotion, yet would notice contortions in their bodies and extremities. My growing professional understanding, which paralleled my own inner discoveries, was that these elements right in front of me were more tools for transformation and growth. Though I wanted to include these insights in therapy sessions, I lacked the skills, education, and confidence to do so. It was this impasse that motivated me to explore the wide variety of body energetic theories and processes now available.

This education focused on yoga, polarity and other massage techniques, the Hands of Light work by Barbara Ann Brennan, the Rubenfeld Synergy Method (derived from the works of Fritz Perls, Milton Erikson, Moshe Feldenkrais and F.M. Alexander) and Stanislav Grof's Holotropic Breathwork. For several years I studied Bioenergetics, Core Energetics and other non-intrusive body energetic interventions with Barry Walker, a master of these techniques. For more than two decades, he has been training psychotherapists internationally for certification. My discovery of Barry, along with his interest and willingness to supervise my learning, was a serendipitous blessing. I learned body exercises to deepen awareness of stress, blockage and energy flows. As a member of a society that advocates living in our heads, it became an exciting adventure to discover the wisdom, secrets, and power that we conceal in our dissociated bodies.

When these body energetic methods are appropriately integrated into Authentic Process Therapy, deeply veiled feelings and traumas are often exposed. I began to realize that traditional psychotherapies could not by themselves correct the compounded effects of post-traumatic stress that many recovering people suffer. The repressed energy configurations are too complex. Without at least some degree of body-sensation awareness, freedom of fuller self-expression would always be limited. What I might have called frozen feelings some years ago, I now see as convoluted or blocked energy patterns in the body.

Today there are many possibilities and options available to gain a richer experience and awareness of our bodies and all the mysteries that lie within. These options include (but are not limited to) body-oriented psychotherapies, massage therapies of many varieties, yoga, dance, stretching, aerobic activity and weight training. When you begin doing bodywork, it is important to bring intentionality to your approach. Make a conscious effort to unite all consciousness together; otherwise the benefits may be limited to the physical realm.

Since the 1800s, our society has held a severely mechanistic view of the body-mind connection; consequently most of us have a mindset that precludes body-mind-spirit consciousness. Some of us in recovery often have a compounded sense of this compartmentalization. Our survival instincts and our determination to make it through difficult childhood histories have made us masters of dissociation. To get through painful or difficult situations while growing up, we creatively removed parts of ourselves from consciousness in order to manage pain, anger, and frustration. There were no other options.

However, today in our search for wholeness and recovery, we must venture back into our body, connecting with and making friends with all the wonders, secrets, and wisdom that wait therein. Bringing more body awareness into consciousness is vital to promote the body-mind-spirit connection that inspires the transcendent forces that lead to holism and shame-free presentation of self.

It is very difficult to describe my own path to holism, or God, or self-love via the two-stage paradigm I speak of. I have used a great deal of yoga, massage and movement exercises from body energetic techniques to make friends with my body. Sometimes it is hard to inspire myself to do this work, as old resistance surfaces again. I try to remind myself that, like it or not, it is my responsibility to reconnect separate aspects of myself and no one else is going to do it for me. I love the way my body feels when I do it. This good feeling often provides me with the impetus to move through my resistance, and then gives me permission to experience a heightened sense of awareness. I encourage everyone to include at least one body awareness process in their healing mix, and remember to have fun doing it. Keep in mind that once we pierce resistance, we reach an inner bliss.

9. Martial Arts and Self-Defense

Martial arts and self-defense are areas of creative expression that share many of the attributes of bodywork. Like yoga, these arts possess great centering qualities. They also help keep you grounded (supported, held-up or existentially connected) in the world. Though the martial arts may not be for everyone, they can be valuable to a recovering person who has a history of physical abuse or of being emotionally and verbally violated. These arts can restore a sense of safety and confidence, and often lead to body-mind-spirit connectedness. Within this framework, we learn to channel our energy, we know what it feels like to "own" the ground on which we stand and say "no." For many of us in recovery, this feeling does not come easily. People who feel fearful and unsafe in the world and whose trauma has been triggered by a recent assault or intrusion might benefit greatly from these modalities. This work, when integrated with Stage Two Authentic Processes, tends to promote a healthy awareness and expression of repressed rage, transforming it into useful boundary defenses.

Knowing martial arts gives you a psychological advantage in the kind of self-defense that's really needed in this modern world: verbal negotiation. Most of us in recovery are really more afraid of being verbally and psychologically abused, and the energetic centering and visualization skills learned from the martial arts can be harnessed to defuse any situation before it gets to the street. Some call it "verbal judo." Practicing the principles of Authentic Process can help. Read self-help books such as *The Verbally Abusive Relationship*, by Patricia Evans. Practice the gentle art of self-respect with those who try to manipulate you verbally. Practice speaking honestly to people by dropping your mask of composure whenever safely possible. In this way, your martial skills may never be needed. Realize that each of us has limitations and are entitled to them, and you will know the secret to negotiation.

In my use of body awareness and energetic exercises with clients, the results are often startling. Clients are often instantly able to perceive a barrier to expression on an emotional and intuitive level, rather than a cerebral level. Often these experiences lead to a quantum leap in therapy. The story of Sandra comes to mind as one of my early Authentic Process experiences with the incorporation of energetic awareness.

Sandra's Story

Sandra was a 53-year-old woman who had been sober for nine years in AA. When she came to my office, she was living in a state of despair and isolation. Historically, she had grown up in a low-income, suburban setting and was the oldest of three children. Professionally, she developed fragrances for the cosmetics industry, drawing on her heightened awareness of scent. Though she was respected by her professional peers, she considered herself an underachieving failure. She had not had an intimate relationship since her drinking days, and she reported that people had run away from her since. In terms of family-of-origin, Sandy reports that they were of Italian heritage and very poor. Her father was remote and placating to her mother, who was intrusive and had a history of mental illness.

When she came for therapy, Sandy was sad and angry. She said, "I don't understand. I did everything they told me to do in AA, and my life is more painful now than before. People ignore me and run the other way. I just need someone to be nice to me, to desire me, to touch me or

even just to be my friend. I couldn't buy all that God stuff in the program. With the childhood that I had, there could not possibly be a God.
Is that what I'm doing wrong? I just can't believe that."

While Sandy spoke these words, she sent out mixed energetic messages. I felt that she was going to suck me up and devour me into a
swell of painful horrors; yet her stiff, rod-like body pushed me eight feet
back if I dared succumb to the seduction. Overall, Sandra looked like a
"sad sack." Though she was physically attractive, the energetic defenses
that kept her locked in painful isolation detracted from her appearance.
As the safety and trust levels built in our relationship, I was able to
share these observations with Sandy. She was aghast and energized at
the same time.

She knew I was telling her the truth. At the same time she was challenging me, as if to say: "Okay, if you are daring enough to bring this
out, you had better be prepared to deal with it."

I suggested that we could do that together, and asked her to lie on
the couch. I told her that we were going to do a simple relaxation exercise, after which I would lead her into these defenses. I asked permission to touch her gently, at an appropriate moment, in a non-sexual way.
She said yes.

After creating a relaxed, mildly hypnotic trance state, I asked Sandy
to imagine that I really wanted to help her and that I could. I suggested
that she already believed this and asked her to imagine that I was coming to her to do just that. I asked her to notice her defenses come up as I
approached, moving my chair closer to the couch. I said, "Let me know
when you begin to feel the steel rod that stiffens you up and wants to
push me away. Share with me the 'friction point' of that engagement."
She did. I told her to breathe into it without judgement. "Just keep
breathing into it and let me know when I can come a little closer."

As she breathed, her body began to twist and turn, almost in convul-
sions. I said simply, "It's okay, keep breathing."

The twisting became very severe at moments and then relaxed.
Slowly I got close enough to ask her if I could take her hand. She said
yes and began to sob uncontrollably. I held her hand gently in both of
my hands and said, "It's still okay, keep breathing. I'm breathing right
here with you." At this point, she asked to go on the floor where she
could move more freely. I said of course. For about five minutes she
rolled and rocked and cried and shook. I witnessed both the torture she
was experiencing and the release. I continued to reassure her that this
was good, and to keep breathing.

As Sandy regained composure, I asked her what images came up during this cathartic release. She immediately offered the graphic details.

"I was in the closet, I practically lived there. I would come home from school and sneak right into the closet. Nowhere else was safe. I would hide there while my psychotic mother screamed around the house looking for me. She would call me such vile names. I would twist and turn in those same ways while sitting in that closet. She used to work me to the bone, cleaning the house and caring for my siblings. She would actually spit at me and deprive me of basic health care. For some reason that crazy woman hated me, and sometimes I just had to hide from her."

In subsequent sessions we reviewed this occurrence, and Sandy was able to experience how her own defense structure and neediness, growing out of childhood abuses and neglects, caused her present loneliness and isolation. She began to realize that the world didn't really hate her after all. Quite miraculously, within weeks after this energetic work, Sandy was dating and beginning to enjoy the first dating relationship in her recovery.

By including some awareness of the body energy, we can begin to cut through logical and theoretical conflict. Feelings and sensations are a true expression of, and a pathway to childhood roots. With this direct experience and some understanding of its origins, we can begin to let go of the shame that leads to isolation and destructive and compulsive behaviors. The growing awareness of body energetics and sensations brings direction and fluidity to our Stage Two awakening.

10
The Uses of Medication in Recovery

The Relationship Between "Applied Psychopharmacology" and Complete Recovery

Using medication to support a more expansive recovery can seem like a paradox to those of us who have been addicted to alcohol and other substances. Yet many of us have been significantly helped by medication at some point in our recovery.

What Is "Applied Psychopharmacology"?

I have preceded the reference to psychopharmacology with the word "applied" out of respect for the community's sensitivity around the use of medication. When I say applied, I mean that all sensitivities and circumstances are taken into consideration by the physician, the client, and possibly the therapist before an individual *chooses* to include medication as a tool in their recovery.

Applied psychopharmacology is the introduction of psychotherapeutic medication to manage the more severe symptoms of complex post-traumatic stress or chemical imbalances that may be inhibiting the fuller recovery of approximately fifty percent of those in recovery today. Medicine can manage the anxiety and depression that are the result of relaxing unconscious defenses created in response to traumatic childhood experiences. This relaxing of defenses is a natural and necessary healing occurrence.

For many years, medication has been a very controversial option among those in the recovering community, to be avoided unless serious mental illness is evident. The fears and misapprehension are understandable and are grounded in at least four issues:

1. Most people recovering from substance abuse diligently practice a life of abstinence from mood-altering chemicals for fear of developing another chemical dependency.
2. Many distrust psychiatry and physicians because before entering recovery, many were misdiagnosed and medicated by doctors who failed to identify their addiction.
3. A stigma still prevails regarding "mental illness," and psychiatric medication conjures up this demon. (Additionally, some recovering people have a mentally ill relative and they fear or resist associating themselves with this concept.)
4. A condemnation of weakness still exists in our society and in pockets of the recovering community, which they risk if they can't "pull their lives together" without medication.

Due to these and similar reasons, there have been instances where it has taken me a year or more of gentle and respectful urging to convince a severely depressed, recovering person to agree to a psychopharmacological assessment. There have also been a few instances where clients have rigidly refused assessment. I have come to respect people's feelings and defenses and trust that they are doing what they need to do. Those who are assessed and who are prescribed appropriate medication by an addiction-savvy psychiatrist, report moderate to dramatic changes in discomfort and growth-limiting symptoms. After several weeks on medication it is not uncommon to hear people express that they feel "better than well." People reported that they "had more energy," "ruminated less," and were "able to let go of anxiety-producing memories." Others said that "an overwhelming sense of dread was gone," that they "began to feel alive for the first time in many years," or that they "became more light-hearted and smiled more." Although not everyone who explores the use of medication reports such dramatic results, these examples are representative.

I have shaped my current opinions on this matter through a five-year clinical study of 112 individuals in Stage Two Recovery and another two-year study with Dr. Rocco Marotta, who was chief psychiatrist at

St. Luke's-Roosevelt Hospital in New York City. In this second study we followed fifteen recovering people who were treated with medication. However, my first and most fundamental study was that of my own experience of using medication to assist my healing at a crucial point. Using these three studies (including observations from my private practice) as templates, I have shaped my current understanding and appreciation that psychopharmacology, when appropriately used, benefits about half the recovering population some time in their healing process. I have had to hone my diagnostic skills as I came to respect applied medication as one color on the palette of creative Authentic Process Therapy in working with the recovering community.

In 1983, six years into my own recovery, when I was diagnosed with "terminal" cancer, a very aggressive lymphoma, the combined emotional and physical devastation of chemotherapy completely overwhelmed, and then collapsed, my emotional defense system. I went into deep depression. Accompanying this darkness was an undercurrent of severe anxiety and agitation that made me want to jump out of the nearest window. When the suicidal urges became overwhelming, I was treated as a psychiatric emergency and pumped full of thorazine. It brought much needed rest to my system.

When I emerged from the bleakest period, I was left completely disabled by this emotional condition. My cancer, which was treated with many alternative and complementary approaches in addition to chemotherapy, appeared to be in remission (to my physician's surprise). My chemotherapy had been discontinued after eight months because I could no longer tolerate the toxicity. I was still crippled by depression. Being a "model" recovering person, I was determined to resolve my depression without medication. I burned out two psychotherapists in the process. While they were extremely helpful in bearing witness to the repressed traumatic episodes that rushed to my awareness every waking hour, my undefended subconscious self frightened them. It looked like psychosis. The fear on their faces in turn further frightened me, flooding me with even more intense feelings. I struggled to cope on my own and with friends and family. Throughout this period I was always strangely and intuitively aware that these horrible feelings were not new, and I felt defeated that they finally caught me.

A year into the depression, I received a phone call from Martha, a nurse I had known from recovery circles. (This is how healing in community works, people network with each other.) She had been sober from alcohol for about twenty years, and had a warm sensitivity about her. She told me that she heard that I was struggling with depression and offered to help by sharing her experience. I was pleased to hear from her and listened carefully. She told me of her own depression, which years earlier had made her a prisoner of her bedroom. She explained how she found relief from the symptoms with a medication prescribed by her psychiatrist. She comforted me and reassured me that the medication was not contradictory to my recovery. I believed her and asked for her doctor's name.

Within several days after starting to take the medication (Ludiomil), I began to feel better.

My sense of interest returned. For the first time in over a year, I could see a light at the end of the tunnel. I was able to do things again. I could hardly believe how dramatically different — and better — I felt. Within several months, I was taking courses to complete my requirement for a counseling certification. I also began to address and take steps toward resolving some of the painful family memories that the breakdown of my defenses had revealed. Within a year, I was creating and directing two new programs for recovering people. It took me a while to trust the change. As I felt more stable in this re-creation of my life, I was able to gradually discontinue the medication.

Three years later, as a professional working with people in longer-term recovery, I realized that I had refined my ability to perceive masked, systemic depression and anxiety in my clients. Because of my own experience with these issues, I was able to read subtleties in my clients eyes, speech and expressions. Slowly, I became confident in my instincts and explored with a few clients my suspicions about how a depression or anxiety condition, sometimes masked in recovering people, could be holding them back. As they began to go for assessment and take medication one by one, the results surprised me as much as it did them. Their therapy began to progress with a new fluidity.

Within two years, almost half the clients that I worked with had, at least for a time, been dramatically helped by psychoactive medication. While these successes pleased me, I was conscious of and concerned about the fact that for an addictions-oriented therapist, a fair percentage of my clients were on medication. Because medication was such a sensitive issue in the community, I questioned myself. Was I being hyper-vigilant? This concern inspired my research into the effectiveness of medication.

A comprehensive literature search revealed many studies of "dual diagnosis" patients — people with a psychiatrically-defined illness who also have a substance-abuse problem. These studies did not address my inquiry for two reasons. One, the studies focused on individuals who had histories of psychiatric problems; second, the studies were framed from the clinician's perspective and lacked the client's point of view, which is vital to recovery work.

I set out to undertake my own study, based on my community practice and interviews with colleagues working in the community. The five-year study included 112 men and women in Stage Two addictions recovery who were consistently committed to psychotherapy for a minimum of six months. By the end of the study period, 57 of the clients showed signs of systemic depression and/or anxiety. While medication was suggested in each of those cases, 8 individuals indicated strong resistance to medication and declined intervention. Of the 49 who were assessed and received appropriate non-addictive medications, all experienced moderate to dramatic relief of symptoms. This group also was able to engage in their therapy with a fuller understanding of their feelings, and their uncovery work seemed to accelerate.

In these cases, I believe medication relieved an unconscious state of being overwhelmed, thereby allowing the individual greater flexibility for all aspects of living. Most of their problems became more manageable, and their ability to tolerate conflict improved. There is another point to emphasize: for 55 of these individuals, no medication was indicated. While medication might be more prevalently indicated than we once thought, it is definitely not appropriate for all recovering people.

In the second study, Dr. Marotta and I closely observed 15 Stage Two clients for two years. In all cases, I had referred them to him for medication management, while I provided individual and/or group Authentic Process Therapy. We monitored them closely and studied their progress. At the completion of the two-year period, each client was asked to respond to a detailed questionnaire evaluating their experiences relative to the medication. All of the participants continually maintained their therapy and proceeded to make healthy, empowering changes in their lives. Their conditions and medications varied. Medications included BuSpar, Desipramine, Lithium, Paxil, Prozac, Wellbutrin, and Zoloft.

Dr. Marotta was challenged by the configuration of symptoms these clients presented. I was fortunate to be working with a physician who displayed such dedication, flexibility and intuitive judgement. Listening to him struggle to match the complex symptoms of my clients to the appropriate medication, I was reminded of the words from an article in the *American Journal of Psychiatry* by Dr. Lawrence Kolb. He suggested that because of its "heterogeneity," post-traumatic stress is to psychiatry as syphilis was to medicine. "At one time or another [post-traumatic stress] which is at the root of all addictions and compulsions, may appear to mimic every personality disorder," he said. No wonder this population has so often been misdiagnosed! Trauma specialist Dr. Judith Herman complements Kolb's theory, noting that "the responses to trauma are best understood as a spectrum of conditions rather than as a single disorder."

Selected responses from the client's evaluations include the following:

Was medication helpful in normalizing feelings of depression and/or anxiety?

Very helpful: 10   Helpful: 5   Not helpful: 0

Was it helpful in giving you clearer perception of your feelings?

Very helpful: 10   Helpful: 4   Not helpful: 1

Did medication help your ability to work through deeper issues in therapy?

Very helpful: 8   Helpful: 5   Not helpful: 3

Did taking medication help you relate better with others?

Very helpful: 9   Helpful: 6   Not helpful: 1

Was it helpful in being able to express yourself more clearly?

Very helpful: 7   Helpful: 7   Not helpful: 1

Was your sleep pattern helped by the medication?

Very helpful: 6   Helpful: 7   Not helpful: 2

Those who reported "not helpful" answers to a particular question consistently had enough other "helpful" and "very helpful" responses to encourage continued use of medication. Seven of the 15 participants, at some point in the study, felt improved and stable enough to discontinue medication. Of those seven, three chose to restart medication when stressful periods became overwhelming.

I have collected comments from some of the study participants. Monica obtained considerable relief from fearful withdrawal and isolation with medication. Thinking back to when I had first suggested she take it, she wrote, "First I thought I didn't need it. I thought I could get through on my own. I felt I had been sober for seven years, and I had survived a lot, so I could survive this, too. Part of me didn't want to believe I was bad off enough to need medicine." After taking medication for a few months, she said, "I feel stronger inside. I am not so afraid of people. I don't feel under attack from everyone. I can better see the reality of situations and don't need to personalize everything. In my encounters with people before, I always came away thinking there was something wrong with me. It's not like that anymore. I now feel like I have a voice, that what I say matters. I also understand other people better and have more compassion for them."

Another study participant, Gregory, tended to be highly intellectual and generally thought feelings made no sense and were too irrational to take seriously. A series of losses in his life began to manifest as body ticks and spasms in his extremities. I recommended assessment for medication. Though he said he "thought it was not necessary," he went along anyway in a spirit of experimentation. Shortly after starting Zoloft, Greg reported, "I've had the first sobbing cry in my life. I've lost so many people and it feels good to be able to grieve them. I seem to be more able to touch a more tender side of myself since taking medication. A long-standing and pervasive feeling of dread is gone."

Nancy, who described herself as a complainer who pushes people away with her negativity, experienced constant anxiety when she was with people, and found it impossible to make friends. After her experience on BuSpar she reported feeling "not so easily excited" and "more laid back." Overall, Nancy proclaimed that she "had less inner fear and was much less inclined to push people away by constantly complaining and being negative. I can now recognize negative thoughts and process them differently."

A gay man in the study named William struggled painfully in his recovery, attempting to reconcile his sexual orientation with his evangelical upbringing. When asked on the survey if he could see medication as part of a holistic approach to recovery for him, he responded: "Definitely, especially when I have a major voice in whether and how the medication is used. This view allowed me to take medication from a position of personal choice or empowerment, rather than from a point of defeat over any failure of mine." William was able to begin a new coming-out process, addressed shameful feelings regarding family and religion, and became more self-respecting and hopeful. In explaining his experience with medication he offered: "It feels like I took off the emergency brake and was able to move on to a new plateau of experience and behavior."

Of the 49 Stage Two clients who used medication as part of their recovery and with whom I personally worked, these remarks are representative. There were some participants, however, who had poor experiences with their first attempt and had to try an alternative medication. They reported various side effects, but most were bearable and were rarely serious enough to offset the positive effects. There were a couple of instances where a person's system was too sensitive for any of the currently available medications. Even in these rare cases I still feel that the experimentation was fruitful to the overall healing and learning process.

I have come to three conclusions from these two clinical studies: First: More than fifty percent of recovering individuals suffer from organic, systemic, sometimes masked, inhibiting anxiety and/or depression. Second: Similar to addiction, these are symptoms of post-traumatic stress triggered from unhealed childhood histories. Third: In most cases, appropriate medication can greatly relieve symptoms, free the individual from a sense of being overwhelmed, and give them the clarity and energy to live more fully and resolve historic conflicts.

I want to make a final (albeit contradictory) comment regarding my experience with these medications in the recovering community. I often wish there was another way. I wish our society was enlightened enough to nourish and be supportive of individuals who need special attention as they work through their spiritual emergence. If our culture understood and supported the sensitive nature of the complete recovery process, we would not need to resort to medication as often. (Even a systemic biological depression can often be worked through with appropriate compassion and support in a safe setting.)

There are times when I can see difficult times coming for my clients, and I encourage them to get away from the everyday challenges and heal in a safe, nurturing place. Often they cannot take time from work or they cannot afford to go away. Even if they could, our culture lacks appropriate, low cost, supportive, rest and renewal environments that facilitate such healing. We need them desperately. Psychiatric facilities are not the answer — they are the last resort. I have come to share the views of transpersonal psychologist Christina Grof and Stanislav Grof, M.D. In their book, *The Stormy Search For The Self,* they suggest that:

> For some individuals. . . the transformational journey of spiritual development becomes a "spiritual emergency," a crisis in which the changes are so rapid and the inner states so demanding that, temporarily, these people may find it difficult to operate fully in everyday reality. In our time, these individuals are rarely treated as if they are on the edge of inner growth.

> 'In a supportive environment, with proper understanding, these difficult states of mind can be extremely beneficial, often leading to physical and emotional healing, profound insights, creative

activity, and permanent personality changes for the better. When we coined the term "spiritual emergency," we sought to emphasize both the danger and opportunity inherent in such states. The phrase is, of course, a play on words, referring both to the crisis, or "emergency," that can accompany transformation, and to the idea of "emergence," suggesting the tremendous opportunity such experiences may offer for personal growth and the development of new levels of awareness.

Based on my own experience, there is great wisdom, understanding and compassion in these words. Until we can provide temporary, safe community environments for healing, we are severely limited. We need creative solutions. During these times of economic constraint and limited health-care resources, it is almost impossible to provide such environments at the levels required. The best we can do is provide as safe, structured and nurturing environments as possible and use our more refined knowledge of contemporary medications to provide symptom management as we coach ourselves and others through this emergence of spirit.

11

Moving Forward
Transforming
Our World

Praying for "The Hundredth Monkey"

Only from a place of total self-acceptance do we stand the real possibility of transforming ourselves and satisfying our thirst for wholeness. When I say "acceptance," I mean "what is," not "how we want it to be." In a similar way, perhaps it is only by accepting our outer world "as it is" that we can change it — not only for ourselves but for generations to follow. How is this possible?

"The Hundredth Monkey," a well-known essay by Ken Keyes, Jr., offers inspiration and hope. He tells the story of how a few young monkeys living among a colony of monkeys on isolated islands tried a new spontaneous behavior and gradually inspired their peers to do the same. A couple of the monkeys accidentally discovered the advantages of washing the sand off of their potatoes at the seashore before eating them. At first, their elders resisted the new ways, continuing to eat the potatoes, sand and all. At a certain point in the study, when enough young monkeys had changed their behavior (symbolized by the hundredth monkey), there was an almost instantaneous shift in consciousness and all of the resistant older monkeys adjusted to the new practice. What was so remarkable was that this shift even occurred on neighboring islands simultaneously.

I believe that if, one by one, we continue to empower ourselves to act in an enlightened, positive way, the critical mass of this growing energy will gradually transform our world. The phenomena that inspired Keyes was taught to him by researcher Marilyn Furguson and psychologist Carl Rogers. They felt that the "hundredth monkey" research story illustrated an important psychological phenomenon: that when enough of us are aware of something, all of us become aware of it. This concept confirms my own intuitive trust in the basic tenet of my work — that the appreciation and love and respect we have for ourselves and others creates an expanding energy field that becomes a growing, transforming power in the world.

This also reflects Carl Jung's teachings on the collective unconscious. These philosophical realities, and the support that they suggest, give us a counterbalance of hope to offset the doomsday feelings and fears that our culture sensationalizes daily. Many of us are healing. The recovery movement lives. The feminist movement lives. The men's movement lives. The gay/lesbian/ bisexual/transgender movement lives. People of all colors continue to create healing communities. An extraordinary force emerges as we heal ourselves and respect the mysteries of our diversity. In the organic, self-organizing whole of the universe, this is a worthy energy to want to live, grow, and play in.

The Twelve-Step programs and other recovery models are doorways to profound growth. If each of us in recovery surrender our lives to a loving spiritual power in a radical and life-altering manner, doesn't it seem possible that we could *inspire* every person in our society in a healing way, without consciously trying to change anything?

Authentic Process Therapy is based on the principle that all people have suffered emotional or physical trauma to their natural emergent energies at some stage in their development; that we all have moments of dissociation and separation from ourselves, and that we are all consciously or unconsciously seeking a more holistic connection with the universe. This then is the common ground with Twelve-Steppers and with others in recovery, with those seeking holism through spirituality and with the general population. We are all working through stages of awakening to recover our lost innocence, our lost joy, our lost place in the universe; and we can help each other succeed, just by speaking our truth as we discover it. We in recovery are in as good a position to be the hundredth monkey for global transformation as any group in history, and the Stage Two process (however you choose to undertake it) offers an opportunity to connect with every other sentient being and to the planet as a whole. Perhaps it is the "missing link" you have been looking for.

Authentic Process is not new. For centuries, Native Americans have gathered in "talking feather" circles to speak from the heart, to express grief and joy (in a truly authentic process) and to pray for help from a higher power to become "one with the Creator" again. Community healing, by whatever name it is called, has always been highly valued by Native Americans and indigenous people all over the globe. It is safe to say that there are many true shamanic healers in these communities, whether they are located in Africa, Asia, or South America, who understand complete recovery without ever reading a book, and some may even share their insights through these "talking circles." They are the oldest school of therapists on the planet. We should honor these elders — they may be praying for *our* healing!

The authors of the twelve steps were divinely inspired individuals as well, and the miracle of their works are still unfolding. Perhaps Stage Two recovery, as an expansion outward from the original program, can help a greater number of people to more fully realize the "promises" originally offered by AA, mentioned in the introduction of this book.

The AA "Big Book" states that these "promises will always materialize if we work for them," and countless recovering people can attest to the validity of that statement. Yet a complete realization of these attributes eludes many Twelve-Steppers I know. These people struggle between feelings of gratitude — thankful to have their lives back in control — and feelings of emptiness that something is still missing. Authentic Process Therapy shows how to respond to these unconscious conflicts and work through the Stage Two issues that isolate us and block us from achieving the state of Complete Recovery.

Recovering people sincerely want to experience the vitality that comes with being fully alive. Many of us have battled — and conquered — a major addiction. Many of us report that we "have been to hell and back." We struggle to adjust our characters; we labor to remove limitations. We are motivated and will usually do whatever hard work it takes, providing we have access to, and respect for, the process.

In order for recovering people to commit themselves at this high level, we must trust the healing process and it must be community-driven. The model must be honest, realistically hopeful, and it must resonate with our specific needs and be as inclusive as possible. Currently more people are looking for this authentic community model than there are opportunities for participation. We need to respond with more community-driven opportunities. Committed organizations, such as The Foundation for Community Encouragement founded by M. Scott

Peck, and The Institute for Staged Recovery, and individuals who have facilitation or organizational skills, can nurture these developments. See the Resource directory in this book.

Moving Forward: A Turn-of-the-Century View

> So in dealing with addicts, the greatest payoff comes from emphasizing not the regressive aspects... but rather the progressive ones — the yearning for the spirit and for God.
>
> I believe the greatest positive event of the 20th century occurred in Akron, Ohio, on June 10, 1935, when Bill W. and Dr. Bob convened the first AA meeting. It was not only the beginning of the self-help movement and the beginning of the integration of science and spirituality at a grass-roots level, but also the beginning of the community movement.
>
> That is... why I think of addiction as the sacred disease.... Very probably, God created... alcoholism in order to create... AA, and thereby spearhead the community movement which is going to be the salvation not only of alcoholics and addicts, but of us all.
>
> M. Scott Peck, M.D.

The 21st Century will bring times of accelerated transition. Just like our own recovery, the coming century will be fascinating, increasingly complex and often chaotic. This is frightening for us, yet it can also be exciting if we incorporate new perceptions. We need to continue to build communities of wisdom to assist us in this appreciation.

We will begin to adopt pluralistic perceptions. We will dissolve right and wrong, good and bad, better than or less than. We will begin to operate out of *respect for self and others*. We need to welcome the multiplicity of our experiences and the experiences of others. We will move from hierarchal relationships to "linking" ones where we will share our authority and power. In giving up black-and-white polarized thinking, we will embody and come from a spiritual grounding that prioritizes respect for individual expression and the lessening of pain (in all its manifestations) for individuals and cultures.

Our society routinely teaches people to hide from negative feelings; and although the process is now unconscious in most of us, this does not absolve us of the responsibility to integrate and neutralize our destructive forces. This hiding of our shadow-self makes us pompous, blind, and irresponsible. We look on as our friends and loved ones experience emotional breakdowns, take up addictive behaviors, act out compulsive urges in one way or another, or slowly self-destruct through illness or gradual suicide. Care is desperately needed, and yet our society seems unwilling to encourage the type of nurturing care that allows people to recover gradually and fully.

APT, with its emphasis on community, offers a centering point. Because the healing available in Staged Recovery can usually take place in groups, the overall cost is less than individual care. Because it defines and promotes a complete recovery and a fuller understanding of the issues that block the holistic experience, it can help us chart a course through the inner wilderness.

APT also helps promote long-term, generational healing, because it addresses cultural ignorance with compassion. In Stage Two, we are able to move on from our fears, our need to place blame on others, and the inclination to fault ourselves. We confront reality and see our own limitations in the enormity of the task. We then seek out community for grounding, and spiritual sustenance. From this place we bring a meaningful degree of understanding and compassion to the consequences of our limited consciousness, our inadequacies, generational ignorances and our culture's lack of preparedness for parenting. We do all this with respect for the mysterious, all-encompassing, evolutionary process.

The Western World embarked on a bold exploration of technology a few centuries ago and it has brought us much, but also at great expense. Too many times it has torn apart our families and our communities. It has at times damaged our bodies, our minds, our hearts, and our spirit. It has made some people into its own image, robot-like beings whose intuitions and emotions are irrelevant to their roles in society. Such people become power modules in corporate and scholastic machines, and may turn these powers on their own families. We are the abused children of these victims of technology and science.

At the same time, we must acknowledge that science led to medicine, which led to Dr. Freud; and Freud led to Jung who led to Dr. Rogers and dozens of others who saw and addressed the growing problems of their high tech environment, and the growing dissociation it was fostering. It is appropriate that this lineage and tradition, when married to the Alcoholics Anonymous lineage and tradition, leads us right back to community healing circles, talking from the heart (in authentic process), and "praying to become one with the Creator" — things which have been around for thousands of years. Everything moves in a circle.

As we individually begin to emerge out of the confusing and chaotic Stage Two processes and experience a holistic, shame-free presentation of self, we change our views. We compassionately reframe words like "relapse" and "acting out" — words that have become shameful, value-laden, and synonymous with failure. We may also want to update and review words like "codependency" and "dysfunctional," which sometimes become pejorative labels, endeavoring to instead articulate the complexities that underlie them, in an effort to find more effective and enjoyable lifestyles. We must learn to welcome the ambiguity and the mystery, because it will bring us closer to the natural world that is reflected in our inner selves.

My colleague Nicholas Cimorelli is an insightful psychotherapist and health journalist whose work has intersected with my own. While trained in repressed trauma therapy, his clients have educated him in addictions. I have the opposite situation: while trained in addictions, my clients have given me an education in repressed traumatic conflicts. Our collegial relationship has been extraordinarily enriching. When Nicholas was asked to comment on this manuscript, he summarized his ideas on Stage Two recovery.

> Recovery in the 21st Century encompasses an active and on-going relationship with our intuitive intelligence. The consciousness of the approaching millennium brings with it a firm request that we access our inner-voices and incorporate this guidance into the everyday workings of our body-mind experiences.

> Initially, the fine-tuning of our human instruments will evolve in the context of healing within our communities through the transformative power of collective group process. Our intuitive intelligence as applied in these settings will allow for an integration of the accelerated changes to come.

From the standpoint of our daily lives, his words may seem other-worldly and prophetic. However, if you stop the action and take a snapshot of our world, his words make more sense. Consider that, in today's world, some of the best-selling musical recordings are Gregorian Chants by the Benedictine monks of Santo Domingo de Silos, and ethereal musical creations (such as Deep Forest), which honors primitive societies by invoking a universal language. Perhaps not by coincidence, today's best-selling books are *Embraced By The Light* by Betty J. Eadie, *The Tibetan Book of the Living and the Dead* by Sogyal Rinpoche, *Conversations With God,* by Neale Donald Walsch, *Care of the Soul* by Thomas Moore, *A Passion for the Possible,* by Jean Houston, and *The Celestine*

Prophecy by James Redfield. All of these books respond to our innermost needs. With this awareness of our inner-thirsts exposed, I concur with Nicholas that our continued recovery requires us to make more conscious the very world in which we are living.

If you read these books or listen to this music, you may experience resonance — an energetic reaction from deep inside. I believe that these expressions all share and draw from our collective intuitive intelligence. While we may not all be ready to experience all of the insights of the Celestine and similar prophecies, other experiences presenting themselves are certainly evolutionary steps in those directions. We recovering people often feel this in the core of our healing hearts. As we look to our future and to the tasks ahead, we are being called upon to ground ourselves in personal creativity, welcoming the ambiguity and the mystery. Individually and collectively we will find the complete recovery that embodies a new and holistic world.

My experiential research and the awareness it provided led to the creation of The Institute for Staged Recovery. Its mission is to provide focused community settings to address issues related to Complete Recovery, intimacy, sexuality, spirituality, personal fulfillment, and our evolutionary process. By pursuing these issues in community, in a safe structure with a facilitator who is skilled in cultural education, we create an opportunity for participants to resolve and clarify complex issues.

As empowered human beings we are testing our ideas in the world rather than internalizing them. As Pulitzer prize-winning playwright Tony Kushner wrote in *Angels in America*, "You need an idea of the world to go out into the world. But it's the going into that makes the idea. You can't wait for a theory, but you have to have a theory." At the Institute we study, share, and reflect on our emergent theories, envision a Complete Recovery, and to the best of our ability, we realize it.

The Goals of The Institute for Staged Recovery

To offer a structure for the Staged recovery process, educating and preparing recovering individuals and professionals for necessary Authentic Processes and community healing .

- To provide Stage Two pyschospiritual workshops for individuals on a journey toward complete recovery.
- To train and certify facilitators in Authentic Process Therapy within the staged model of recovery.

- To help create opportunities for making the Stage Two recovery processes more available to culturally disenfranchised people.
- To offer psycho-education about and encourage supportive environments for individuals on the verge of, or in, spiritual emergency. The Institute will continue to help people manage and demystify experiences of flooded feelings and internal conflicts that can be part of the recovery process.
- To encourage continued research and education on the community recovery process and how it engages with and helps to shape our larger world.
- To acknowledge, respect, and address special considerations in recovery.

The Institute teaches that complete recovery is possible and supports recovering people in creating that image and possibility. We realize together that our thoughts determine what we perceive of this world, our beliefs create our experience.

And so perhaps the greatest of all the responsibilities we face as we approach the new millennium is to raise our level of consciousness. This means understanding not only our abstract mental processes, but understanding how our thoughts condition, and are conditioned in turn, by our emotions, and how our emotions are conditioned by patterns of reaction reinforced by habit within our bodies, habits learned by our muscles and even by our cells. It means understanding exactly how we create our experience of this world and assuming responsibility for that creation.

But it means more than understanding; it means *acceptance*, acceptance of the given conditions of human existence — that we have bodies, that we live in a material world. For without embodiment, without acceptance and grounding in this physical world of flesh and earth, trees and stones, cement, cardboard, and chrome, our thoughts are but mere illusions; they carry no life. To honor and truly fulfill the challenge of being human, we must embrace *both* mind and body, an achievement far beyond logic or will or muscle power, an achievement that only the full, unconditional embrace of the heart can accomplish. It is a big job, but as each of us sets ourselves to it, we can be sure it will become that much easier for everyone else. We heal ourselves while simultaneously creating a sense of life purpose!

I want my final words in this text to be the ones that propel me and help me to energize my own commitment and enthusiasm. I feel that if we seize this moment in time and bring our intuition and an expanded complex view to recovery, we will be able to powerfully influence the positive growth of our world. We will be able to assist each other in making smoother, more efficient recoveries of "self." Authentic community respects that our external realities seem to be changing faster than our internal systems. Moving through Stage Two Recovery together enables us to protect our inner selves while taking fuller self-responsibility for our outer selves and the planet on which we live.

Awakening this morning to write this last chapter, I randomly opened the book *Earth Prayers From Around the World*. These are the words, by Rumi, on that page:

The breezes at dawn have secrets to tell you.
Don't go back to sleep!
You must ask for what you really want.
Don't go back to sleep!
People are going back and forth
Across the doorsill where the two worlds touch;
The door is round and open.
Don't go back to sleep!

Closing Words

Now you come to yet another gateway. As you close this book, go back in your mind and think about all that you've seen and experienced within yourself during this psychological and spiritual journey. I hope it has been transformational. Now you must begin a new phase of the same journey, the one that leads to the holistic state and the complete recovery of the spiritual self. This time, the map is the world around you. The door is round and open. Don't go back to sleep!

Where you go from here is up to you, but if while sinking into this material you found yourself working in a powerful new mode of operation that you never experienced before, one which opened your eyes, connected you to your core energy and bore fruit for you in your life, hold onto that. Although nothing lasts forever, remind yourself of that transformational feeling now and then. That's the healer within.

With the awareness of impermanence I know that this work will continue to change and evolve. That is why we developed the Institute, to create an environment where we can continue to teach each other and expand our understanding of inner healing. I invite you to participate. Each of the concepts and healing modalities you have just read about are limited by my own current perceptions, time and energy. Your questions and experiences will be what continues the expansion of these concepts and makes them available to more of our brothers and sisters in recovery.

Please advise us if you would like to receive the institute's newsletter and the mailing address you would like it sent to, there is a $25 annual subscription charge, so please include your check. There is no charge to be on our mailing list for workshops and retreats. Address your questions, suggestions or healing contributions to:

> Michael Picucci
> THE INSTITUTE FOR STAGED RECOVERY
> 85 Fifth Avenue, Suite 900
> New York, NY 10003
> or e-mail the institute at: www.theinstitute.org

Acknowledgments

This revised and expanded version of my earlier book, *Complete Recovery: An Expanded Model of Community Healing*, primarily rests on the shoulders of those who have extended themselves to me since that publication.

Nicholas Cimorelli, Jim Cusack, John McCormack and Barbara Warren will always be the four cornerstones in my foundation as a healing professional. I am grateful for all of their loving energy and guidance. My colleagues at The Institute for Staged Recovery consistently present opportunities for my personal growth and for the expansion of the Complete Recovery phenomena. Thank you: Sandra Benziger, Doug Goldschmidt, Elias Guerrero, John McCormack, Barry Walker, and Matthew Whaley.

For helping me bring this work out into the world and contributing to that process in so very many ways, I want to gratefully acknowledge Cathy Lewis and her colleague P.J. Lorenz. I want to extend heartfelt thanks to Vicki Hickman who in many ways helps us communicate our message in words and graphic images and who designed the text of this book. I am appreciative of the detailed professional critique of the first edition and special contributions to this book by Susan Ray. Richard Grossinger, Lindy Hough, Antonio Cuevas and everyone at North Atlantic Books get cheers for their confidence, support and guidance. I thank Chuck Stein for bringing to the manuscript a fresh-eyed perspective which encouraged important improvements and for his copy-editing the final text. Susan Quasha's artistic mastery is to be applauded for the outstanding cover design. Very special kudos to my editor, Evan T. Pritchard. In the most delightful and inspiring way, Evan continuously helped me find the words that were in my heart and mind and arrange them in a way that could be best comprehended. He brought with him keen insights that added richness to my ideas.

Appreciation also goes to go Gerald Epstein, Stan and Christina Grof, Teri Litman and Joyce Reinitz, all of whose dedicated teachings in the past few years have impacted my work with new tools and deeper understanding of my own discoveries.

And special thanks to those who have been inspirational in my personal and professional development and in the ability to face the challenges before me: my family-of-origin, the whole Picucci clan, Robert Axel, Sue Cusack, Beth Hagens, Tom Kane, John T. Koss, Mary Mc-Donald, Mary Mandis, Paul Matwiow, David Shaw, Harold Dennis Schmidt, Peter Simmons, Robbie Tucker, and Jerry Ward.

In memorial, I want to acknowledge the following people who gave me love, support, foundation, and wisdom: Ken Axel, David Goodstein, Mel Hammock, Richard Lacarda, Sensei Sandra Jishu Holmes, Michael McMahon, Sheila Picucci and Gil Rubin-O'Keefe.

To all my clients and workshop participants through the years — you know who you are — I sincerely thank you for your trust and confidence in me, and for your support in helping me develop this work as part of our shared journey. It has been and continues to be a rare privilege. Together we have co-created the essence for the healing described herein.

I also want to acknowledge all the great contributors (many of whom are mentioned in the book, as well as those who are not) in the recovery, transpersonal, and humanistic psychology fields, who have come before me and have so generously informed this vision of Complete Recovery.

The completion of this text demonstrates the steadfast love and grounding provided by my life-partner, Elias Guerrero, who sustains and comforts me through these extraordinary challenges and adventures. Bravo, Elias. I love you dearly.

Lastly, to the higher powers and spiritual world that guides me, protects me, and ultimately graces all of my challenges, I express humble gratitude.

Resources

The resources listed below are just a sampling of those that have come my way over the past few years. Each resource has stood the test of time and reputation and has surely assisted many people on their own authentic journey toward wholeness. However, for clarity's sake let me add that none are directly affiliated with APT or The Institute for Staged Recovery, except its own listing, nor is this an endorsement for their services or products. The list is limited to those which either I or those around me have had positive and enriching experiences.

The recovery community today is undergoing rapid transformation, perhaps you could call it a Recovery Renaissance. Because of this, some resources listed are undergoing tremendous change, some are growing rapidly, some disappearing, others merging together for a common cause. It's all part of the global creative process.

Let this be a starting point and a well of inspiration for the next phase of your healing. I urge you to be flexible and intuitive as you use this directory as a guide for starting or continuing your own research, allowing your own inner compass or inner voice to point the way. Once you have a foothold in this work, one contact will lead to another, one clue will lead to many, one seed will bear fruit and become many seeds. Trust in the holistic process.

The letter codes in parenthesis after each organization's name will indicate the nature of resource(s) being offered in the listing. *Most have catalogs or brochures for the asking.*

A=Healing Primary Addictions – Primarily Treatment Centers
B=Psychospiritual (P/S) Workshops/Retreats/Seminars for Healing
   Toward Complete Recovery
C=Crisis Intervention and Spiritual Emergency
D=Professional Facilitation Training
E= Educational Institution
F= Resourceful Information

Related Publications and Websites that each provide additional resources are listed separately. 12-Step Programs (Alcoholics Anonymous, etc.) are listed in local telephone directories.

Organizations

Betty Ford Center (A), 39000 Bob Hope Dr., Rancho Mirage, CA, 92270, 800-854-9211. Primary Addictions Treatment

Body Electric School (B,D), 6527-A Telegraph Ave., Oakland, CA 94609, 510-653-1594. Sexual Healing Workshops and Massage Training. Sex Enrichment Videos.

California Institute of Integral Studies (E), 9 Peter Yorke Way, San Fran., CA 415-674-5500. Graduate Programs: Psychology, Human & Organizational Transformation, etc.

Caron Foundation (A,B), Galen Hill Road, Box A, Warnersville, PA 19565, 800-678-2332. Adult/Adolescent/Family Primary Addictions & 5-Day Codependency Program.

Dawn Manor Retreat/Study Center (B), 621 Cattail Rd., Livingston Manor, NY, 914-439-5815. P/S Retreats & Workshops for Gay/Bisexual Men.

Esalen Institute (B,D,E), Highway 1, Big Sur, CA 93920, 408-667-3000 Founded 1962. Pioneering Institution in P/S Workshops & Training. Major Program.

Eupsychia Institute (B), PO Box 3090, Austin, TX 78864, 512-327-2795. Founded by Author Jacqueline Small. 3, 6 and 10 day P/S Intensives.

The Fortune Society, 39 W. 19th St., New York, NY 10011, 212-206-7070. Life Reclamation and Recovery for Ex-Offenders.

The Foundation for Community Encouragement, PO Box 17210, Seattle, WA 98107, 888-784-9001. Founded by M. Scott Peck. Conducts Nationwide Workshops on Community Building.

Grof Transpersonal Training (B,D), 20 Sunnyside Ave., #A314, Mill Valley, CA 415-721-9891. Founded by Author Stanislav Grof. P/S Holotropic Breathwork Workshops and Training.

Hazelden Foundation and Renewal Center (A,B), Box 11, Center City, MN 55012, 800-833-4497. Primary Addiction Treatment/P/S Renewal Workshops

Hope Spring, (B), Charleston, SC 800-342-9655. P/S Workshops with Well Known Authors and Healers.

The Institute for Staged Recovery (B,D), 85 Fifth Ave., Ste. 900, N.Y., NY 10003, 212-242-5052. Authentic Process Therapy. P/S Workshops/Retreats / Facilitator Training in APT.

Institute of Transpersonal Psych. (E), 744 San Antonio Rd, Palo Alto CA 94303, 650-493-4430. PhD/Masters Experiential Programs. Well Known Faculty. Off-Campus Program.

Institute of Noetic Sciences (B,E, F), 475 Gate Five Rd, Sausalito, CA 94965 415-331-5650. Membership Org. Study of Mind/Consciousness/Spirit. Excellent Quarterly Review (see Publications).

Kalani Ocean Retreat (B), RR 2, Box 4500, Pahoa-Beach Rd., Hawaii 96778, 800-800-6886. Big Island. P/S, Yoga, Wellness, R&R Getaway.

Kirkridge Retreat Center (B), 2495 Fox Gap Rd., Bangor, PA 18013, 610-588-1793. P/S Retreats – Individuals, Couples, Gay/Les/Bi, with Known Healers

Kripalu Center (B,D), PO Box 793, Lenox, MA 01240, 800-741-7353. Yoga, P/S Workshops/Retreats. Individually Structured R&R program.

The Learning Annex (B), 16 E. 53 St, New York, NY 10022, 212-371-0280. Seminars with Well Known Authors, Healers and Local Specialists.

Life Enhancement Series (B,D), 2180 Park Ave North, Winter Park, FL 32789, 407-740-7610. P/S Workshops, Professional Training.

Living Arts (F), 2434 Main Street, Venice CA 90291, 800-254-8464. Resourceful Catalog. Sexual Enrichment Videos. Breathwork, Yoga, Massage, etc.

The Meadows (A,B,C), 1655 North Tegner St, Wickenburg, AZ 85390, 800-632-3697. Primary Addictions Treatment – P/S Workshops/Psych. Crisis Intervention

Namaste Retreat Center (B), 29500 Grahams Ferry Rd, Wilsonville, OR 800-893-1000. P/S Retreats / Workshops with Well Known Authors and Healers.

The Naropa Institute (E), 2130 Arapahoe Ave, Boulder, CO 80302, 303-546-3572. B.A & M.A. Degree Programs integrating psychology and spirituality.

New York Open Center (B), 83 Spring Street, New York, NY 10012, 212-219-2527. P/S Workshops with Well Known Authors and Healers / Conferences

Omega Institute (B,E), 260 Lake Drive, Rhinebeck, NY 12572, 800-944-1001 Center for Holistic Studies. Well Known Authors/Healers. Retreats/Travel/Conferences

Onsite Inc. (B), 10 Court Square, PO Box 272, Charlotte, TN 37036, 800-341-7434. Founded by Author Sharon Wegscheider-Cruse. Offers 5 & 7 Day P/S Intensives.

Pavillon International (A,B), 500 Pavillon Pl, PO Box 189, Mill Spring, NC 800-392-4808. Primary Addiction Treatment and Advanced Recovery P/S Workshops

Pride Institute (A, C) 14400 Martin Drive, Eden Prairie, MN 55344, 800-54PRIDE. Gay/Les/Bi/Trans Primary Addictions Treatment. Crisis/Psych in Add'l Locations.

Project Connect, Lesbian & Gay Community Services Center (A,D,F), Little West 12th Street, New York, NY 10014, 212-620-7310. Intervention, Referral & Education – Addictions, Bereavement, Mental Health.

ReSource Guide: Books/Audio/Video Tapes (F), Box 909, Sausalito, CA 94966, 800-383-1586. Body/Mind/Spirit Resource Catalog from Institute of Noetic Sciences.

Rowe Conference Center (B), Kings Highway Road, Rowe, MA 01367, 413-339-4216. P/S Workshops/Retreats with Well Known Authors/Healers and Local Specialists.

Rubenfeld Synergy Method (B,D), 115 Waverly Place, New York, NY 800-747-6897. Founded by Ilana Rubenfeld. Body Therapy Training Program. P/S Workshops.

Seminar Center (B), 1776 Broadway, #1001, New York, NY 10019 212-655-0077. Varied Seminars/Workshops with Well Known Authors and Local Specialists.

Shavano Institute (D), Box 17904, Boulder, CO 80308, 303-440-4153. Training for Transformational Leadership for Social Change. Well Known Faculty.

Shalom Mtn. Retreat/Study Center (B,D), 664 Cattail Rd., Livingston Manor, NY, 914-482-5421. P/S and Sacred Sexuality Retreats for Individuals & Couples. Process Therapy Training.

Sierra Tucson (A,B,C) 16500 N. Lago del Oro Pkwy, Tucson, AZ 85737, 800-842-4487. Primary Addiction Treatment / Psych. Crises Intervention / P/S Workshops.

Sky Dancing Tantra Int'l. (B,D), 524 San Anselmo Ave., San Anselmo CA 415-456-7310. P/S Workshops, Retreats and Trainings in Sacred Sexuality.

Star Foundation (B), PO Box 516 Geyserville, CA 95441, 888-857-STAR. Offers Two Week Intensive P/S Healing Workshops.

The Union Institute (E), 440 East McMillan Street, Cincinnati, OH 45206, 800-456-7688. PhD and Undergrad Programs, Distance Learning, Indiv. Designed P/S Programs.

Veritas Villa, (A,D), RR 2, Box 415, Kerhonkson, NY 12446, 914-626-3555. Primary Addiction Treatment, Training Workshops for Counselors.

Publications

Body Mind Spirit, PO Box 701, Providence, RI 02901, 401-351-4320. Bi-Monthly Mag. Inspirational Articles on Personal/Spiritual growth.

Body Positive, 19 Fulton Street, Suite 308B, NY, NY 10038, 212-566-7333. Monthly Publication for HIV-Positive Individuals – Inspirational Profiles/Information

Common Boundary, PO Box 445, Mt. Morris, IL 61054, 800-548-8737. Monthly Mag that Explores Relationship of Psychology, Spirituality & Creativity.

The Counselor, 1911 North Fort Myer Drive, Arlington VI 22209, 703-741-7686. Bi-Monthly Counselor Mag by Nat'l Assoc. of Alc. and Drug Abuse Counselors

Hope Magazine, PO Box 160, Naskeag Rd, Brooklin, ME 04616, 207-359-4651. Bi-Monthly Mag Focusing on People Making Positive Difference. Full of Recovery.

In The Family, PO Box 5387, Takoma Park, MD 20913, 301-270-4771. Quarterly Mag Exploring Gay/Les/Bi/Trans Relational Issues.

Intuition Magazine, 275 Brennan Street, 3rd Fl, San Fran, CA 94107, 415-538-8171. Monthly Mag on Developing Relevancy of Intuition, Synchronicity and Healing.

Many Voices Newsletter, PO Box 2639, Cincinnati, OH 45201, E-Mail. LynnWatMV@aol.com. Hope and Healing for Trauma Survivors Since 1989

New Age, PO Box 488, Mount Morris, IL 61054, 815-734-5808. Monthly Mag Focusing on New Age Phenomena.

Noetic Sciences Review, 475 Gate Five Road, Suite 300, Sausilito CA 94965, 800-383-1394. Quarterly Mag Exploring Mind, Consciousness and Spirit Beyond Physical Phenomena.

Poz Magazine, 349 West 12 Street, New York, NY 10014, 800-883-2163. A Magazine of Health, Hope & Empowerment for People Living With HIV/AIDS

Professional Counselor, 3201 S.W. 15th St, Deerfield Beach, FL 33442, 954-360-0909. Bi-Monthly Mag by Health Communications for Addiction/Mental Health Professionals

Treating Abuse Today, PO Box 3030, Lancaster, PE 17604, 717-291-1940. Bi-Monthly Publication for Professional Focused on Healing Post Traumatic Stress.

Tricycle, The Buddhist Review, 92 Vandam Street, New York, NY 10013, 800-950-7008. A Current Buddhist Perspective on Aspects of Human Enlightenment.

Websites

The sites below provide a large variety of articles, references, poems, stories, email lists, chat lines, and most importantly, links to other sites relating to recovery. The list is a fragment of the range of sites currently on the Internet.

Alcohol and Substance Abuse
National Institute on Alcohol Abuse and Alcoholism: www.niaaa.nih.gov
National Institute on Drug Abuse: www.nida.nih.gov/NIDAwelcome.html

12-Step Groups
Alcoholics Anonymous (AA): www.alcoholics-anonymous.org
Sexaholics Anonymous: www.sa.org
Debtors Anonymous: www.debtorsanonymous.org/
Codependents Anonymous (CODA): www.ourcoda.org/

Recovery/Pyschospiritual
The Institute For Staged Recovery: www.theinstitute.org
Honest-Open-Willing (HOW) Recovery Resources Online:
    www.whitemtns.com/~tsa/recovery
Mollykat's Resources for Survivors: www.geocities.com/hotsprings/1872
The National Council on Sexual Addiction & Compulsivity: www.ncsac.org
Recovery Online: recovery.netwiz.net/
Sue's Information Zone: www.pilot.infi.net/~susanf/
Survivors Line Around the World: www.dhearts.org/
Self Injury Pages: crystal.palace.net/~llama/selfinjury/
Survivorship Home Page: www.cts.server.com/~svship/
Voices of Wellness: www.vow.com
National Victim Center: www.nvc.org
Wisdom Channel: www.wisdomchannel.com

Sexual Assault/Trauma
Incest Survivors Resource Network: www.zianet.com/isrni/
National Organization on Male Sexual Victimization: www.nomsv.org
Wounded Healer: www.idealist.com/wounded_healer
Sexual Assault Information Page: www.cs.utk.edu/~bartley/
    sainfopage.html

Trauma — General
David Baldwin's Trauma Information: www.trauma-pages.com
Traumatic Stress Home Page: www.long-beach.va.gov/ptsd/stress.html

This list will be updated in future editions of this book and updates can also be found at The Institute for Staged Recovery's website: www.theinstitute.org and in its quarterly newsletter *Authenticity*. To subscribe to the newsletter, send your name, mailing address, phone number, and a check for $25 to cover production/mailing costs to: The Institute for Staged Recovery, 85 Fifth Avenue, Suite 900, New York, NY 10003.

Bibliography

Almaas, A.H. *Diamond Heart: Book One*. California: Diamond Books, 1987

Anonymous. *As Bill Sees It*. New York: Λ. A. World Services, Inc., 1967.

ibid. Alcoholics Anonymous. New York: A. A World Services, Inc., 1955.

Bell, Peter. *Cultural Pain and African Americans*. Minnesota: Hazelden, 1992.

Bradshaw, John. *Bradshaw On: The Family*. Florida: Health Communications Inc., 1988.

ibid. *Healing The Shame That Binds You*. Florida: Health Communications Inc., 1988.

ibid. *Homecoming*. New York: Bantam Books, 1990.

Brennan, Barbara Ann. *Hands of Light*. New York: Bantam Books, 1987.

ibid. *Light Emerging*, New York: Bantam Books, 1995.

Butterworth, Eric. *Discover The Power Within You*. New York: Harper & Row, 1968

Carnes, Patrick. *Don't Call it Love*. New York: Bantam Books, 1992.

Cruise, Sharon Wegscheider, Joseph R. Cruise and George Bougher. *Experiential Therapy of Co Dependency*. CA: Science and Behavior Books, 1990.

Eisler, Riane. *The Chalice & The Blade*. New York: HarperSanFrancisco, 1987

Epstein, Gerald. *Healing Into Immortality*. New York: Bantam Books, 1994

First, Michael B. (Text Editor). *Diagnostic And Statistical Manual Of Mental Disorders*. (4th Edition). Washington, DC: American Psychiatric Association, 1994.

Foehr, Stephen. "Joan Halifax and her Robe of Many Tears." *Shambhala Sun*, November, 1997

Forward, Susan with Craig Buck. *Toxic Parents*. New York: Bantam Books, 1990.

ibid. *Betrayal Of Innocence*. New York: Penguin Books, 1988.

Foster, Diane S. (Editor). "Research Design and Methodology," Heuristic Research. CA: Sage Publications, Inc., 1990.

Fox, Matthew. *WHEE! We, Wee All The Way Home: A Guide To The New Sensual Spirituality*. n.p.: Consortium Books,

Frankl, Viktor E. *Man's Search For Meaning*. (2nd Edition). New York: Touchstone, 1984.

Garfield, Charles, Cindy Spring and Sedonia Cahill. *Wisdom Circles*. New York: Hyperion, 1998

Gass, Robert with On Wings of Song. "Living With Loss." Colorado: Spring Hill Music, 1993.

Gilligan, S.G. *Therapeutic Trances.* New York: Brunner/Mazel, Inc., 1987.

Grof, Christina and Stanislav Grof. *The Stormy Search for The Self.* New York: G. P. Putnam's

Grof, Christina. *The Thirst for Wholeness.* CA: Harper SanFrancisco, 1993.

Grof, Stanislav and Christina Grof (Editors). *Spiritual Emergency.* CA: Jeremy P. Tarcher/Perigee,

Grof, Stanislav. *The Adventure of Self-Discovery.* New York: State University of New York Press

Hayles, Katherine N. (Editor). *Chaos and Order: Complex Dynamics in Literature and Science.* Chicago: University of Chicago Press, 1991.

Hendrix, Harville. *Keeping the Love You Find.* New York: Pocket Books, 1992

Herman, Judith Lewis. *Trauma And Recovery.* New York: Basic Books, 1992.

Hopcke, Robert H. *There Are No Mistakes: Synchronicity and the Stories of our lives.* New York: Riverhead Books, 1997

Houston, Jean. *A Passion for the Possible.* New York: HarperCollins, 1997

Ibid. *The Life Force.* Illinois: Quest Books, 1993

Ibid. *The Possible Human.* New York: Tarcher/Putnam, 1982

James William. *The Varieties of Religious Experience.* New York: Touchstone, 1997

Ibid. *Pragmatism.* New York: Prometheus Books, 1991

James, John W. and Frank Cherry. *The Grief Recovery Handbook.* New York: Harper & Row, Publishers, 1988.

Johnson, Robert A. *Owning Your Own Shadow.* CA: Harper San Francisco, 1991.

Johnson, Stephen M. *Characterological Transformation: The Hard Work Miracle.* New York: Norton Books, 1985.

Jung, C. G. *Modern Man In Search Of A Soul.* (W. S. Dell and C. F. Baynes, Trans.) New York: Harcourt, Brace & World,

ibid. *Psychology and Religion.* CT: Yale University, 1938.

Keyes, jr., Ken. *The Hundredth Monkey.* Coos Bay, Oregon: Vision Books, 1985.

Kushner, Tony. *Angels In America, Part Two: Perestroika.* New York: Theatre Communications Group, Inc., 1992.

Larsen, Earnie. *Stage II Recovery: Life Beyond Addiction.* New York: Harper & Row, 1985.

Levine, Stephen. *Healing Into Life And Death.* New York: Doubleday, 1987.

Lew, Mike. *Victims No Longer.* New York: Nevraumont Publishing Co., 1988.

Lowen, Alexander. *Bioenergetics.* New York: Penguin Group, 1975.

Maslow, A. *Toward a Psychology of Being.* New York: D. Van Nostrand, 1968.

ibid.*The Farther Reaches of Human Nature.* (2nd Edition). New York: Viking Penguin, 1971.

Miller, Alice. *Thou Shalt Not Be Aware.* New York: Meridian, 1984.

ibid.*Pictures Of A Childhood.* Toronto: Collins Publishers, 1986.

ibid.*The Drama Of The Gifted Child.* New York: Basic Books, Inc., 1981.

Peck, M. Scott. *The Road Less Traveled.* New York: Touchstone, 1978.

ibid. *Further Along The Road Less Traveled*. New York: Simon & Schuster, 1993.

Perry, Robert. *An Introduction To A Course In Miracles*. CA: Miracle Distribution Center, 1987.

Picucci, Michael. "Planning an Experiential Weekend Workshop." *Journal of Chemical Dependency Treatment*. The Hayworth Press, Inc., Volume 5, Number 1.

Pierrakos, Eva. *The Pathwork of Self-Transformation*. New York: Bantam Books, 1990.

Pritchard, Evan T. *No Word For Time: The Way of the Algonquin People*. Oklahoma: Council Oak Books, 1997

Redfield, James. *The Celestine Prophecy*. New York: Warner Books, 1993.

Reich, W. *Character Analysis*. New York: Farrar, Straus and Giroux, (1933 1st Ed., 1980 3rd Ed.)

Roberts, Elizabeth and Elias Amidon. *Earth Prayers: From Around the World* CA: Harper San Francisco, 1991.

Rogers, Carl. *A Way Of Being*. MA: Houghton Mifflin Company, 1980.

Schaef, Anne Wilson. *When Society Becomes An Addict*. New York: Harper & Row, 1987.

ibid. *Beyond Therapy, Beyond Science*. New York: Harper Collins, 1992.

Sills, Franklyn. *The Polarity Process*. Great Britain: Element Books, 1989.

Small, Jacquelyn. *Embodying Spirit*. New York: HarperCollins, 1994

ibid. *Awakening In Time*. New York: Bantam Books, 1991

Tilleraas, Perry. *The Color of Light*. New York: Harper & Row, 1988.

Whitfield, Charles L. *Healing the Child Within*. Florida: Health Communications.

Wilber, Ken. *The Spectrum of Consciousness*. Illinois: Quest, 1997

Williams, Walter L. *The Spirit and the Flesh*. Massachusetts: Beacon Press, 1986

Woititz, Janet G. *Adult Children Of Alcoholics*. Florida: Health Communications.

ibid. *Healing Your Sexual Self*. Florida: Health Communications, 1989.

ibid. *Struggle For Intimacy*. Florida: Health Communications, 1985.

Woodman, Marion and Elinor Dickson. *Dancing in the Flames*. Massachusetts: Shambhala, 1997

Yalom, Irvin D. Existential Psychotherapy. New York: Basic Books.

Zambucka, Kristin. *The Keepers Of The Earth*. Hawaii: Harrame, 1985.

ibid. *Ano, Ano: The Seed*. Hawaii: Harrane, 1985.

Index

About the Author
MICHAEL PICUCCI, PH.D., M.A.C.

Michael Picucci is one of the growing number of people today who have gone from surviving to "thriving." From a childhood of trauma, abandonment, loss, and continuous uprooting, he reached his teens already addicted to alcohol and drugs. In 1983, he was diagnosed with a fast-growing lymphoma, now recognized as an AIDS- classified cancer. As well as being a long-term survivor of HIV, he has endured the deaths of two life partners, countless friends, and a recent heart attack. In struggling to heal himself both physically and spiritually he has discovered many powerful methods of healing that he now shares with others.

A nationally credentialed Master Addiction Counselor with a doctorate in The Psychology of Addictions Psychotherapy, Michael discovered a method that combines psychotherapy, the wisdom of the maturing recovery movement, and his own personal healing strategies. The result is a bold new form of healing for *all* people called Authentic Process Therapy. It allows deep feelings, longings for intimacy, and spiritual yearnings to emerge and become integrated, creating the experience of Complete Recovery.

Through his workshops, lectures, seminars, professional training program, and writing, Dr. Picucci brings forth a new and timely vision of joy and personal realization, one which shows how our most challenging personal hardships can be catalysts which guide us to and through our "life purpose." This psychospiritual approach to healing has helped many find their way to fulfillment. He has a private practice in New York City and is co-founder of The Institute for Staged Recovery and Institute Psychotherapy Associates.

To order additional copies of
The Journey Toward Complete Recovery
by Michael Picucci
visit your local bookstore
or order direct from the publisher:

(800) 337-2665

NORTH ATLANTIC BOOKS
P.O. Box 12327
Berkeley, CA 94712
www.northatlanticbooks.com